Other Books by Gary North

Marx's Religion of Revolution (1968, 1989)
An Introduction to Christian Economics (1973)
Puritan Economic Experiments (1974, 1988)
Unconditional Surrender (1981, 1988)
Successful Investing in an Age of Envy (1981)
The Dominion Covenant: Genesis (1982, 1987)
Government by Emergency (1983)
Backward, Christian Soldiers? (1984)
75 Bible Questions Your Instructors Pray You Won't Ask (1984)
Coined Freedom (1984)
Moses and Pharaoh (1985)
The Sinai Strategy (1986)
Conspiracy: A Biblical View (1986)
Honest Money (1986)
Fighting Chance (1986), with Arthur Robinson
Unholy Spirits (1986)
Dominion and Common Grace (1987)
Inherit the Earth (1987)
Liberating Planet Earth (1987)
Healer of the Nations (1987)
The Pirate Economy (1987)
Is the World Running Down? (1988)
When Justice Is Aborted (1989)
Political Polytheism (1989)
The Hoax of Higher Criticism (1990)
Tools of Dominion: The Case Laws of Exodus (1990)
Victim's Rights (1990)
Westminster's Confession (1991)
Christian Reconstruction (1991), with Gary DeMar
The Coase Theorem (1992)
Politically Incorrect (1993)
Salvation Through Inflation (1993)

RAPTURE FEVER
Why Dispensationalism Is Paralyzed

Gary North

Institute for Christian Economics
Tyler, Texas

copyright, Gary North, 1993

Library of Congress Cataloging-in-Publication Data

North, Gary.

  Rapture fever: why dispensationalism is paralyzed / Gary North
    p. cm.
  Includes bibliographical references and index.
  ISBN 0-930464-67-2 : $25. – ISBN 0-930464-65-6 (pbk.) : $12.95
  1. Dispensationalism – Controversial literature 2. Millennialism – United States – History – 20th century. 3. Rapture (Christian theology) – Controversial literature. 4. Walvoord, John. 5. House, H. Wayne. Dominion theology: blessing or curse? 6. Dominion theology. 7. Dallas Theological Seminary.
I. Title

BT157.N67 1993   93-444
230'.046–dc20   CIP

Institute for Christian Economics
P. O. Box 8000
Tyler, Texas 75711

This book is dedicated to

Kenneth L. Gentry, Jr.

whose books would have paralyzed the dispensational theologians of this generation, had it not been for one thing: their constant revisions to the system had already paralyzed each other.

TABLE OF CONTENTS

Foreword ix
Preface xxiv

Introduction 1

1. Endless Unfulfilled Prophecies Produce Paralysis 19
2. Fear of Man Produces Paralysis 40
3. Pessimism Produces Paralysis 61
4. Dispensationalism Removes Earthly Hope 76
5. A Commitment to Cultural Irrelevance 91
6. A Ghetto Eschatology 110
7. House of Seven Garbles 129
8. Revising Dispensationalism to Death 145
9. Dispensationalism vs. Six-Day Creationism 163
10. Dispensationalism vs. Sanctification 172
11. Theological Schizophrenia 180
12. When "Babylon" Fell, So Did Dispensationalism 188
13. The Strange Disappearance of
    Dispensational Institutions 195

Conclusion 202

Bibliography 222
Scripture Index 235
Index 238
A Challenge to Dallas Theological Seminary 247
A Three-Year Strategy for Pastors 248
A Three-Year Strategy for Laymen 249
About the Author 250

AT GOD'S RIGHT HAND, UNTIL . . . .

A Psalm of David.

The LORD said unto my Lord, **Sit thou at my right hand, until I make thine enemies thy footstool.** The LORD shall send the rod of thy strength out of Zion: **rule thou in the midst of thine enemies.** Thy people shall be willing [*volunteer freely*: New American Standard Bible] in the day of thy power, in the beauties of holiness from the womb of the morning: thou hast the dew of thy youth. The LORD hath sworn, and will not repent, Thou art a priest for ever after the order of Melchizedek. **The Lord at thy right hand** shall strike through kings in the day of his wrath. He shall judge among the heathen, he shall fill the places with the dead bodies; he shall wound the heads over many countries. He shall drink of the brook in the way: therefore shall he lift up the head (Psalm 110:1-7; emphasis added).

But now is Christ risen from the dead, and become the firstfruits of them that slept. For since by man came death, by man came also the resurrection of the dead. For as in Adam all die, even so in Christ shall all be made alive. But every man in his own order: Christ the firstfruits; afterward they that are Christ's at his coming. **Then cometh the end, when he shall have delivered up the kingdom to God,** even the Father; **when he shall have put down all rule and all authority and power.** For he must reign, till he hath put all enemies under his feet. **The last enemy that shall be destroyed is death. For he hath put all things under his feet.** But when he saith, all things are put under him, it is manifest that he is excepted, which did put all things under him. And when all things shall be subdued unto him, then shall the Son also himself be subject unto him that put all things under him, that God may be all in all (I Cor. 15:20-28; emphasis added).

FOREWORD
(to be read)

> *For which of you, intending to build a tower, sitteth not down first, and counteth the cost, whether he have sufficient to finish it? Lest haply [it happen], after he hath laid the foundation, and is not able to finish it, all that behold it begin to mock him, Saying, This man began to build, and was not able to finish (Luke 14:28-30).*

Count the costs, Jesus said. But we must also remember to count the benefits. In this Foreword I present three major gifts that are available to all Christians through their membership in God's New Testament Church. The existence of these stupendous gifts has been denied by many theologians. Millions of Christian laymen have therefore been unwilling to accept these benefits from the hand of God. I concluded that it was time for a Christian layman to protest. I can read the Bible, too, and I am convinced that all three of these gifts are not only available to God's people, but also that He is highly displeased when we deny their existence and thereby reject them.

There is a reason for Christians' hesitancy to admit the availability of these gifts. They know that with all blessings inevitably come duties and obligations. We never get something for nothing. Even salvation requires men to live new lives that break with their evil past (I Cor. 6:9-10; Eph. 5:1-5). Millions of Christians think they can evade many duties and obligations if they just refuse to accept God's blessings. This is a terrible mistake. It is analogous to the person who refuses the gift of eternal life because he knows he will have to live differently after he receives this gift. He prefers to turn down the gift of salvation rather than allow God to change his life for the better.

The Gift of Eternal Life

In July, 1959, a man sat down with me after a church meeting. He opened a Bible. I had never read the entire Bible; I was 17 years old, and I lived in a non-Christian home. Here is the first verse he showed me:

> For all have sinned, and come short of the glory of God (Rom. 3:23).

I knew this was true. Men are not God, and God is perfect. Back in 1959, a pagan could go through the U.S. government school system and still know this much. I knew that I was included under the words "for all." But then he showed me another verse:

> For the wages of sin is death; but the gift of God is eternal life through Jesus Christ our Lord (Rom. 6:23).

That verse drew a conclusion from the earlier verse: all men are going to die. My friend told me that I had better believe the Bible's conclusion regarding the wages of sin if I believed the Bible's premise about all having sinned. I did draw this conclusion. My father had been a military policeman and was at the time an F.B.I. agent, one of J. Edgar Hoover's men. I knew there is cause and effect in breaking laws and receiving punishment. So, I accepted the truth of the warning: "For the wages of sin is death." But there is a way to escape death. The second half of the verse is crucial, "but the gift of God is eternal life through Jesus Christ our Lord." Jesus Christ is Lord. He offers a gift. I had better take it, my friend warned, and so I did.

There was a cost in not taking it: death. There was a valuable benefit in taking it: eternal life. But what he did not tell me – what so few fundamentalist-dispensationalists ever tell those with whom they share the message of salvation – is that *there are costs in accepting the gift*. It is a free gift in the sense that it is offered freely to those who do not deserve it, but it is not a free gift in the sense that it does not require changes in a person's life – a lifetime of changes. For example:

> Know ye not that the unrighteous shall not inherit the kingdom of God? Be not deceived: neither fornicators, nor idolaters, nor adulterers, nor effeminate, nor abusers of themselves with mankind, Nor thieves, nor covetous, nor drunkards, nor revilers, nor extortioners, shall inherit the kingdom of God (I Cor. 6:9-10).

Clear, isn't it? It was surely clear to those who received Paul's warning, for some of them had come out of such a lifestyle: "And such were some of you: but ye are washed, but ye are sanctified, but ye are justified in the name of the Lord Jesus, and by the Spirit of our God" (I Cor. 6:11).

There are some benefits available to you as a Christian that you have not been willing to claim as a dispensationalist. Like the free gift of grace that must be acknowledged and accepted by the recipient in order to complete salvation's transaction, so must these other gifts be acknowledged and accepted by the recipient in order to be completed. But millions of Christians have been told by their teachers and friends that these gifts are not for Christians. These gifts are supposedly only for those people who will be converted to Christ during a future millennium. Until then, dispensational theologians insist, it is "hands off!" These gifts are supposedly not for this dispensation.

With this book, I intend to persuade you to accept both the reality of these gifts and their obligations, just as my friend in 1959 persuaded me to accept the gift of eternal life.

Gift #1: Our Participation in God's Earthly Kingdom

Jesus said of eternal life that it does not begin at the time of a redeemed person's physical death. It begins when a person accepts as his possession Jesus Christ's perfect life, His bodily death and resurrection, and His ascension in glory to the right hand of God *in history*. Eternal life begins in history:

> He that believeth on the Son hath everlasting life: and he that believeth not the Son shall not see life; but the wrath of God abideth on him (John 3:36).

Similarly, Jesus told us that as members of His eternal Church, we are the heirs of the Old Covenant kingdom that God had given by grace to the Jews. *The Church receives the kingdom inheritance of Israel.* Not only did Jesus tell this to His disciples, He also told it to the Jews of His day, who hated Him for saying it:

> Therefore say I unto you, The kingdom of God shall be taken from you, and given to a nation bringing forth the fruits thereof (Matt. 21:43).

This new "nation" is not some geographical, political entity; it is an international, spiritual entity: His Church. But the Church is more than spiritual; it is an institution, made up of real, live human beings. God's kingdom is broader than His Church.

Benefits

As members of Christ's kingdom, born-again Christians are heirs of all the promises attached to such membership. Jesus said in His famous Sermon on the Mount: "But seek ye first the kingdom of God, and his righteousness; and all these things shall be added unto you" (Matt. 6:33). *All these things*: food to eat, liquids to drink, and clothes to wear (Matt. 6:31). Meek before almighty God, Christians can be bold before men. This is why Jesus had promised earlier in this sermon: "Blessed are the meek: for they shall inherit the earth" (Matt. 5:5). He did not mean meek before men; He meant meek before God.

Dispensationalists until quite recently denied that this promise was given to Christians. Yet they also taught that the kingdom of God in Matthew 6:33 is the same kingdom promised in Matthew 21:43. You can see this in Note 1, page 1029, of the original *Scofield Reference Bible* (1909). It says that the kingdom which was about to be transferred to the gentiles was the kingdom of God. The note refers the reader to another note at Matthew 6:33: identical kingdoms.

But then Scofield discussed the "beatitudes" – the "blessed are" verses. He said they refer only to the kingdom of heaven (Note 2, which begins on page 999). "In this sense the Sermon on the Mount is pure law. . . ." (p. 1000). Scofield then removed both the duties and the inheritance from the Church: "For these reasons the Sermon on the Mount in its primary application gives neither the privilege nor the duty of the Church" (p. 1000). He made a distinction between the kingdom of God (for the Church) and the kingdom of heaven (for millennial Jews): "The kingdom of heaven will yet be set up" (p. 1029). Thus, *the external blessings of God's kingdom will return to a Jewish Church during the millennium; the New Testament Church never receives them as part of her lawful inheritance.*

What very few dispensationalists realize is that more recent dispensational theologians have abandoned the distinction between the kingdom of God and the kingdom of heaven. Professor Craig Blaising of Dallas Theological Seminary writes in the Seminary's journal, *Bibliotheca Sacra*: "Many contemporary dispensationalists deny that there is any *one* dispensational interpretation of the Sermon on the Mount."[1] Referring to the distinction between the kingdom of God and the kingdom of

---

1. Craig Blaising, "Development of Dispensationalism by Contemporary Dispensationalists," *Bibliotheca Sacra* (July-September 1988), p. 259.

heaven, he says that this idea goes all the way back to John Nelson Darby, who is generally regarded as the founder of dispensationalism.[2] It was taught by Scofield and by the founder of Dallas Seminary, Lewis Sperry Chafer.[3] But then he adds: "Subsequent publications by dispensationalists show signs of revision." He cites J. Dwight Pentecost, Alva McClain, and John F. Walvoord. "Other dispensationalists have essentially abandoned any distinction between the kingdom of heaven and the kingdom of God." He cites the *Ryrie Study Bible*, Clarence E. Mason, Jr., Stanley Toussant, and Robert Saucy. He concludes: "Again this shows that dispensationalism is not a fixed set of confessional interpretations but that development is taking place."[4] A theological distinction which for over a century was regarded as crucial to the dispensational system is now optional.

This means that there is now no good theological reason for dispensationalists not to accept the magnificent inheritance that all other branches of the Christian Church have accepted since the early Church: the kingdom of God, which is the same as the kingdom of heaven. These are two terms used to describe the kingdom of Jesus Christ, both in history and in eternity.

The kingdom of God is not some purely internal experience; it is the realm of God's authority in history, the true civilization of God, where our churches, our families, our schools, our businesses, and our governments are all operated in order to please God, according to His will. As Jesus taught us to pray: "Thy kingdom come. Thy will be done in earth, as it is in heaven" (Matt. 6:10). *This prayer is answered progressively in history, not merely in heaven,* just as "Give us this day our daily bread" is also answered in time. This is why H. Wayne House, a dispensational theologian and social activist, can write the following about God's kingdom:

---

2. *Idem.*
3. *Ibid.*, p. 260.
4. *Ibid.*, p. 262.

Moreover, as we Christians spread the good news of Christ to others and share the compassion and love of God to others, the kingdom to come becomes the kingdom on this earth. Heaven gradually comes to earth, though certainly one day this will be so in fullness and glory.[5]

What a tremendous opportunity: a benefit! But what a tremendous responsibility: a cost!

Costs

There can be no escape from making responsible ethical decisions in this kingdom. Obviously, this transfer of ownership from Old Covenant Israel could not skip to some future Jewish society at least 1,960 years after Jesus announced it. He told them that their kingdom would be removed from them and given to someone else, not held in a kind of deep freeze for two millennia. It would be given to a rival nation that would bring forth the fruits of the kingdom. So, we must abandon the fruits of unrighteousness. Paul wrote to the church at Ephesus:

> Be ye therefore followers of God, as dear children; And walk in love, as Christ also hath loved us, and hath given himself for us an offering and a sacrifice to God for a sweetsmelling savour. But fornication, and all uncleanness, or covetousness, let it not be once named among you, as becometh saints; Neither filthiness, nor foolish talking, nor jesting, which are not convenient: but rather giving of thanks. For this ye know, that no whoremonger, nor unclean person, nor covetous man, who is an idolater, hath any inheritance in the kingdom of Christ and of God (Eph. 5:1-5).

There are laws governing this kingdom inheritance. We must obey God through the empowering of the Holy Spirit. If

---

5. H. Wayne House, "Creation and Redemption: A Study of Kingdom Interplay," *The Journal of the Evangelical Theological Society* (March 1992), p. 11.

we do not keep His commandments, we are not Christ's redeemed, holy people:

> And hereby we do know that we know him, if we keep his commandments (I John 2:3).

> And whatsoever we ask, we receive of him, because we keep his commandments, and do those things that are pleasing in his sight (I John 3:22).

> By this we know that we love the children of God, when we love God, and keep his commandments (I John 5:2).

So, there we have it: as Christians, we participate in a great inheritance: *the whole earth*. We lawfully claim this inheritance in two ways: (1) by trusting in the perfect obedience of Jesus Christ, a perfection which is imputed to us judicially by God; and (2) by working out our salvation in history: "Wherefore, my beloved, as ye have always obeyed, not as in my presence only, but now much more in my absence, work out your own salvation with fear and trembling" (Phil. 2:12). In short, we must *trust and obey, for there's no other way*. Christians sing this in church, but do they believe it after they leave church? Does singing this in church testify against their theology?

Gift #2: Our Authority Over Satan and His Kingdom

Satan has a kingdom in history, just as Christ does. Christians are part of an army – angelic and human – that struggles against Satan's army: demonic and human. Christians have been given authority over the troops in Satan's army, both demonic and human:

> And he called unto him the twelve, and began to send them forth by two and two; and gave them power over unclean spirits (Mark 6:7).

There came also a multitude out of the cities round about unto Jerusalem, bringing sick folks, and them which were vexed with unclean spirits: and they were healed every one (Acts 5:16).

Benefits

When men are saved by grace, they are given power through the Holy Spirit. "But ye shall receive power, after that the Holy Ghost is come upon you: and ye shall be witnesses unto me both in Jerusalem, and in all Judaea, and in Samaria, and unto the uttermost part of the earth" (Acts 1:8). This is what enables the Church to overcome the power of Satan in history: "And the God of peace shall bruise Satan under your feet shortly. The grace of our Lord Jesus Christ be with you. Amen" (Rom. 16:20). In the early days of the Church, this grant of power included the power to do signs and wonders, but long-term, the most important aspect of this power is wisdom: the ability to discern truth from falsehood.

> That the God of our Lord Jesus Christ, the Father of glory, may give unto you the spirit of **wisdom and revelation** in the knowledge of him: The eyes of your understanding being enlightened; that ye may know what is the hope of his calling, and what **the riches of the glory of his inheritance in the saints**, And what is the exceeding greatness of his power to usward who believe, according to **the working of his mighty power**, Which he wrought in Christ, when he raised him from the dead, and **set him at his own right hand in the heavenly places**, Far above all principality, and power, and might, and dominion, and every name that is named, not only in this world, but also in that which is to come: And **hath put all things under his feet**, and gave him to be the head over all things to the church (Eph. 1:17-22; emphasis added).

Costs

With power always comes responsibility. We must obey God. We are empowered by the Holy Spirit to obey God.

> There hath no temptation taken you but such as is common to man: but God is faithful, who will not suffer you to be tempted above that ye are able; but will with the temptation also make a way to escape, that ye may be able to bear it (I Cor. 10:13).

Biblical wisdom therefore includes obedience: not merely to know what is right but to have the courage to do what is right. Knowing what is right is not good enough. "Therefore to him that knoweth to do good, and doeth it not, to him it is sin" (James 4:17). We are empowered to do good works *in history*, which is part of our glorious inheritance *in history*. Why?

> That ye might walk worthy of the Lord unto all pleasing, being **fruitful in every good work,** and increasing in the knowledge of God; **Strengthened with all might, according to his glorious power,** unto all patience and longsuffering with joyfulness; Giving thanks unto the Father, which hath made us meet to be **partakers of the inheritance of the saints** in light: Who hath delivered us from the power of darkness, and hath translated us into **the kingdom of his dear Son** (Col. 1:10-13; emphasis added).

So, God gives His people power and wisdom, but He also gives them responsibility. Because He gives us power over Satan and his kingdom, we must exercise this authority in terms of Jesus Christ and His kingdom. In short, *we are required by God to work hard to replace Satan's kingdom in history with God's kingdom in history.* We must defeat something evil with something good. Is this possible in history? Of course:

> And I say also unto thee, That thou art Peter, and upon this rock I will build my church; and the gates of hell shall not prevail against it (Matt. 16:18).

Note: it does not say that the gates of heaven shall prevail against Satan's kingdom (defensive imagery for Christianity);

rather, the gates of hell will not prevail against God's Church (offensive imagery).

Gift #3: Our Victory in History

Did Jesus triumph over Satan when He rose from the dead? Of course. Did He triumph over history when He ascended into heaven to sit at God's right hand? Of course. *Jesus is not a loser in history.* But if this is true, then we have to conclude: *neither are His earthly servants.* That means us!

Jesus extends His rule in history through His Church. He extends his rule *representatively*, just as Satan does. Satan does not need to sit on an earthly throne in order to extend his kingdom; neither does Jesus. Nothing can stop this extension of His kingly rule in history. David wrote:

> Serve the LORD with fear, and rejoice with trembling. Kiss the Son, lest he be angry, and ye perish from the way, when his wrath is kindled but a little. Blessed are all they that put their trust in him (Psalm 2:11-12).

This Old Testament commandment is fulfilled in Christ:

> But now is Christ risen from the dead, and become the firstfruits of them that slept. For since by man came death, by man came also the resurrection of the dead. For as in Adam all die, even so in Christ shall all be made alive. But every man in his own order: Christ the firstfruits; afterward they that are Christ's at his coming. Then cometh the end, when he shall have delivered up the kingdom to God, even the Father; when he shall have put down all rule and all authority and power. For he must reign, till he hath put all enemies under his feet. The last enemy that shall be destroyed is death (I Cor. 15:20-26).

Jesus Christ must continue to reign over history until all His enemies are put under His feet. That is what the text says. But we know that He sits today at His Father's right hand. Thus,

He must remain seated on His heavenly throne until the day that He returns in final judgment to end death. That is what Paul taught. It could not be any clearer.

Benefits

We are Christ's representatives in history. We therefore are His agents to extend His rule. When Jesus celebrated Passover with His disciples, He gave them this promise regarding their authority in history:

> And I appoint unto you a kingdom, as my Father hath appointed unto me; That ye may eat and drink at my table in my kingdom, and sit on thrones judging the twelve tribes of Israel (Luke 22:29-30).

Scofield adds this heading: "The apostles' place in the future kingdom."[6] The problem is, this interpretation depends on making an absolute distinction in history between the kingdom of heaven and the kingdom of God, a distinction that modern dispensationalists no longer insist on.

As the Church matures, we gain greater experience and greater confidence in our ability to rule. We do this as parents in our families. We do this as leaders in our churches. On what basis can this be restricted to families and churches? What about education? What about our businesses? Don't we extend our dominion in history here? Then why should Christians expect to be losers in history? The Bible teaches no such thing.

Costs

With greater success comes greater responsibility. Jesus warned sinners that this is the case; how much more for His people, who have greater knowledge than sinner do! He warned:

---

6. *Scofield Reference Bible*, p. 1108; see notes 1 and 2, p. 1026.

And that servant, which knew his lord's will, and prepared not himself, neither did according to his will, shall be beaten with many stripes. But he that knew not, and did commit things worthy of stripes, shall be beaten with few stripes. For unto whomsoever much is given, of him shall be much required: and to whom men have committed much, of him they will ask the more (Luke 12:47-48).

Just as a parent has more responsibility before God than his child does, so do those who become successful. They receive greater blessings, and so they bear more responsibility. But our successes are supposed to establish our confidence in the fulfillment in history of God's covenantal promises, which should produce greater obedience, which increases our confidence, and so on, until He comes again in final judgment. This is *positive feedback*: progress. But beware, God warned, that

> thou say in thine heart, My power and the might of mine hand hath gotten me this wealth. But thou shalt remember the LORD thy God: for it is he that giveth thee power to get wealth, that he may establish his covenant which he sware unto thy fathers, as it is this day (Deut. 8:17-18).

God offers us the possibility of marching from victory unto victory, if we obey Him by obeying His law. But there are many Christians who prefer to believe in the Church's defeat in history so that they can live under humanist man's laws instead of God's law. They even proclaim this subservience to humanist politicians, judges, and lawyers as God's plan for His Church.

I say there is a better choice. That is why I wrote this book.

Ask Yourself These Three Questions

First, do you hope that your work on earth will leave a positive legacy to future generations, no matter how small the legacy is, even if no one in the future remembers who you were or what you did? Of course you do. *Second*, does God's Word return to Him void? No. *Third,* as a covenant-keeper before God, can you legitimately expect that your good words and good deeds will have more impact in the future than your evil words and evil deeds? I am not speaking merely of building up treasures in heaven; I am speaking also of your legacy in history to your earthly heirs. I am speaking here of *inheritance* in the broadest sense.

If you answer *yes,* I think you have the right attitude about yourself and your work in God's kingdom. If you answer *no,* I think you are in need of professional Christian counseling. You are headed for a mental crisis. First, you have a problem with your lack of self-esteem (and covenant-keepers have a right to self-esteem as legally adopted sons of God: John 1:12). Second, you have a problem with your lack of confidence regarding God's willingness to bless your work. You have neglected God's promise: "Wherefore the LORD God of Israel saith, I said indeed that thy house, and the house of thy father, should walk before me for ever: but now the LORD saith, Be it far from me; for them that honour me I will honour, and they that despise me shall be lightly esteemed" (1 Sam. 2:30).

The three questions I have asked here with respect to your legitimate expectations about the historical outcome of your *personal* efforts also need to be asked with respect to Christianity in general: *the kingdom (civilization) of God.* When we begin to seek Bible-based answers to these three questions regarding the kingdom of God in history, we have necessarily raised the issue of a biblical philosophy of history.

If all of our personal efforts will inevitably be swallowed up and wiped out during a future Great Tribulation, then of what earthly use are they? Similarly, if all of the Church's good works are wiped out during that same Great Tribulation, what is the use of trying? Why should Christians sacrifice to build universities and other great institutions if they will all be stolen or ruined after the Rapture (and maybe before)? This is what millions of Christians conclude. That is because they are worried about the costs of working hard today: the benefits will not endure the Great Tribulation. Yes, His people will be safe in heaven after the Rapture, but their inheritance will be destroyed. What a terrible, debilitating effect this belief has on people's hopes and dreams! Fortunately, this is an incorrect belief, as this book will prove.

The Bible tells us that those who are redeemed by God's grace are assigned a task: to extend His dominion in history (Gen. 1:28; 9:7). That is both our great honor and our great responsibility. It is time for Christians to cease looking for theological loopholes to escape this responsibility.

Conclusion

This book presents the case against just this aspect of dispensationalism: the deliberate evasion of responsibility through the invention of a false doctrine: the "secret" Rapture. This evasion of responsibility comes at a very high cost: the public denial of God's earthly blessings on His people. It is time for Christians to count this terribly high cost of evading their responsibilities as God's designated agents in history, the ambassadors of His kingdom, which progressively extends across the face of the earth through missionary work and evangelism. It is time for God's people to acknowledge the greatness of Christ's Great Commission[7] and to stop fretting about the so-called Great Tribulation, which was *the great tribulation for Israel in A.D. 70*, not a future event.[8] Our work will not be destroyed by the Antichrist or the Beast (died: A.D. 68) in a future seven-year tribulation period. Our work will persevere: an inheritance to future generations. And thus will God's promise be fulfilled: "A good man leaveth an inheritance to his children: and the wealth of the sinner is laid up for the just" (Prov. 13:22).

---

7. Kenneth L. Gentry, Jr., *The Greatness of the Great Commission: The Christian Enterprise in a Fallen World* (Tyler, Texas: Institute for Christian Economics, 1990).

8. David Chilton, *The Great Tribulation* (Ft. Worth, Texas: Dominion Press, 1987).

PREFACE
(also to be read)

Seeing many things, but thou observest not; opening the ears, but he heareth not. The LORD is well pleased for his righteousness' sake; he will magnify the law, and make it honourable. But this is a people robbed and spoiled; they are all of them snared in holes, and they are hid in prison houses: they are for a prey, and none delivereth; for a spoil, and none saith, Restore. Who among you will give ear to this? who will hearken and hear for the time to come? (Isaiah 42:20-23).

It is time for Christians to begin to restore. But what, exactly, are Christians morally obligated by God to restore? And how are they supposed to do this? On these two crucial questions, dispensationalism is self-consciously silent. This is why it is paralyzed. This is why it has entered its terminal phase. Let me offer some indirect evidence.

Except in the historically rare instance when a nation goes to war to defend an idea and then loses the war, movements do not give up their ideas overnight. Large numbers of people do not march out of a movement, nor do they as a unit openly abandon their former belief systems. Then why do movements disappear? *Attrition.* They fail to recruit new followers, either from the outside or from the youth within their ranks.

This is now happening to dispensationalism. It is not that millions of die-hard dispensationalists have openly abandoned premillennialism for either amillennialism or postmillennialism.

It is that the children of dispensationalists are being sent to state universities by their parents, where they abandon their parents' religion. From the 1870's until the 1970's, dispensationalists self-consciously withdrew from the world into a kind of cultural and emotional ghetto. But, beginning in the years following World War II, they began sending their children off to college, which generally meant tax-funded humanist colleges. They want their children to climb the ladder of upward economic mobility, and this means college. There is a heavy price to pay for this mobility – the risk of an eternal tuition payment. Christian parents vaguely recognize this, but they think, "My child is ready for this challenge." It is a safe guess to say that half of them are not ready for it, and this may be much too low an estimate.

Surviving College

To survive the gauntlet of the secular college, an intelligent student needs defenses: emotional, institutional, and intellectual. He is not provided with these defenses in his high school years unless he has been subjected to a Christian curriculum. Few fundamentalists send their children to Christian high schools. Fewer still home school their children. In his excellent two-week summer seminars, David Nobel asks each group of 150 students how many attend or attended public high schools. At least 80% of the students raise their hands. Nobel says two of his sessions have a much lower percentage: the first one, held before schools normally get out, since this one is attended by home schoolers; and the last one, on six-day creationism.[1]

This information reinforces my main point: dispensationalism is losing the war to humanism. There must be a systematic effort on the part of Christian parents to train up their children in the way they should go, but dispensational parents are unwilling to do this. They voluntarily turn their children over

---

1. Summit Ministries, 935 Osage Ave., Manitou Springs, Colorado 80829.

to the humanists to educate them. Then they send their children to tax-funded colleges or heavily humanist-influenced Christian colleges, which finish the process.

An Intellectual Inferiority Complex

In the battle for the minds of educated men, dispensationalists have always seen themselves as outclassed and headed for inevitable defeat. This is what dispensational premillennialism teaches: the defeat of the Church in this, the so-called Church Age, the dispensation of the mystery, the Great Parenthesis. In earlier years, prior to World War II, few high school graduates went to college and far fewer fundamentalists, who rarely had the money, the required academic background, or the push from parents and peers to attend. This changed after World War II, when the G.I. bill opened up colleges to returning servicemen. Tax-funded higher education became universal, and fundamentalists began to take advantage of the subsidy. The result has been the attrition process.

When bright fundamentalist students hit college, humanism hits them. A lot of them do not survive the ordeal. They have no body of dispensational-based scholarship to help them through their courses in psychology, philosophy, economics, education, and the arts. Dispensationalism has yet to produce any academic materials in these fields. Humanist professors take full advantage of this well-known lack of defenses. The freshman course in Western Civilization is designed to separate Christians from their parents' prejudices. I know. I studied under the two scholars who co-authored one of the most popular Western Civilization textbooks in the post-World War II era. One of them, a historian, hated Christianity with all his heart; the other, a philosopher, was merely amused by it.

There is no money in Christian scholarship. There is only a lifetime battle. To produce Christian scholarship in the so-called secular realm – secularism is in fact highly religious – it takes a lifetime of study and a willingness to challenge publicly the bureaucratically certified, highly educated, well-funded academic masters of this age. To make this challenge, a Christian needs a uniquely Christian world-and-life view, which includes a rival system of law and truth. Dispensationalists possess the rival view of truth, but they do not possess a rival view of law. They have adopted the view of law espoused by pre-Darwin humanism and no longer taken seriously in academia or politics: natural law. Dispensationalists have yet to develop their own view of law based on biblical creation. Darwinists had captured law, political science, history, and the arts within three decades after the appearance of *The Origin of Species* (1859). Dispensationalists have yet to make the attempt to conquer these fields in terms of their anti-Darwinian view of the origin of the universe. (See Chapter 9.)

The Goal of This Book

I wrote this book for the same reason that I have written about two dozen books of Christian scholarship and published dozens of others with my own money or money I have raised: I am determined to offer Christians, especially college students, a biblical alternative to humanism. I want to provide them with something that no one provided me.

I was converted to saving faith in Jesus Christ in July, 1959, in the summer between my senior year in high school and my first year in college. This took place when a friend invited me to attend a local Bible church: premillennial, dispensational, and fundamental. I had been a very good student in high school. I had won a California State Scholarship to attend the most prestigious undergraduate liberal arts college in the West Coast, Pomona College. My faculty advisor at Pomona College was later to come within one percentage point of defeating Jerry Brown ("Governor Moonbeam") for the governorship of California. So, I was tossed into the middle of humanism's gauntlet at age 17. I had been a Christian all of two months.

In the second semester of my freshman year, I transferred to the University of California, Riverside, which at the time was the only four-year liberal arts college in the University of California system. It did not add a graduate school for another four years. I studied there, on and off, for the next dozen years, taking my doctorate in 1972. But what changed me the most was my realization in the second semester of my freshman year that there had to be a Christian approach to economics. I realized that free market economics is true and socialist economics is not true. I knew that the Bible is true. Therefore, I concluded that the Bible must have something unique to say about economics.

I spent the next three years searching for someone who had written on Christian economics. I found nothing. There was nothing.[2] Today, three decades later, things are a lot better. There are a few books that deal with Christian economics, including a dozen written by me. There is even an Association of Christian Economists, although its hundreds of members rarely write explicitly Christian economics; rather, they are Christians who write academically acceptable articles on topics that are occasionally interesting to other Christians academicians. But, in 1959, there was nothing.

There was also nothing in the other fields. No one was talking about an explicitly Christian world-and-life view except a handful of Dutch-American Calvinist scholars whose work was unknown outside of Michigan. Henry Van Til's *Christian Concept of Culture* appeared in 1959, but I did not come across it until I enrolled at Westminster Theological Seminary, a Calvinist institution, in 1963. For a fundamentalist scholar, there was nothing available in 1959. There was not even *The Genesis Flood*, which appeared in 1961, and only because Calvinist scholar R.

---

2. The twice-monthly tabloid newspaper called *Christian Economics* was in fact a humanist free market newspaper that was financed by a billionaire Calvinist: J. Howard Pew. There was no attempt by its writers to use the Bible to provide the content of their economic opinions and analysis.

Preface

J. Rushdoony intervened to persuade Presbyterian & Reformed, a small Calvinist publishing firm, to publish the book after fundamentalist Moody Press had turned down the manuscript because of its complete opposition to theistic evolution and age-day creationism.[3]

For a fundamentalist in 1993, there is still nothing, except in creationism, where Henry Morris and other dispensationalists have broken with C. I. Scofield's "gap" theory. (See Chapter 9.) The fundamentalist student is still dependent on others for his academic defenses.

Dispensationalism vs. Scholarship

What I argue in this book is that inherent in dispensationalism's view of law is a worldview that denies the possibility of Christian scholarship in "secular" fields. To challenge humanism in any field, you must possess a uniquely biblical view of God, man, law, and time.[4] The dispensationalist's denial that Old Testament law is valid in New Testament times strips him of any uniquely biblical view of law. He is then forced to adopt one or another of the humanist views of law. But this is only the beginning of his intellectual dilemma. The dispensational view of the future of the Church in this dispensation completes the burial of Christian scholarship. The dispensationalist insists that there is not enough time for Christians to work out alternatives to humanism, let alone actually substitute them for humanist culture. This has paralyzed dispensationalists who have the intelligence and the technical academic skills to produce biblical alternatives. Their refusal to take up the academic plow has in turn left fundamentalist college students intellectu-

---

3. Henry M. Morris, *History of Modern Creationism* (San Diego: Master Book Pubs., 1984), p. 154.
4. Gary North, *Unconditional Surrender: God's Program for Victory* (3rd ed.; Tyler, Texas: Institute for Christian Economics, 1988), Part I.

ally and conceptually defenseless against humanists in the classrooms where their parents naively and trustingly send them.

And then Billy Bob and Jenny Sue are deliberately assigned to sexually mixed dorm floors, or worse, mixed dorm rooms. If you think the humanists are not self-conscious in their methods of breaking down intellectual resistance to their worldview, you are suffering from terminal naiveté. It is fundamentalists who are not self-conscious, not the humanists.

In 1985, I hired Gary DeMar to write a manuscript which later became a book, *Surviving College Successfully: A Complete Manual for the Rigors of Academic Combat* (1988). In 1993, I finally completed a manuscript I had written in 1975: *Politically Incorrect: A College Survival Manual for Parents and Students*. I could not find a Christian publisher for the original version of this book in 1975: not spiritual enough, no visible market, obviously irrelevant to "the normal Christian life." The one company that did express some interest in it then sent the manuscript to be rewritten by a man who had spent seven years trying to earn a bachelor's degree but finally quit school. This was, and remains, the world of fundamentalism.

I am the co-founder with R. J. Rushdoony of what is known as Christian Reconstruction.[5] Christian Reconstructionism offers alternatives to humanism: intellectual, academic, and cultural. We are self-consciously in the battle for the minds of men, and not just their minds: their lifetime commitment. We are scholars. What I am saying is that dispensationalists are not – not in their capacity as dispensationalists.

Dispensational Scholarship: A Permanent Missing Link

Dispensationalists can and do produce works of scholarship in certain narrowly defined fields of biblical studies, but they rarely do so as dispensationalists. They may be proficient in the

---

5. Gary North and Gary DeMar, *Christian Reconstruction: What It Is, What It Isn't* (Tyler, Texas: Institute for Christian Economics, 1991).

biblical languages or some related technical field, but when they produce their scholarship, these works are rarely explicitly dispensational. Rarely in our day do they even attempt to define and defend the broad categories of dispensational theology. The classic works of dispensationalism are at least a generation old and are going out of print.

This is not random. This is the result of a specific view of time and law. Dispensationalism in the 1990's has become intellectually paralyzed. This book shows why and how this happened. I believe, though do not attempt to prove here, that this intellectual paralysis will lead to a more general paralysis within two decades. To avoid this paralysis, today's intellectual leaders within the dispensationalist camp must rethink the categories of traditional dispensationalism and make the system relevant. I believe this cannot be done without scrapping dispensationalism and inventing something new. It may be called dispensationalism, but it will not be dispensationalism. It will have abandoned every theological distinctive that the founders of the various dispensational seminaries sacrificed so much to defend. This abandonment has already begun, as I show in this book. More than this: this process of abandonment is now in its final stages. This is the "dirty little secret" that the leaders of dispensationalism have done their best to hide from donors since 1985.

The Silence of the Sacrificial Lambs

This intellectual defection began in 1945. That was the year that O. T. Allis, America's premier Old Testament scholar at the time, wrote *Prophecy and the Church*. That book was relentless and thorough in its refutation of dispensationalism's eschatology, point by point. Academic dispensationalists adopted a doomed strategy to deal with Allis: a conspiracy of silence. They played "let's pretend": let's pretend our students will never read this book, our supporters will never hear of it, and our critics will never spot the nature of our defensive strategy.

Forty years later, they were still using this strategy. There is no doubt that the most vocal critics of dispensationalism have been the Christian Reconstructionists. Our view of law and the future – theonomy and postmillennialism – is the antithesis of dispensationalism. Where dispensationalism flourishes, the vision and goals of Christian Reconstruction cannot prosper. I therefore decided in the early 1980's to devote whatever amount of money it would take to refute in print every aspect of dispensational theology.

I decided in 1984 that I would like to be known in Church history as the man who financed the intellectual demise of dispensationalism in its time of greatest crisis. *Institutionally, dispensationalism is committing suicide in broad daylight*: by failing to produce a single systematic theology in this generation; by failing to respond to its published critics from O. T. Allis (1945) to the present; by failing to provide alternatives to humanism, even in the field of education; and above all, by its seminaries' terrified silence on the controversial issue of abortion. *Roe v. Wade* was a case that began in the city of Dallas, but Dallas Theological Seminary has adopted the three-monkey approach: hear no evil, see no evil, and speak no prophetic word of warning. In 1973, Dallas Theological Seminary committed moral suicide by its silence. So did every other seminary that remained silent. This means most of them.

Evangelicalism cannot identify mass murder when it sees it. Evangelicalism is therefore morally bankrupt. *Evangelicalism has become the silent partner of humanism*. When the inevitable collapse of humanism comes, it will drag down evangelicalism with it. Dispensationalism is the largest branch of evangelicalism. That is why I decided to finance an alternative to dispensationalism. I have financed a two-prong strategy: positive and negative. "You can't beat something with nothing."

I have financed the following anti-dispensational books since 1984: my own *75 Bible Questions Your Instructors Pray You Won't Ask* (1984), followed by David Chilton's *Paradise Restored: A*

Biblical Theology of Dominion (1985), *Days of Vengeance: An Exposition of the Book of Revelation* (1987) and his smaller book, *The Great Tribulation* (1987). In succession came Greg Bahnsen and Ken Gentry's *House Divided: The Break-Up of Dispensational Theology* (1989), a devastating reply to (then) Dallas Seminary professor H. Wayne House and his research assistant, Thomas D. Ice. (House left Dallas soon thereafter.) Then came Gentry's *Before Jerusalem Fell: Dating the Book of Revelation* (1989), *The Beast of Revelation* (1989), *The Greatness of the Great Commission* (1990), and his massive exposition, *He Shall Have Dominion: A Postmillennial Eschatology* (1992). Also published in this period were Gary DeMar and Peter Leithart's *The Reduction of Christianity: A Biblical Response to Dave Hunt* (1988), DeMar's *The Debate Over Christian Reconstruction* (1988), *Last Days Madness* (1991; not published by me), and my *Millennialism and Social Theory* (1990). Above all, there was *That You May Prosper: Dominion By Covenant* (1987), written by a Dallas Seminary Th.M., Ray Sutton. Dr. Sutton today is the president of Philadelphia Theological Seminary and the chancellor of education for the Reformed Episcopal Church. In the face of all of this, Dallas Seminary has remained silent, except for an occasional brief book review by John Walvoord or Robert Lightner.

Only two dispensationalist authors have replied in detail to Christian Reconstruction: House and Ice. (Dave Hunt never devoted more than a few pages to us, and the ill-fated attempt by Hal Lindsey to identify all non-dispensational theologies as inherently anti-Semitic is representative of neither dispensationalism nor scholarship.[6]) Since his departure from Dallas Seminary, Dr. House has not put anything into print about theonomy or Christian Reconstruction, which is not surprising, given what Dr. Bahnsen did to him in full public view for over 130

---

6. Hal Lindsey, *The Road to Holocaust* (New York: Bantam, 1989). For a response, see Gary DeMar and Peter Leithart, *The Legacy of Hatred Continues: A Response to Hal Lindsey's **The Road to Holocaust*** (Tyler, TX: Institute for Christian Economics, 1989).

pages in *House Divided*. This leaves only Rev. Ice, who publishes several monthly newsletters from his Austin, Texas, Bible church. The theologians of Dallas Seminary, by their steadfast silence regarding Christian Reconstruction's numerous critiques of dispensationalism, have by default transferred the unofficial role of dispensationalism's spokesman to Rev. Ice. What it boils down to is this: *the intellectual defense of the traditional dispensational system as an integrated whole now rests solely on the shoulders of Tommy Ice.* This does not bode well for traditional dispensationalism.

In 1945, this strategy of silence worked because dispensational laymen paid no attention to an academic book such as Allis' *Prophecy and the Church*. Dispensationalists still believed they could live in safety inside their psychological and ecclesiastical ghettos. The moral decline of American culture after 1965 has made this assumption appear ludicrous. As they have begun tentatively to defend Christian and conservative views of how society should operate, dispensational laymen have been drawn out of their ghettos and into the arena of political conflict. This has led to a division within dispensationalism: the activists vs. the pessimists. As I have said repeatedly, a dispensational activist has become psychologically an operational postmillennialist. He does not fight in order to lose. This division within dispensationalism can be seen even in the brief and ill-fated partnership that produced *Dominion Theology: Blessing or Curse?* (1988). Dr. House is a Christian activist who has publicly debated Dave Hunt on the legitimacy of Christian activism; Rev. Ice is a self-conscious pietist and a cultural retreatist who joined Hunt to debate Gary DeMar and me on this same question in 1988.

Since 1965

This post-1965 division within the dispensational camp – social activism vs. pietistic passivism – has called into question the academic theologians' strategy of silence. When dispensationalists become socially and politically active, many of them begin to search for a theological justification for their activism. They cannot find this in dispensationalism; it exists only in Christian Reconstructionism and liberation theology. But liberation theology is liberal or radical; also, the failure of Communism, 1989-91, has left it without much support anywhere, let alone in conservative dispensational circles. This is why activist dispensationalists have begun to adopt the conclusions and, sometimes, much of the theology of Christian Reconstruction. This is why academic dispensationalists need to reply to us in print: *we theonomists are picking off the best and the brightest of their followers*. Yet the leaders are afraid to challenge us, for a public attack on our theologically consistent social activism will make them appear to be exactly what they are, namely, theologically consistent defenders of the historical necessity of Christianity's cultural and political surrender to humanism.

I will put it as plainly as I can: this silence of the theologians has now become suicidal. It is the silence of sacrificial lambs. Silence in the face of humanism, silence in the face of Christian Reconstruction, silence in the face of both six-day creationism and Darwinism, silence in the face of public education, and above all, *silence in the face of legalized abortion*: this is not the strategy of a movement that expects to survive. It is the strategy of a movement that waits and prays constantly for a supernatural deliverance from the realities and limits of history. This deliverance never comes. Its delay has produced paralysis.

Conclusion

Dispensational theology leads to moral paralysis. Moral paralysis produces intellectual paralysis. Intellectual paralysis produces institutional paralysis. Institutional paralysis produces extinction through attrition. Dispensationalism is now at this final stage. We appear to be witnessing the birth of the terminal generation – not the terminal generation of the Church of Jesus Christ but of dispensationalism.

Give me an opportunity to prove my case. Keep reading.

FIND THE MISSING RAPTURE . . . .

Another parable put he forth unto them, saying, The kingdom of heaven is likened unto a man which sowed good seed in his field: But while men slept, his enemy came and sowed tares among the wheat, and went his way. But when the blade was sprung up, and brought forth fruit, then appeared the tares also. So the servants of the householder came and said unto him, Sir, didst not thou sow good seed in thy field? from whence then hath it tares? He said unto them, An enemy hath done this. The servants said unto him, **Wilt thou then that we go and gather them up?** But he said, Nay; lest while ye gather up the tares, ye root up also the wheat with them. **Let both grow together until the harvest:** and **in the time of harvest** I will say to the reapers, **Gather ye together first the tares,** and bind them in bundles to burn them: but gather the wheat into my barn (Matt. 13:24-30; emphasis added).

Then Jesus sent the multitude away, and went into the house: and his disciples came unto him, saying, Declare unto us the parable of the tares of the field. He answered and said unto them, He that soweth the good seed is the Son of man; **The field is the world**; the good seed are the children of the kingdom; but the tares are the children of the wicked one; The enemy that sowed them is the devil; **the harvest is the end of the world**; and the reapers are the angels. As therefore **the tares are gathered and burned in the fire; so shall it be in the end of this world**. The Son of man shall send forth his angels, and they shall gather out of his kingdom all things that offend, and them which do iniquity; And shall cast them into a furnace of fire: there shall be wailing and gnashing of teeth. Then shall the righteous shine forth as the sun in the kingdom of their Father. **Who hath ears to hear, let him hear** (Matt. 13:36-43; emphasis added).

INTRODUCTION

Ye are the salt of the earth: but if the salt have lost his savour, wherewith shall it be salted? it is thenceforth good for nothing, but to be cast out, and to be trodden under foot of men (Matt. 5:13).

In 1970, Hal Lindsey and ghostwriter C. C. Carlson wrote a book, *The Late Great Planet Earth*. It was eventually to sell over 35 million copies. It became the best-selling nonfiction book of the 1970's. Prior to the publication of this book, Lindsey had been known, if at all, only as a successful southern California college-age youth pastor in the UCLA area. After its publication, he became the premier international spokesman for dispensationalism.

This placed dispensationalism in a dilemma. Its best-known representative was not a theologian. He had to employ an assistant to write his books.[1] The basis of his reputation was a sensational paperback book that made a series of predictions regarding the nation of Israel and the imminent return of Christ in secret to pull Christians into heaven: the doctrine of the pre-tribulation Rapture. The book dealt with contemporary prophecy, not permanent theology. It made Lindsey a fortune. (If Lindsey is an honest man, C. C. Carlson made one, too.)

---

1. This is not inherently a bad idea. There is a division of labor in life (I Cor. 12). A lot of authors could dearly use an openly acknowledged ghost writer. But employing one has never been regarded as academically acceptable.

Lindsey and Carlson wrote two more prophecy books: *Satan Is Alive and Well on Planet Earth* (1972) and *The Terminal Generation* (1976). Two other books by Lindsey had only his name on the title page: *There's a New World Coming* (1973) and *The 1980's: Countdown to Armageddon* (1980). He set the pattern: huge royalty income through prophecy book sales. Throughout the 1970's and right up to the present, there have been many imitators. They continue to write sensational paperback prophecy books. Problem: the prophecies never come true.

The public silence of those who trained Lindsey at Dallas Seminary has testified for over two decades that they have voluntarily surrendered leadership to him, and are content to have it that way. In the case of Dallas Seminary's former president John Walvoord, who wrote *Armageddon, Oil and the Middle East Crisis* (1974; revised edition, 1990), he not only deferred to him, he imitated him. Lesson: "If one set of false prophecies doesn't come true, just re-package it and try again!"

This is the curse of Rapture fever. It is highly contagious.

Rapture Fever: The Inside Dope

Rapture fever is a deliberately induced psychological condition. The number of its victims has escalated rapidly since 1970. Millions of readers repeatedly inject themselves with what can best be described as a psychologically addicting drug: the expectation of the imminent return of Jesus Christ, which will remove them from their troubles by removing them from history. The results of this addiction are predictable: an initial "high," followed by a debilitating letdown, followed by painful withdrawal symptoms (mentally re-entering the hum-drum world), followed by another injection. Again and again, millions of emotionally vulnerable Christians return to their "pushers" for another "fix."

Yet there is hope. Some of them do "get clean." They say to themselves, "Never again!" They refuse to allow themselves to be subjected to another round of the fever. Of course, as with alcoholics and other addicts, a lot of well-meaning dispensationalists swear off the addictive prophetic substance, only to return to it again as soon as the next pusher shows up with a paperback book with a gleaming, multi-color cover. "Only $9.95. Be the first in your church to know the inside dope!" Everyone wants the inside dope; again and again, millions of them become the inside dopes.

Hal Lindsey is the most successful pusher in dispensationalism's comparatively brief history. He made a fortune and a reputation by selling inside dope. As part of his "prophecy poppers," Lindsey has written about the terminal generation. That is also an underlying theme in *Rapture Fever*. We are now witnessing the birth of dispensationalism's terminal generation. The torch being passed to it is burning very low. Over its tombstone should be placed these words: "Overdosed on Sensationalism."

A Brief History of Dispensationalism's Brief History

Dispensationalism was invented around 1830, either by 20-year-old Margaret Macdonald, who received a vision regarding the pre-tribulation Rapture while in a trance,[2] or by John Nelson Darby.[3] It escalated in popularity in the United States after the Civil War (1861-65), especially when William E. Blackstone (W.E.B.) wrote *Jesus Is Coming* in 1878. Prophecy conferences became the order of the day. Then came C. I. Scofield's immensely successful *Scofield Reference Bible* (1909). After the widely publicized embarrassment of the Scopes' "Monkey Trial" of 1925, Protestant evangelicals retreated into a kind of cultural shell. Dispensational theology was used to justify this withdrawal. The creation of the State of Israel in 1948 seemed to prove that the prophetic message of dispensationalism was on track:

---

2. Dave MacPherson, *The Unbelievable Pre-Trib Origin* (Kansas City, Missouri: Heart of America Bible Society, 1973).
3. This is the conventional view.

there was at long last a nation for the army of the invader from the North to surround. The post-Rapture Great Tribulation of the Jews now became geographically possible. During the Great Tribulation, according to dispensational theology, two-thirds of the world's Jews will surely perish.[4]

But a change in outlook began in 1976 with the nomination of Jimmy Carter as the Democratic Party's candidate for President. Initially, he seemed to many voters to be an evangelical. Bob Slosser, who later became Pat Robertson's ghost writer,[5] co-authored *The Miracle of Jimmy Carter* (1976), and Logos Books published it. When Carter's Presidency turned out to be just another humanist experiment in internationalism, just as conservatives and libertarians had predicted, the evangelicals did not retreat back into political isolation. The Reagan candidacy in 1980 galvanized them. Thus was born the Christian Right. Its premier manifestation was the Religious Roundtable's National Affairs Briefing Conference, held in Dallas in August, 1980, when thousands of Christians came to the Reunion Arena for three days of political education. (See Chapter 11.)

With the return of fundamentalists to politics came a quiet, almost embarrassed shelving of the doctrine of the Rapture. This doctrine had long served them as a theological justification for passivity. After all, if all of a man's good works and all of the church's efforts to reform this world will inevitably be smashed by the Antichrist during the seven-year Great Tribulation, then there is no earthly payoff. Conclusion: concentrate on passing out gospel tracts instead.

We have seen very few gospel tracts being passed out by North American Christians since the 1970's. The era of the gospel tract appears to be over. The gospel tract has been re-

---

4. John F. Walvoord, *Israel in Prophecy* (Grand Rapids, Michigan: Zondervan Academie, [1962] 1988), p. 108.

5. Pat Robertson (with Bob Slosser), *The Secret Kingdom* (Nashville: Nelson, 1982). Slosser later wrote (with Cynthia Ellenwood) *Changing the Way America Thinks* (Dallas: Word, 1989).

placed by the newsletter, the audio cassette tape, and the desktop-published magazine. Short little messages written on tiny tracts no longer suffice; it takes a great deal of copy to fill up a newsletter, let alone a magazine. You cannot fill a monthly magazine with 24 pages of brief "how to get saved" messages. The same is true of 24-hour a day cable or satellite television networks. *Technology has forced a change on American fundamentalism.* Technological change has produced a quiet but significant shift in fundamentalist tactics, and therefore fundamentalist theology. This theological shift lags behind the technological changes, but it is now becoming obvious to those who pay attention to what is being written and spoken in public, and also what is no longer written or spoken in public.

The Disappearance of Academic Leadership

In 1980, there were three major seminaries that taught dispensationalism: Talbot (La Mirada, California), Grace (Winona Lake, Indiana), and Dallas. By 1988, Talbot had quietly abandoned the older dispensationalism. In December, 1992, the president of Grace announced a restructuring of the seminary. Not one of the existing seven full-time faculty members will have their contracts renewed. The Th.D. and Th.M. programs will end. There will be a new mission for what little remains of the old seminary. The president wrote to Grace supporters:

> *Its mission is to: "develop Christian ministry leaders who can influence culture with an integrated biblical world and life view."*

Among the Big Three, only Dallas Seminary now remains in the fold. But it remains remarkably silent. Its faculty members no longer write detailed academic books that defend dispensationalism. Today, scholarly publications written by Dallas Seminary faculty members have almost no impact in the broad dispensational community. Charles Ryrie departed from the faculty in the early 1980's under a cloud. A few retired members of the faculty still occasionally update books that they wrote in their days of influence, but they no longer direct the seminary. Occasionally, one of them writes a non-scholarly paperback book, but little comes out of Dallas Seminary that can be regarded as both scholarly and dispensational. Thus, there is virtually no intellectual leadership in dispensationalism. There are only writers of sensational paperback prophecy books.

Dispensationalism's academic leaders are now on the defensive within the Christian community. (They have rarely been involved in confrontations with the non-Christian community, except over the question of biological and geological evolution, and then only after 1960.) This was not true in 1970 or earlier, but it is true today. *Because dispensationalism's academic leaders are on the defensive, dispensationalism is now experiencing a paradigm shift.* Within a generation, this paradigm shift could easily complete the demise of dispensationalism. Like Soviet Marxists, who were supremely confident of victory over the capitalist West in 1970, so the dispensationalists in 1970 were supremely confident in the failure of the gospel in the Church Age. They were supremely confident that the Rapture would ratify their prophecy of Christianity's inevitable historical defeat and therefore the prudence, and perhaps moral obligation, of cultural retreat by Christians. What happened to Soviet Marxism within a twenty-year period, 1970-1990, could also happen to dispensationalism. It depends on how rapidly the paradigm shift moves to the people in the pews.

What Is a Paradigm Shift?

In his important book, *The Structure of Scientific Revolutions* (1962),[6] historian of science Thomas Kuhn argued that a paradigm is an intellectual system which focuses an investigator's attention so that he can solve certain narrow problems. The investigator asks only certain questions and applies a narrowly

---

6. University of Chicago Press. Revised edition, 1970.

Introduction

circumscribed system of investigation to solve these problems. In other words, we are limited creatures. We cannot understand everything about everything, so we narrow our questions, our approaches, and the range of acceptable answers in our attempt to learn something accurate about anything.

A kind of academic guild imposes penalties on anyone who keeps asking questions that the guild's existing paradigm cannot readily solve. When younger members of the academic guild, or especially gifted outsiders, raise new questions that are increasingly embarrassing to the guild's leaders, a battle for control of the guild begins. The existing leaders have to provide believable, practical answers, or at least provide investigative strategies that may conceivably provide answers, to these embarrassing but pressing questions. If they cannot provide them, they will attempt to suppress anyone who asks them, and they will dismiss as unprofessional (i.e., heretical) or misguided those whom they cannot suppress.

When the guild's leaders can no longer persuade younger members of the guild that the received strategy of investigation – the paradigm – can adequately handle these new and important questions, a paradigm shift occurs. Rarely do the older members accept the new paradigm, but eventually they retire. As the older members retire, they are replaced by men who no longer share the faith in the old paradigm. Thus, the sign of a looming paradigm shift is the inability or unwillingness of the guild's leaders to address the new questions that younger members regard as crucial.

If the leaders find it institutionally impossible to suppress or ridicule those who pursue embarrassing questions, they adopt a fall-back strategy. This strategy is marked by the willingness of the guild's older leaders to accept (usually only in private correspondence) changes in the details of the paradigm that would never have been acceptable before. The leaders believe that they can defend the integrity of the overall paradigm by surrendering piecemeal on certain fronts. These lost fronts are then redefined by the leaders as peripheral. The reason why this strategy usually fails is that the paradigm is inevitably surrendered by a thousand qualifications and revisions. (See Chapter 7.)

The sign that the strategy of piecemeal surrender has been adopted by the leaders is the absence of any overall presentation of a "revised and updated" paradigm which incorporates all of the suggested new revisions while maintaining the coherence of the original system. The older textbooks are rarely cited in contemporary writings. They are allowed to go out of print, but nothing is offered to replace them. The original system has in fact been abandoned in everything except name. I contend in this book that this is where dispensationalism is in the early 1990's.

Pressures for a Paradigm Shift

A paradigm is a way of thinking, an approach to finding solutions to problems. For about a century, 1875-1975, the fundamentalist world's solution to problems was to withdraw from most problems outside of the narrow confines of the local church, the family, and personal ethics. Politics, education, literature, the arts, and culture in general were all dismissed as at best irrelevant to the Christian way of life and at worst a threat to spiritual growth. "Politics is inherently dirty" was the rallying cry, especially after 1925, and everything else was viewed as at least in need of a good scrubbing – in a ghetto community that was short of soap. Fundamentalists deliberately narrowed the definition of evangelism's Great Commission in order to reduce their perceived zones of personal and institutional responsibility.

This attitude of necessity required a broad transfer of authority to non-Christians, a step that made life easier for non-Christians. No longer would they face challenges from fundamentalists and pietists. They would be given increasingly free rein (or reign) to do what they wanted, and, best of all, do it with taxes extracted from Christians. *The major institutions of American humanism have been built with Christians' money.* The Christians never complained about this publicly until the late 1970's, when they finally began to perceive three things: (1) the growing failure of humanist institutions to "deliver the goods"; (2) the size of their own tax bills; and (3) the non-neutrality of humanism – humanism's war on the Christian faith.

Today, American fundamentalism is sharply divided. There are many who still hold the old theology and the old worldview – not in the Big Three seminaries, but in the pulpits and pews. Their solution is reminiscent of the tactic used by the wagon trains on the Great Plains in 1870: "Form a circle with the wagons!" They hope and pray for the imminent arrival of Calvary's cavalry: Captain Jesus and His angelic troops, trumpet blaring, who will carry them safely to their final destination – not California; heaven. The problem is, this psychological and institutional tactic is not a valid strategy, since nobody really wants to spend his whole life inside a circle of covered wagons, with a horde of howling savages – many of them with Ph.D. degrees from prestige universities – attacking the perimeter of the camp.

More and more of those who are trapped inside fundamentalism's tight little defensive circle are becoming fed up, both with the savages outside the camp and the leaders inside. They are becoming ready psychologically to take the war directly to the enemy. But they don't know how. They have not been trained to fight an offensive campaign. At best, they are specialists in defense. They have long been denied the weapons needed to conduct an offensive campaign, most notably *comprehensive, self-consciously biblical higher education*.

Questions that have long been dismissed as irrelevant for Christians to ask are now being asked by younger fundamentalists. The main question is the one that premillennial but non-dispensational Calvinist Francis Schaeffer asked in 1976: *How should we then live?* Schaeffer never offered an answer, but his question remains. As the humanist savages continue to shoot their flaming arrows into the highly flammable wagons of fundamentalism, it is becoming clear to a minority of those trapped inside that fundamentalism's traditional defensive tactic is no longer working. Captain Jesus has not visibly arrived. But those in leadership positions who steadfastly refuse to consider the alternative – an offensive breakout – have only one response: "Captain Jesus is coming soon! This time, He will! Trust us!"

This is Rapture fever. Rapture fever destroys the will to extend God's principles of justice and restoration beyond the narrow confines of a religious ghetto. Its public manifestation is a series of increasingly frantic appeals for everyone to believe that "history belongs to the savages, and there is not much history remaining." Its philosophy of history is simple to summarize: "All efforts of Christians to build a world that will increasingly reflect Christ's glory and righteousness are doomed in our dispensation." What is the proof? There is no proof. There is only an appeal: "Trust us!"

An increasing number of younger fundamentalists are saying to themselves, and occasionally to their peers: "Why should we trust them? They have been wrong about the imminent Rapture for over a century and a half. Why shouldn't Christians go on the offensive for a change? Why must we live out our lives inside this little circle, with both the wind and these savages howling in our ears until we die or get raptured, whichever comes first?" These questions demand answers. This is why a paradigm shift has begun, in evangelicalism in general and dispensationalism in particular.

Questions Producing Dispensationalism's Paradigm Shift

In the pews of fundamentalist churches, faithful, simple people still accept the broad outlines of the received dispensational paradigm, even though they are incapable of sitting down, Bible in hand, and explaining to a nondispensationalist the evidence for their belief, verse by verse. When they search for specific verses – a rare event in their lives – they get totally confused very fast. But they nevertheless cling to the received faith, just so long as they do not become active in politics or the battle against abortion or the battle against pornography. Just so long as they don't get involved in home schooling. Just so long as they refuse to commit time and money to the activities recommended by Phyllis Schafly's Eagle Forum or Beverly LaHaye's Concerned Women of America. In other words, *just so long as they remain content to lose every major battle in history*, they will continue to cling to the received dispensational faith. It comforts them. It reassures them that their personal commitment to do nothing to improve society is God's way of getting nothing done, since all that God plans for His people to accomplish in this dispensation is nothing.

So, I am not talking here about the loyal troops sitting in the pews, sitting at home, and above all, sitting on their checkbooks. I am talking about theological leaders. I am talking about a series of ideas and those academic institutions that are expected to deal with these ideas. I am operating on the assumption that ideas have consequences, that men become increasingly consistent with what they believe, and societies become increasingly consistent with what a majority of their members have become. I also believe that people do change their minds – sometimes lots of people. This is what evangelism is all about: offering people the opportunity to change their minds, and then, when they do change their minds, persuading them to live consistently with their new beliefs.

Here are a few questions that North American Christians have been asking themselves over the last two or three decades. Because of the one intellectual battle that a few fundamentalist spokesmen have entered into – the public defense of the six-day creation account found in Genesis 1 – some fundamentalists have been forced to begin considering some of these questions. These questions demand specific answers, but the search for these specific answers is steadily undermining the received dispensational paradigm. So are the *self-conscious evasions* by the few remaining academic theologians who are willing to defend traditional dispensationalism in print. These theologians have rarely been six-day creationists, especially those who have taught at Dallas Theological Seminary, which, following Scofield's notes, has never made the six-day creation a test of orthodoxy. (Scofield was a "gap" theologian: an indeterminate gap of time between Genesis 1:1 and 1:2. See Chapter 9.) Here are just a few of the questions that demand answers but which receive no responses in print from dispensationalists.

- Is evolution the religious faith which undergirds every humanist institution in today's world?
- Does the Bible teach evolution or creation?
- Should biblical creationism also have comparable effects in every human institution?
- What are these creationist alternatives to evolutionism in social thought?
- Where do we find information about them?
- Have dispensational creationists ever discussed these creationist social alternatives in detail?

- Is humanism religiously neutral?
- Is humanism morally neutral?
- Are the public schools religiously neutral?
- If they aren't, where do we find dispensational schools and especially colleges that provide comprehensive alternatives to humanism in every classroom?
- Is intellectual neutrality a myth?
- If intellectual neutrality is a myth, does the Bible provide real-world intellectual alternatives?

- Is sin comprehensive, affecting everything in history?
- Are all men completely responsible to God for every sin they commit?
- Is the gospel as comprehensive as sin?
- Is the healing power of the gospel as comprehensive as sin?

Introduction 13

• Are there biblical alternatives for sinful thoughts and practices in every area of life?
• If so, what are they, specifically?
• Where do we discover them, specifically?
• Who has taught in detail about these alternatives?
• Have any of these teachers been dispensationalists?
• Does the phrase "we're under grace, not law" apply to criminals? To policemen and civil judges? To lawyers?
• Is politics dirty?
• Could the gospel of Jesus Christ clean up politics?
• If most politicians were converted to saving faith in Jesus Christ today, what changes could we expect tomorrow? In a century? In a millennium?
• If the answer is "none," is Christianity politically irrelevant?
• If the answer is "many," where in the Bible should we look to discover the actual content of these specific changes?

• If Old Testament law is not valid in the New Testament era, where do we find New Testament legal standards for social ethics?
• What dispensational author has written a detailed study of New Testament law and social ethics?
• What dispensational institution teaches courses in New Testament social ethics?

• Is abortion a sin?
• Is abortion grounds for excommunication?
• Is abortion a crime?
• Where do we look in the Bible to find a law against abortion, other than Exodus 21:22-26?
• What public stand did the seminaries take in 1973 when *Roe v. Wade* was handed down? In 1983? In 1993?
• Should seminary professors actively preach against abortion in classes on ethics?
• Do dispensational seminaries provide classes on ethics?

• Is homosexuality a sin?
• Is homosexuality said to be a crime in the Bible?

- Where is it said to be a crime in the Bible?
- Should we regard the arrival of AIDS in 1981 as an "ethically random event," the way we regard chicken pox?
- Is bestiality a sin?
- Is bestiality said to be a crime in the Bible?
- Where is it said that bestiality is a crime in the Bible?

- If we cannot find New Testament legal standards, could dispensationalism be wrong about Old Testament law?
- Has dispensational theology become irrelevant?

These questions are never addressed in print by the older dispensational theologians. They are rarely addressed by the younger ones, since they fear losing their jobs. If they make a wrong answer – a wrong answer being one which clearly breaks with one of the official tenets of the dispensational system – they could be fired. Not at Talbot, of course. And there are no longer any full-time positions remaining at Grace. But at Dallas you could lose your job. So the wise faculty member at Dallas Seminary follows Solomon's advice: "A prudent man concealeth knowledge" (Prov. 12:23a). He keeps his mouth shut and his published work focused on some topic not inherently dispensational. So, dispensationalism today has no intellectual leaders.

Traditional dispensational textbooks and theological treatises are going out of print. The surviving professors who wrote them, now in their eighties, no longer write new ones. Neither do the younger men. In this sense, the theological leaders of dispensationalism have adopted a strategy of prudent deferral. Like those terrorized pilgrims cowering inside the perimeter of those forever-circled wagons, they pray that Captain Jesus will arrive before word gets out that dispensationalism is terminal.

Evidence of a Paradigm Shift

I have already discussed one of the main signs of the shift: the quiet, unpublicized demise of dispensationalism in the traditional dispensational seminaries. First, without institutions to train up the next generation of preachers in the received theology, there is little likelihood that the academically qualified Church leaders of the future will proclaim, or at least enthusiastically defend, the traditional dispensational system. Second, the faculties have cut off their own future. If they no longer are willing and able to invest the money required to train up their successors, then dispensational seminaries will soon completely lose their faculties, if they haven't already lost them. The demise of dispensationalism in the seminaries testifies to the accuracy of my prediction (not a prophecy): we are seeing the birth of dispensationalism's terminal generation.

There are other signs of the paradigm shift that is undermining traditional dispensationalism. I will list them here briefly. Understand, I am not talking about declining numbers of those who say they are dispensationalists. Not yet. I am talking about seemingly subtle shifts that have taken place within the dispensational camp, especially parachurch ministries, the ones in the front lines of confrontation with humanism.

- Those activists who still say they are dispensationalists no longer discuss the Rapture and its anti-motivational implications.
- They continually speak of the possibility of victory, especially in their fund-raising appeals.
- They recruit their followers into a long-term confrontation with humanism and rival religions.
- They speak about "the next generation" of Christian activists.
- They have adopted the phrase, "biblical principles" as a verbal cover for "Old Testament law."
- They have adopted the phrase, "Christian world and life view."
- They proclaim: "The Bible has answers for all of life's problems."
- Then they search the Old Testament to find answers for problems outside the local church and the family.

- They speak positively of "Christian America," or at least of "returning America to her Christian roots."
- They speak of the coming judgments of God against America unless there is national repentance, and then cite Old Testament passages governing Israel to prove their case.
- They speak of the possible blessings for national repentance and national obedience, and then cite Old Testament passages governing Israel to prove their case.
- They no longer proclaim the inherent fruitlessness of Christian social action.
- They rarely quote from the traditional textbooks and theological manuals of dispensationalism.
- They are rarely graduates of dispensational seminaries.
- When they are graduates of dispensational seminaries, they complain about the unwillingness of their former professors to get involved in their particular reform projects.
- They speak of the inherent weaknesses of secular humanism.
- They encourage some of their disciples to attend graduate school, to prepare them for social combat.
- They keep using the word "accountability."
- Some of them even use the word "covenant."
- They keep introducing their recommended social action programs with the phrase, "I am not a Christian Reconstructionist, but. . . ."

We see the leaders of Christian activist organizations adopting the time frame of postmillennialism and the social ethics of theonomy, but never in the name of either. We see official dispensationalists adopting strategies appropriate to Christian Reconstructionism. Yet almost no one wants to admit publicly what is going on. Those inside the organizations do not want to scare off existing members. Dispensationalist leaders outside – other than Dave Hunt – no longer want to appear to be what dispensationalists have always been in principle: pietistic defeatists. So, the paradigm shift is rarely self-conscious. But a paradigm shift is in progress. The new leaders refuse to proclaim their dependence on either traditional dispensationalism or

Christian Reconstruction. The dispensationalists of 1970 had no problem identifying their theology and its social implications. Today's dispensationalists do. *This is evidence of their quiet abandonment of traditional dispensationalism.*

Conclusion

First, I ask six very simple questions regarding the world's premier dispensational institution of theology, Dallas Theological Seminary: (1) What is Dallas Theological Seminary's position on abortion? (2) What is its position on the legitimacy of public education? (3) Where is its textbook on New Testament social ethics? (4) Where is its systematic theology? (5) Why did the seminary in 1988 refuse to republish Lewis Sperry Chafer's *Systematic Theology* (1948)? (6) Why has no one on the faculty written a point-by-point refutation of O. T. Allis' *Prophecy and the Church*? (I omit Charles Ryrie, whose attempted refutation in *Dispensationalism Today* in 1965 was both partial and brief, and who subsequently disappeared from the faculty.)

Second, I ask five questions regarding dispensationalism in general: (1) Where is a dispensational, Ph.D. degree-granting university (other than family-operated Bob Jones University)? (2) Where is a dispensational college whose faculty members in every department place the Bible as the foundation and final court of appeal for the actual content of their courses? (3) Where are college-level textbooks that present a dispensational view of philosophy, education, psychology, economics, civil government, architecture, the arts, mathematics, biology, geology, and paleontology? (4) Where is a non-charismatic dispensational law school? Medical school? (5) Why have charismatic dispensationalists dominated cable television rather than traditional dispensationalists?

Here is my main question: Is the absence of dispensational leadership in every area of life related to dispensationalism's theology? I think it is. Some readers may not. What other explanation makes sense except the theology of dispensationalism

– its view of God, man, law, and time? In short, is the absence of dispensational intellectual positions related to Rapture fever?

Here is a very practical question: Has Rapture fever played itself out among those fundamentalist leaders who seem most likely to command the allegiance of a majority of the next generation of fundamentalists? If the answer is *yes* – as I think it is – then this new leadership will soon inherit the dispensational movement by creating something entirely new, although the leaders probably will not call it anything different for several years. This replacement process is already going on. A new generation of leaders will replace traditional dispensationalists who proclaim inevitable defeat in history and then do nothing in order to achieve it.

Traditional dispensationalists believe that until things get really terrible, the Rapture will not occur; therefore, they conclude, "Let us rejoice in the inevitable decline of the once-Christian West. If we can speed up the process of decline by doing nothing, let us do nothing with conviction." But what is their earthly future, according to their own belief? *Disinheritance in history by God*. This is completely just on God's part, for they proclaim a theology of God's historical disinheritance of His Son's church. They receive exactly what they expect: *historical defeat*. Theirs is a self-fulfilling prophecy.

Today, are witnessing dispensationalism's terminal generation: all those self-conscious, culturally isolated people who, as a matter of principle, choose not to play a significant role in the wave of the future – Christianity's technological, intellectual, and moral future. Hal Lindsey is the prophet of this terminal generation. This does not bode well for dispensationalism.

1

ENDLESS UNFULFILLED PROPHECIES PRODUCE PARALYSIS

When a prophet speaketh in the name of the LORD, if the thing follow not, nor come to pass, that is the thing which the LORD hath not spoken, but the prophet hath spoken it presumptuously: thou shalt not be afraid of him (Deut. 18:22).

During the 1970's, when The Late Great Planet Earth *was outselling everything, the rapture was the hot topic. Pastors preached about heaven, and Christians eagerly anticipated being taken up at any moment to meet their Lord in the air. When Christ didn't return after 40 years since the establishment of a new Israel in 1948 without the fulfillment of prophesied events, disillusionment began to set in.*[1]

In 1977, a book written by premillennial historian Dwight Wilson appeared: *Armageddon Now!: The Premillennial Response to Russia and Israel Since 1917.*[2] This book recorded the teachings of hundreds of books and pamphlets regarding the Antichrist, the Beast, and similar prophetic themes in the Bible, all of which had been applied to current events – unsuccessfully, as it

---

1. Back cover copy, Dave Hunt, *Whatever Happened to Heaven?* (Eugene, Oregon: Harvest House, 1988).
2. Reprinted in 1991 by the Institute for Christian Economics.

turned out – by premillennial, dispensational authors. The book received guarded praise from the dean of dispensational scholars, John F. Walvoord, who for three decades served as the president of Dallas Theological Seminary. He said modern dispensationalists can "learn from it many important lessons applicable to interpretation today."[3] But one dispensational scholar failed to learn a single lesson from Wilson's book: John F. Walvoord.

As a U.S. war with Iraq loomed in late 1990, Walvoord revised his 1974 book, *Armageddon, Oil and the Middle East Crisis*, and it sold over a million and a half copies – a million by February, 1991.[4] It did so by rejecting Dr. Wilson's warning: do not use sensational interpretations of Bible prophecy in order to sell books. If you do, he warned, you will look like a charlatan in retrospect, and you will also injure the reputation of Christ and His Church. But the tremendous lure of sensationalism's benefits – book royalties and fame – was too great for Dr. Walvoord. A dispensational feeding frenzy for prophecy books was in full force as war loomed in the Middle East in the second half of 1990. Dr. Walvoord decided to feed this frenzy.

It was at that point that Walvoord publicly rejected his earlier belief in the "any-moment Rapture" doctrine. This was proof that he had abandoned traditional scholarly dispensationalism and had adopted the pop-dispensationalism of Hal Lindsey, Dave Hunt, and Constance Cumbey – what I like to call *dispensensationalism*. (Most of his colleagues at Dallas Theological Seminary remained, as usual, discreetly silent. They know exactly how their bread is buttered: by donations from laymen who are thoroughly addicted to sensational prophecies.)

The leaders of American dispensationalism have not resisted the lure of huge book royalties and a few moments in the pub-

---

3. J. F. Walvoord, "Review of *Armageddon Now!*," *Bibliotheca Sacra* (April/June 1981), p. 178.

4. *Time* (Feb. 11, 1991).

lic spotlight which the doctrine of "today's ticking clock of prophecy" offers to them. In an interview in the national newspaper, *USA Today* (Jan. 19, 1991), three days after the U.S. attacked Iraq, a theologically well-informed reporter asked Dr. Walvoord: "So the prophetic clock is ticking?" Walvoord answered emphatically, "Yes." He had begun the interview with this assertion: "Bible prophecy is being fulfilled every day." This was an about-face of astounding proportions on his part. He threw out a lifetime of scholarship for a moment of fame. He sold his theological birthright for a pot of message – a sensational message that sells newspapers and paperback books. He sold out orthodox dispensationalism in general and what little remains of orthodox dispensationalism at Dallas Theological Seminary.[5] He bought pop-dispensationalism's ticking clock.

Orthodox Dispensationalism's Silent Clock of Prophecy

The doctrine of the clock of prophecy is central to dispensational theology. This idea rests on dispensationalism's interpretation of the 69th week of Daniel (Dan. 9:24-27). Walvoord wrote in 1979 that "The interpretation of Daniel 9:24-27 is of major importance to premillennialism as well as pretribulationism."[6] Why should this be the case?

Dispensationalism hypothesizes a gap of an indeterminate period of time after the fulfillment of the prophecies of the 69th week at the crucifixion of Christ and the (supposedly) as-yet unfulfilled prophecies, which they say will be fulfilled during the 70th week, which they define as the Great Tribulation era which begins after the Rapture, i.e., after the Christians are removed from the earth and pulled secretly into heaven by

---

5. The revised curriculum at Dallas, introduced in the fall of 1991, indicates how little of that tradition remains.

6. John F. Walvoord, *The Rapture Question*, revised and enlarged edition (Grand Rapids, Michigan: Zondervan, 1979), p. 25.

Jesus. As Walvoord insisted, "a parenthesis of time involving the whole present age is indicated."[7] That is to say, *from the crucifixion of Christ to the Rapture, the clock of prophecy cannot tick, let alone tock.* This means that not a single Bible prophecy can be fulfilled during this gap, which dispensationalists call "the parenthesis" and the "Church Age." (Non-dispensational theology insists that the entire New Testament period is the Church's age. The doctrine of the Church Age is one of the central pillars of dispensational principles of Bible interpretation – perhaps the central pillar. If some blind "Samson" inside dispensationalism's temple ever puts his hands on this pillar and pushes it down, that will end dispensationalism.)

What no paperback dispensationalist prophecy book of the *This Time, Armageddon Really Is Near!* variety ever discusses is that orthodox dispensationalism officially affirms a non-ticking clock in this, the so-called Church Age. If the clock of Old Testament prophecy begins ticking again in the Church Age (pre-Rapture), then there has to be *judicial continuity* between Old Testament Israel and the New Testament Church. Specific judgments of God in history, announced by the prophets of Israel, would have to be fulfilled in the era of the Church.

What does Hal Lindsey teach? He writes in *The Late Great Planet Earth*: "The astonishing thing to those of us who have studied the prophetic Scriptures is that we are watching the fulfillment of these prophecies in our time. Some of the future events that were predicted hundreds of years ago read like today's newspaper."[8] This is "newspaper exegesis." Psychologically, this is the heart of "pop-dispensationalism." This is the heart of Rapture fever.

Theologically, it is the denial of orthodox dispensationalism. Such a view of fulfilled prophecy undermines the original the-

---

7. *Ibid.*, p. 26.

8. Hal Lindsey (with C. C. Carlson), *The Late Great Planet Earth* (Grand Rapids, Michigan: Zondervan, 1970), p. 20. I am quoting from the 35th printing, November 1973.

ology of dispensationalism, which stresses the Church as a "Great Parenthesis" which was neither known nor prophesied about in the Old Testament. The New Testament Church (pre-Rapture) supposedly has no connection whatsoever with the dispensation of the Mosaic law. Therefore, if the prophecies of the Old Testament apply to the Church in any sense rather than exclusively to national Israel, the entire dispensational system collapses.

C. I. Scofield understood this clearly. Dispensationally speaking, there can be no biblically prophesied event in between the founding of the Church and the Rapture. Citing Matthew 4:17b, "Repent: for the kingdom of heaven is at hand," Scofield wrote: "'At hand' is never a positive affirmation that the person or thing said to be 'at hand' will immediately appear, but only that no known or predicted event must intervene."[9] Therefore, the Rapture can take place *at any moment*. But if this is true, then its corollary is also necessarily true: the Rapture cannot be said to be *imminent for our generation*. It may be, but it may not be. An orthodox dispensationalist cannot legitimately say when it will be, one way or the other. The Rapture cannot legitimately be said to be *almost inevitable* tomorrow, next month, or next year. Edgar Whisenant's 88 reasons for the Rapture in September, 1988, were wrong – all 88 of them.[10] So were his (revised) 89 reasons for 1989.[11] (As Stayskill put in a cartoon, how many will reasons will he offer in the year 2000?) Yet the mass appeal of the system is its near-term date-setting.

---

9. *Scofield Reference Bible* (New York: Oxford University Press, 1909), p. 998, note 3.

10. Edgar C. Whisenant, *88 Reasons Why the Rapture Will Be in 1988*. It was also published as *The Rosh Hash Ana 1988 and 88 Reasons Why* (1988). The name is pronounced "WHIZnant."

11. A 1989 Associated Press story reported on Whisenant's revised predictions. The Rapture was due in September, 1989. He published *The Final Shout: Rapture Report – 1989*. "The time is short," he said. "Everything points to it. All the evidence has piled up." *Tyler Morning Telegraph* (Aug. 25, 1989). Something had indeed piled up, but it was not evidence.

Walvoord's Warning in 1979

It was this traditional dispensational doctrine of *no intervening prophesied events* that Walvoord emphatically taught his students in the 1970's.[12] In Walvoord's book, *The Rapture Question* (1979), he openly rejected the "ticking today" interpretation of Bible prophecy, and for a very good theological reason: it denies the traditional dispensational doctrine of the any-moment Rapture. If any prophecies are being fulfilled today, he wrote, this would mean that there are events in the Church Age that must come true prior to the Rapture. Therefore, the Rapture could not come at any moment prior to the fulfillment of these prophecies. Such a view of "signs being fulfilled in our day" denies the doctrine of the any-moment Rapture.

Walvoord saw clearly in 1979 that the doctrine of intermediate prophetic events leads to mid-tribulationism or post-tribulationism, or even worse, to postmillennialism. In a subsection, "No Intervening Events," in a chapter called "The Imminency of the Rapture," Walvoord wrote: "The hope of the return of Christ to take the saints to heaven is presented in John 14 as an imminent hope. There is no teaching of any intervening event. The prospect of being taken to heaven at the coming of Christ is not qualified by description of any signs or prerequisite events."[13] This is the heart of the formal theology of pre-tribulational, premillennial dispensationalism: *no ticking clock*.

Nevertheless, there is a major problem with the doctrine of the any-moment Rapture: it reduces sales of books that promote the idea that Bible prophecy is being fulfilled today. These "hot news, ticking clock" paperback prophecy books sell well, sometimes very well. No dispensational author who writes one of these popular books – and these days, those who write them become the movement's spokesmen – is ever willing to devote the Introduction or the first chapter of his book to a

---

12. I was told this by a DTS graduate, Dr. Ray R. Sutton.
13. Walvoord, *Rapture Question*, p. 73.

theological discussion of why the events of his day cannot possibly be fulfillments of Bible prophecy if orthodox dispensational eschatology is correct. At most, they are shadows of things to come. But such a discussion would kill the excitement of the reader in hearing "the latest dope" about fulfilled prophecy. Scholarly books on eschatology do not become best-sellers.

Oswald T. Allis, a postmillennial critic of dispensationalism, commented in 1945 on this schizophrenic aspect of dispensational authors: "One of the clearest indications that Dispensationalists do not believe that the rapture is really 'without a sign, without a time note, and unrelated to other prophetic events' [he cited Scofield, *What Do the Prophets Say?*, p. 97] is the fact that they cannot write a book on prophecy without devoting a considerable amount of space to 'signs' that this event must be very near at hand. . . . This is of course quite incompatible with their any moment doctrine."[14] In late 1990 and early 1991, a huge increase in the sales of "ticking clock" dispensational prophecy books once again proved him correct on this point.[15] The addiction continues. It also debilitates.

A Publishing Coup in the First Half of 1991

In 1974, the year following the beginning of the oil crisis, Dr. Walvoord wrote one of these paperback potboilers, *Armageddon, Oil and the Middle East Crisis*. Eventually, it went out of print. In late 1990, it was resurrected from the dead.[16] The headlines about the imminent war in Kuwait were too powerful

---

14. Oswald T. Allis, *Prophecy and the Church* (Philadelphia: Presbyterian & Reformed, 1945), pp. 174, 175.
15. Scott Baradell, "Prophets of Doom: We're a leg up on Armageddon," *Dallas Times Herald* (Sept. 8, 1990); Edwin McDowell, "World Is Shaken, and Some Booksellers Rejoice," *New York Times* (Oct. 22, 1990); "Prophecy Books Become Big Sellers," *Christianity Today* (March 11, 1991); Nancy Kruh, "The End," *Dallas Morning News* (Feb. 17, 1991).
16. I like to think of this as Dr. Walvoord's "Lazarus" book. Paraphrasing Martha's comment to Jesus: "But after 16 years in the tomb, it stinketh!"

a temptation. They offered him a unique opportunity to revive his career at age 80. Since the first version of the book had not cost him his academic reputation within dispensational circles (he had none outside these circles), there seemed to be no reason not to try to cash in again. Feeding frenzies must be fed, after all. Apparently, publishing highly specific interpretations of Bible prophecy – interpretations that are disproved within a year or two, and possibly six months – has something important to do with spreading the gospel. So, Dr. Walvoord allowed Zondervan to republish this revised 1974 potboiler, and it sold (as of late August, 1991) 1,676,886 copies.[17] The theological cost of this publishing *coup* was high: Walvoord's explicit abandonment of the "any moment Rapture" doctrine of traditional dispensational eschatology. Yet in the July/September 1990 issue of *Bibliotheca Sacra*, Walvoord had dismissed Gentry's statement in *House Divided* that dispensationalists are date-setters: "[V]ery few of its adherents indulge in this procedure."

To complete Walvoord's move to dispensensationalism, his publisher announced his latest book, *Major Bible Prophecies: 37 Crucial Prophecies That Affect You Today*, in August, 1991. The timing, as we shall see, was perfect . . . for anti-dispensational critics of the system.

If John Walvoord, who at age 80 was the last of the old-line dispensational theologians, could not resist the siren call of sensationalism in his own "last days," then what dispensationalist can? As Dr. Wilson proves, not many dispensational authors have resisted it since 1917. Dispensationalists have been visibly addicted to sensationalism. It is an addiction that is not easily broken. The "highs" that sensationalism briefly provides during any Middle Eastern crisis are just too alluring. Gary DeMar identifies this devastating addiction as "last days mad-

---

17. Press Release, "Kudos," Zondervan Publishing House (August, 1991). This figure may not include returned copies which ought to be quite high, given what happened in the USSR in August.

Endless Unfulfilled Prophecies Produce Paralysis 27

ness."[18] The addicts never remember their last round of withdrawal pain, when their confident expectations of imminent deliverance once again failed to come true. Dr. Wilson's book, *Armageddon Now*, is an attempt to remind them of those many failed prophecies. It offers them an example of academic integrity, as well as a helping hand psychologically. Addicts of prophecy sensationalism need both: integrity and psychological help.

A Soviet Coup in the Second Half of 1991

In early 1991, Walvoord told the world that the biblical clock of prophecy was ticking. He was wrong. It was not the clock of prophecy that he heard ticking; it was a time bomb for popular dispensationalism. It exploded on August 21, 1991: the defeat of the Communist *coup* in the Soviet Union, unquestionably the most startling three-day geopolitical reversal of the twentieth century.

When the *coup* began on August 19, geopolitical affairs still looked as though dispensensational prophecy books could conceivably be salvaged. But when this *coup* failed, it ended any immediate or even intermediate threat to the State of Israel from Russia ("Magog"). The Soviet Union has disintegrated. The republics declared their independence. During the *coup*, the Soviet KGB[19] and the Red Army's military masters could not even control downtown Moscow, let alone invade the State of Israel. Today, whatever military resources Russia has at its disposal must be reserved for a possible civil war. Unless the

---

18. Gary DeMar, *Last Days Madness* (rev. ed.; Atlanta, Georgia: American Vision, 1993).
19. The Soviet KGB must be distinguished from the Russian KGB, which was at odds with the Soviet wing. I have been informed that the opposition of the Russian KGB is what saved Yeltsin's life. The head of the Russian KGB gave an ultimatum to the *coup*'s leaders on Monday morning: if Yeltsin dies, there will be immediate consequences. Since he was the General in command of the air force bases surrounding Moscow, he had the clout to enforce this ultimatum. This is all hearsay, but it is worth pursuing by some historian.

State of Israel should, for some suicidal reason, attack Russia, there is not going to be a Russian-Israeli war. (See Chapter 12.)

The failed *coup* placed a tombstone on top of a huge pile of utterly inaccurate prophecies made by the leaders of popular dispensationalism, a pile of errors that had been growing since 1917. (Actually, long before: John Cumming's book, *The End: Or, The Proximate Signs of the Close of This Dispensation*, published in 1855, is evidence. Lecture 7 was: "The Russian and Northern Confederacy.") This tombstone's inscription reads: "Died of a Self-Inflicted Wound: Sensationalism." While a dispensational theologian today might conceivably be able to speculate about a Russian invasion of the State of Israel a century from now, or a millennium from now, the fact remains that the basis of the popularity of paperback dispensational books on prophecy (there have been no hardbacks) has always been the doctrine of the imminent Rapture. The Rapture is just around the corner, the faithful have been told, because Russia is building up its military machine, and the State of Israel is simply sitting there. Defenseless. Waiting to be surrounded by Russia. Now what?

Today, Russia is being surrounded: by seceding republics. What possible incentive does a military confrontation with the State of Israel offer anti-Communist Russian leaders today, now that expansionist Soviet Communism is deader than a doornail? Even if a military autocracy takes over in what is now the Russian republic, what threat would this pose to the State of Israel? What would be the incentive for a military junta to engage in a distant military confrontation with Israel and the United States? What would be the payoff? The Soviets in 1990 and 1991 used Jewish emigration to the State of Israel as a pressure-release valve. Why would any military junta want to close off this valve? Why would a junta want to create Jewish resentment within Russia and worldwide opposition against Russia?

Three and a half years before Russia surrounds the State of Israel, dispensational laymen have been publicly assured for over seven decades, the Rapture will pull all Christians out of their miserable, culturally impotent, present condition – the wretched of the earth. They will meet Jesus secretly in the sky. But if Russia is not in a position to invade the State of Israel, then the Rapture cannot be imminent. In short: *no imminent Russian invasion, no imminent Rapture.* Put another way, to the extent that a dispensationalist is longing for the Rapture, he is longing for Russia to invade the State of Israel. He longs for the beginning of the Great Tribulation of Israel in which, according to Walvoord, two-thirds of the nation of Israel's population will perish.[20] Because this dispensationally inevitable holocaust will begin 3.5 years after the Rapture, he longs for the Rapture. An imminent Rapture, if it is sufficiently imminent, means that he will not have to die, even though millions of Jews will. But now this "blessed hope" is gone for our generation; the invasion by Russia has been postponed indefinitely. This means that *the Rapture has been postponed indefinitely*.

The Rapture Has Been Postponed Indefinitely

This, I believe, is a logical, theological, but utterly unacceptable conclusion for most dispensationalists. It is too hard a pill for them to swallow. They will either identify a new potential invader of the State of Israel or else abandon dispensensationalism completely. If most of the movement's leaders take the former course, as is likely, they will have to act very fast. They must quickly locate a potential invader that can and will bring a gigantic army of millions of men against tiny Israel. They will also have to agree with each other if they are to maintain their contention that Bible prophecies about the Great Tribulation and Armageddon are: (1) future, (2) literal, and (3) clear.

Will it be Iraq? After what the United States did to Iraq? This seems highly improbable. Then who? What nation is large enough, mobile enough, and determined enough to invade the

---

20. John F. Walvoord, *Israel in Prophecy* (Grand Rapids, Michigan: Zondervan Academie, [1962] 1988), p. 108.

State of Israel? Arab nations, perhaps, but do they constitute the long-predicted unified army of invasion? Arabs? Unified? Will they launch a massive attack without meeting nuclear resistance from the Israelis? Without the resistance of the industrialized West? Does anyone seriously believe that the combined military forces of the United States and the State of Israel will be helpless to defeat a military alliance of Arabs anytime soon?[21] Any dispensensationalist who offers this scenario will have a lot of trouble persuading his followers. Conclusion: *Rapture postponed indefinitely*.

Of course, there is always the "New Europe." This seems to be an obvious initial choice. But there are problems with this thesis. First, there are more than ten nations in the New Europe, but there were presumably only ten toes on the Nebuchadnezzar's dream image (Dan. 2:34).[22] Second, the New Europe is as yet only a humanistic dream, not a political reality. In any case, the New Europe would have to employ NATO troops against the State of Israel, and the United States is a member of NATO. This raises a major question: Are American writers of sensational dispensational prophecy books prepared to identify the United States of America as the prophesied co-persecutor of tiny Israel? Are they going to say, as Pogo Possum said, "We have met the enemy, and he is us"? This is pop-dispensationalism's dilemma today. Such a view of prophecy would force upon all morally responsible dispensationalists a new and uncomfortable political assignment: civil disobedience. It would challenge the legitimacy of any pro-American patriotism among dispensationalists. (Can you imagine the church

---

21. George Otis, Jr., *The Last of the Giants* (Old Tappan, New Jersey: Revell, 1991) makes the case that the USSR will break up, and Islam will become the major force in the region. He has abandoned the traditional "the North vs. Israel" scenario. The thesis makes more sense than any standard pop-dispensational theory, but the question now is timing: When will the Arabs be able to destroy the State of Israel? When will they be able to assemble the long-predicted army of millions of invaders?

22. The marginal note in the *Scofield Reference Bible* (p. 901) refers us to Daniel 7:24: ten horns and ten kings.

splits that this would cause?) At the very least, this interpretation of prophecy would force American dispensationalists to demand our abandonment of NATO and the creation of a new, anti-European U.S. foreign policy. Is this likely? Hardly. Conclusion: *Rapture postponed indefinitely.*

Wanted: New Scenarios

Perhaps we will see a dispensational scenario like this one. There will be a civil war in Russia. Or maybe there won't be. The "New Russia" will join the "New Europe." Or maybe it won't. But the important thing is that the Rapture will take place in the year 2000. Then the surviving Russians will join with the U.S. and the U.N. to invade the nation of Israel. The Great Tribulation will begin. This is all inevitable – either one scenario or another. There is nothing a Christian can do to stop it. There is nothing a Christian *should* do to stop it. If the technological or geopolitical possibility of the invasion of national Israel is postponed indefinitely, then the Rapture is also postponed indefinitely, and *nothing must be allowed to postpone the Rapture indefinitely, especially current events.* Nothing – not failed prophecies, not implausible scenarios, not the defeat of Iraq, not the failed *coup* in Russia, and surely not the necessary rejection of orthodox dispensational theology – will be tolerated if it postpones the Rapture. *The clock of prophecy must be allowed to keep ticking.* Signs must testify to the imminent Rapture. Sensationalism must be sustained. Christians' present-day cultural irresponsibility must be defended. There is just too little time remaining to change anything for the better. In short, *Rapture fever is good for the soul!* (It is great for book royalties, too.)

How could such scenarios as these be rewritten and widely sold? Is it psychologically acceptable to millions of dispensationalists to abandon, almost overnight, over 75 years of supposedly certain interpretations of prophecy that have identified Russia as the invader of the State of Israel? If so, then how seriously should anyone take any future "certain" identifications? More to the point, how long will vulnerable premillennial Christians allow themselves to be subjected to the fires of eschatological sensationalism – prophecies that never come true? How many best-selling, "ticking clock," paperback prophecy books will they buy before they catch on to what is being done to them?

The dispensational world deliberately ignored Dr. Wilson's superb chronicling in 1977 of the wildly false predictions about Russia and the State of Israel that began after the October Revolution of 1917. Can today's dispensationalists also ignore the obvious implications of the failed *coup* of August 19-21, 1991? How? Will they argue that the millions of Bibles shipped to the Soviet Union after 1985 had no impact? That God does not honor in history those who honor His written word? If dispensationalists argue this way, what does this say about their view of God?

Wanted: Revised Editions

Dozens of paperback prophecy books were published in the U.S. from 1981 to 1991. None of the pre-1989 books forecasted the fall of the Berlin Wall in 1989; none of the 1990 and 1991 books forecasted the failed Soviet *coup* of 1991. Were these two events relevant prophetically? If the answer is "yes," the paperback prophets should have foreseen both events. If the answer is "no," why were Communism and Russia said for decades to be relevant prophetically? These "experts" never foresee accurately. *They bury their previous prophecies in unmarked graves.*

Usually, these authors do not bother to revise their books. They just publish new books. Revisions are just too embarrassing. Think of Grant Jeffrey's book, *Armageddon: Appointment With Destiny* (1988), published by an obscure press in Ontario, Canada, which proclaimed "144,000 in print" just before the book was picked up by Hal Lindsey's secular publisher, Bantam Books (located at **666** Fifth Avenue, New York City). Section 3 of Mr. Jeffrey's book is titled, "Russia's Appointment With God." Chapter 7 is "Russia's Day of Destruction on the Moun-

Endless Unfulfilled Prophecies Produce Paralysis 33

tains of Israel." This was followed in 1991 by Mr. Jeffries' *Messiah: War in the Middle East & the Road to Armageddon*. It included such "hot off the press" chapters as these: "Russia's Appointment With Destiny" and "The Rise of Babylon, The War in the Gulf." He warned his readers: "Watch for Iraq to recover and return to the project of rebuilding mighty Babylon" (p. 109). This is the dispensationalist's equivalent of a never-ending, thrill-packed serial called, "The Perils of Paulene Eschatology," which always ends: "Continued Next Book!" Fundamentalists just cannot seem to get enough of these books: the literary equivalents to romance novels. The addiction never ends.

Failed visions require extensive revisions. Let me list a few of what I call the "harvest" of soon-to-be-revised books:

Dave Hunt, *Global Peace and the Rise of Antichrist* (Harvest House, 1990)

E. Davidson, *Islam Israel and the Last Days* (Harvest House, 1991)

Jerry Johnson, *The Last Days on Planet Earth* (Harvest House, 1991)

Peter Lalonde, *One World Under Anti-Christ* (Harvest House, 1991)

Chuck Smith, *The Final Curtain* (Harvest House, 1991)

To this list we can add:

Thomas S. McCall and Zola Levitt, *The Coming Russian Invasion of Israel, Updated* (Moody Press, 1987)

Robert W. Faid, *Gorbachev! Has the Real Antichrist Come?* (Victory House, 1988)

Erwin W. Lutzer, *Coming to Grips with the Role of Europe in Prophecy* (Moody Press, 1990)

Gary D. Blevins, *The Final Warning!* (Vision of the End Ministries, 1990)

Paul McGuire, *Who Will Rule the Future? A Resistance to the New World Order* (Huntington House, 1991)

Edgar C. James, *Armageddon and the New World Order* (Moody Press, 1991)

Ed Hindson, *End Times, the Middle East and the New World Order* (Victor Books, 1991)

Who are these people? Have they devoted their lives to careful biblical scholarship? Where are the scholars of dispensationalism in this discussion of Bible prophecy? Where is the head of the department of Old Testament at Dallas Theological Seminary, for example? Or the department of New Testament at Talbot Theological Seminary? Or any department at Grace Theological Seminary? The trained Bible scholars of dispensationalism are all conspicuously silent. They do not comment on these paperback potboilers, either pro or con. But they refuse to provide scholarly support. This is the significant fact. The only academic figures among the camp of the dispensensationalists are John Walvoord, who abandoned all pretence of scholarship when he wrote his potboiler and then gave his interview to *USA Today*, and his Dallas colleague Charles Dyer. Dyer's book, *The Rise of Babylon: Sign of the End Time* (1991), offered the thesis that Iraq's Saddam Hussein was literally rebuilding the prophesied Babylon. The book appeared in January, 1991, a few days before its tenuous thesis was blown to bits during the 30-day air war against Iraq that began on the night of January 16. That war left unmarked graves in Dallas, not just Kuwait.

This spirit of eschatological immediacy has deeply damaged the American evangelical Church, especially the premillennial, fundamentalist wing, which has been swept again and again by waves of expectations regarding Christ's imminent return to "rapture" His people to heaven. What happened after August 2, 1990, with the invasion of Kuwait by Iraq, is simply the latest example of this phenomenon. The Christian bookstores of America were filled with books on prophecy, including the reprint of John Walvoord's. Decades of false predictions about the imminent return of Christ to "rapture" His saints have made no visible impression on the vast majority of the victims. Few of the victims learn from experience. They keep getting misled, both by charlatans and by well-meaning promoters who honestly believe that they have uncovered some neglected key to Bible prophecy. In the case of John Walvoord, he merely picked up a rusting prophetic key that he had discarded years earlier, shined it up, and sent it to his publisher. It sold like hotcakes. Briefly.

But the Church is still here, isn't it? So is the State of Israel. But Soviet Communism isn't. Who, then, is "Magog"?

Should We Evangelize Jews in Israel?

If the Jews of Israel were ever converted to saving faith in Jesus Christ, there could be no Rapture. There could be no Rapture because there would be no Jews in Israel to surround. There could be no Great Tribulation following the Rapture, since all the former Jews would go to heaven at the Rapture. But dispensationalists want the Rapture to deliver them from all of their earthly responsibilities. Thus, they have taken this view of evangelism: "Let's not bring the gospel to the Israelis, thus insuring that two-thirds of them will be killed during the Great Tribulation and roast in hell eternally." This view of evangelism is hidden behind a lot of rhetoric about concern for the State of Israel. There is indeed concern: *to have millions of Israelis die horrible deaths and spend eternity in the lake of fire for the sake of the pre-tribulation Rapture.* This is why dispensationalists refuse to send missionaries to Israel to evangelize Jews.

The preservation of the State of Israel is basic to the eschatology of the pre-tribulational dispensationalist. Why? So that the Antichrist will be able to wipe out two-thirds of Israel's population after the Rapture of the Church and during the Great Tribulation.[23] *The Jews of the State of Israel are to serve as*

---

23. This scenario of slaughter is found in former Dallas Seminary president John Walvoord's book, *Israel in Prophecy* (Grand Rapids, Michigan: Zondervan Academie,

God's cannon fodder in the inevitable war of Armageddon. Without the Jews' service as future sitting ducks, pre-tribulational dispensationalists would lose all faith in the imminent Rapture. The Antichrist would have no ducks in a barrel if there were no barrel. *The State of Israel is the Antichrist's barrel.* The leaders of dispensationalism do not say in public that this is what their support for Israel is all about, but it is.[24] Based on Zechariah 13:8-9, among other passages, dispensationalists conclude that two-thirds of the Jews are doomed. This is standard teaching from the dispensational pulpits.[25]

Dispensational fundamentalism's support for the State of Israel is governed by this unique presupposition: "No national Israel, no Armageddon; no Armageddon, no imminent Rapture." This is *three-stage apocalypticism*: the Rapture of the Church (cosmic discontinuity), followed by the holocaust of Israel's Jews (historical discontinuity), followed by the return of Christ to set up His millennial kingdom seven years after the Rapture (cosmic and historical discontinuity). The Church's work in history has nothing to do with any of this.

One piece of evidence for my contention is the almost total absence of evangelism by dispensational groups in or to the State of Israel. They do not beam Christian broadcasts in from

---

[1962] 1988), p. 108.

24. In their essay for a conservative secular magazine, dispensationalists Ed Dobson and Ed Hindson try to sugar-coat this concern for national Israel. They admit that "The Tribulation will largely consist of the Antichrist persecuting the Jews and the nation of Israel." They quote Dallas Seminary's J. Dwight Pentecost: "God's purpose for Israel in this Tribulation is to bring about the conversion of a multitude of Jews, who will enter into the blessings of the kingdom and experience the fulfillment of Israel's covenants." What they do not discuss is that according to pre-tribulational dispensationalism, this conversion of the Jews only takes place in the midst of the slaughter of two-thirds of the entire population of the State of Israel. Dobson and Hindson, "Apocalypse Now?" *Policy Review* (Fall 1986), pp. 20-21.

25. Grace Halsell, a non-Christian who went on two of Jerry Falwell's tours to the State of Israel, got into a discussion with one young man on the tour who assured her that two-thirds of all Jews would be killed during the battle of Armageddon: Grace Halsell, *Prophecy and Politics: Militant Evangelists on the Road to Nuclear War* (Westport, Connecticut: Lawrence Hill & Co., 1986), p. 26.

Cyprus or other areas, the way they beam programs to the Islamic world. They do not advertise any such campaigns, the way that the "Jews for Jesus" and similar "Messianic Jews" organizations do. They are happy to evangelize Jews outside of the State of Israel, but not inside. Why not? One reason is that if the Jews of the State of Israel were converted before the Rapture, there could be no Armageddon.[26] The Antichrist could invade Palestine, but there would be no national Jewish State of Israel there. If the bulk of the Jews of the State of Israel were converted to saving faith before the Rapture, it would destroy dispensationalism, both pre-tribulational and post-tribulational.

Dispensational theology creates a major incentive to write off the State of Israel as a target of mass evangelism. This is a direct consequence of a particular millennial viewpoint. Here is my contention: *any millennial viewpoint that in any way writes off any group or nation at any point in time is a defective eschatology.* Today is the day of salvation (II Cor. 6:2), not at the beginning of the millennium but after Armageddon.

When the postmillennialist cites Romans 11 and argues that the Jews will be converted in history, leading to unprecedented blessings for the Church,[27] the dispensationalist dismisses this view of the future as utopian. Why is it utopian? Is it because in postmillennialism, not enough Jews get slaughtered before a handful of survivors are converted? Is it because we refuse to single out the Jews as the targets of persecution in a coming era

---

26. Another is that the Israeli government frowns on such evangelism. It would not cooperate with dispensational tour programs if this kind of evangelism were conducted by the leaders. This systematic ignoring of Christians in the State of Israel by the Falwell tours was noted by Halsell, *ibid.*, pp. 55-58. The local Baptist minister in Bethlehem was introduced by Falwell to his tour. He is an evangelist only to Arabs, according to Halsell's report of her interview with the man. The Israelis, he said, do not permit him to share the gospel with Jews (p. 64).

27. Charles Hodge, *Commentary on the Epistle to the Romans* (Grand Rapids, Michigan: Eerdmans, [1864] 1950), p. 365; Robert Haldane, *An Exposition of the Epistle to the Romans* (Mac Dill Air Force Base, Florida: MacDonald Pub. Co., [1839] 1958), pp. 632-33; John Murray, *The Epistle to the Romans*, 2 vols. (Grand Rapids, Michigan: Eerdmans, 1965), II, pp. 65-103.

of tribulation? Is it because we deny that the Great Tribulation is in the future? I think so. Yet Lindsey calls us anti-Semitic![28]

A defective view of evangelism testifies to a defective theology. This is why dispensationalism is in a state of near-paralysis. It cannot make sense of the Bible. It cannot make sense of what Christians' responsibilities are in history, even the responsibility of a narrowly defined form of evangelism. Rapture fever is morally paralyzing. It is therefore culturally paralyzing.

Conclusion

There is a heavy price to be paid for all of this, and the fading reputation of the American evangelical Church is part of that price. Dispensational fundamentalists are increasingly regarded by the humanist media as "prophecy junkies" – not much different psychologically from those supermarket tabloid newspaper readers who try to make sense of the garbled writings of Nostradamus, whose name is also selling lots of books these days. When secular newspaper reporters start calling Christian leaders to expound on Bible prophecy and its relationship to the headlines, and then call occultists and astrologers for confirmation, the Church of Jesus Christ is in bad shape. Read *Armageddon Now!* to find out just what bad shape this is, and has been for over seven decades.

John Walvoord's "ticking clock" book and others just like it in 1991 were the equivalent of General Norman Schwarzkopf's saturation bombing strategy: they flattened orthodox dispensationalism. Almost immediately after theses books' publication, General Schwarzkopf's strategy in Iraq buried the very short-lived "Babylon Literally Rebuilt" dispensationalism. Then, six months later, the failed Soviet *coup* buried "Magog from the North" dispensationalism. What is left? Not much. Dispensationalists must now begin to rebuild the ruins. It will do no good to deny the existence of these ruins. They are much too

---

28. Hal Lindsey, *The Road to Holocaust* (New York: Bantam, 1989).

Endless Unfulfilled Prophecies Produce Paralysis 39

visible. It will do no good to remain silent, either. But dispensationalists will remain silent. This is the only strategy they know.

The sad thing is that fringe Rapture scenarios are becoming wilder and wilder, mixed with pyramidology, UFO's, and other occult materials.[29] As the year 2000 approaches, this "invasion by the fringe" will escalate. This escalation of expectation of the Rapture will tend to paralyze the Church as an institution of salt and light as the 1990's unfold. When this expectation is also fueled by occultism, it cannot have anything but negative consequences for dispensationalism.

A clock is indeed ticking. It is the clock of responsibility. We have all been given assignments by God and enough time to complete them in life (Eph. 2:10). Christian institutions have been given assignments by God through their officers. This is why eschatology matters. This is why the Institute for Christian Economics sometimes publishes books on eschatology. A person's time perspective is important for the tasks he begins, the capital he invests, and the rate of return he seeks. The shorter the time remaining, the more capital we need when we begin our tasks and the higher the rate of return we need to complete them. This is also true of God's Church. Each person, each church, each family, each civil government, and each organization must decide how much available time seems to remain. Our goals and plans, both personal and institutional, should reflect this assessment. False prophecies, decade after decade, regarding an inevitably imminent Rapture distort this assessment.

Christianity has lots of time remaining. Dispensationalism doesn't. This is the message of *Rapture Fever*.

---

29. William M. Alnor, *Soothsayers of the Second Advent* (Old Tappan, New Jersey: Revell, 1989), Part IV.

2

FEAR OF MEN PRODUCES PARALYSIS

And the officers of the children of Israel did see that they were in evil case, after it was said, Ye shall not [di]minish ought from your bricks of your daily task. And they met Moses and Aaron, who stood in the way, as they came forth from Pharaoh: And they said unto them, The LORD look upon you, and judge; because ye have made our savour to be abhorred in the eyes of Pharaoh, and in the eyes of his servants, to put a sword in their hand to slay us (Exodus 5:19-21).

. . . as the secular, humanistic, demonically-dominated world system becomes more and more aware that the Dominionists and Reconstructionists are a real political threat, they will sponsor more and more concerted efforts to destroy the Evangelical church. Unnecessary persecution could be stirred up.
David Allen Lewis (1990)[1]

What frightens some dispensational critics of Christian political action is their fear of persecution. Mr. Lewis is representative of this fear-driven outlook. He assumes that all politics is inherently humanistic – outside the legitimate rule of Christ's kingdom. Because politics is humanistic by nature, any attempt

---

1. David Allen Lewis, *Prophecy 2000* (Green Forest, Arkansas: New Leaf Press, 1990), p. 277.

by Christians to speak to political issues as people — or worse, as *a* people — who possess an explicitly biblical agenda will invite "unnecessary persecution." He recommends silence.

We see once again dispensationalism's concept of *evangelism as tract-passing*, a narrowly defined kingdom program of exclusively personal evangelism that has one primary message to every generation, decade after decade: *flee the imminent wrath to come*, whether the Antichrist's (the Great Tribulation) or the State's ("unnecessary persecution"). This is a denial of the greatness of the Great Commission,[2] but in the name of the Great Commission: "Our vision is to obey and fulfill the command of the Great Commission."[3]

Mr. Lewis says that we can legitimately participate in politics *as individuals*, since our government is democratic: ". . . we encourage Christians to get involved on an individual basis, in all realms of society, including the political arena." Should our goal be to change society fundamentally? Hardly. This is an impossible goal. Our goal is to gain new contacts in order to share the gospel with them. "This is partly to insure that Christians are in place in every strata of society for the purpose of sharing the gospel message."[4] The purpose of political and social involvement is not to reform the world; it is to tell people about the imminent end of this pre-millennium world. We are apparently not supposed to say anything explicitly Christian or vote as an organized bloc (the way that all other special-interest groups expect to gain political influence).[5] "To be involved in

---

2. Kenneth L. Gentry, Jr., *The Greatness of the Great Commission: The Christian Enterprise in a Fallen World* (Tyler, Texas: Institute for Christian Economics, 1990).

3. Lewis, *Prophecy 2000*, p. 282.

4. *Idem.*

5. This is traditional democratic theory, but it has never really come to grips with the reality of political power. The Council on Foreign Relations and the Trilateral Commission do not organize voters into blocs. They simply make sure that they control who gets appointed to the highest seats of power and what policies are enacted. This raises other questions, which, being political, are not the focus of my concern here. See Gary North, *Conspiracy: A Biblical View* (Ft. Worth, Texas: Domin-

our governmental process is desirable; however, it is quite another matter for the Church to strive to become Caesar."⁶

Mr. Lewis does not understand politics: one does not get involved politically in order to lose; one gets involved in order to win. He also does not understand society: one does not make the necessary sacrifices in life that it takes to be successful if one is told that his efforts will not leave anything of significance to the next generation, if in fact there will be a next generation, which is said to be highly doubtful. Mr. Lewis and his pre-tribulational dispensational colleagues have paraphrased homosexual economist John Maynard Keynes' quip, "In the long run we are all dead." They say, "In the short run, we Christians will all be raptured, and the Jews in Israel will soon wish they were dead, which two-thirds of them will be within seven years after we leave." As we saw in Chapter 1, this view of the Jews is taught by the leading dispensational theologian of our era.⁷

Mr. Lewis' position on politics and social involvement is one more example of the long-term operational alliance between the escape religion and the power religion.⁸ Both sides are agreed: Christians should not seek office as civil magistrates, except as *judicially neutral agents*. Yet at the same time, all but dispensational, natural law philosopher Norman Geisler (a former Dallas Theological Seminary professor) and academic political pluralists (e.g., Roman Catholic priest Richard John Neuhaus) admit there is no neutrality. This is schizophrenic.⁹ This schizophrenia has left Christians intellectually helpless in

---

ion Press, 1986; co-published by Crossway Books, Westchester, Illinois). See also Philip H. Burch, *Elites in American History*, 3 vols. (New York: Holmes & Meier, 1980-81); Carroll Quigley, *Tragedy and Hope: A History of the World in Our Time* (New York: Macmillan, 1966), pp. 946-56.

6. Lewis, *Prophecy 2000*, p. 277.

7. John F. Walvoord, *Israel in Prophecy* (Grand Rapids, Michigan: Zondervan Academie, [1962] 1988), p. 108.

8. North, *Moses and Pharaoh*, pp. 2-5.

9. Gary North, "The Intellectual Schizophrenia of the New Christian Right," *Christianity and Civilization*, I (1983).

the face of an officially neutral, officially pluralistic humanist juggernaut. This has been going on for over three centuries.[10] (An Islamic juggernaut may yet provide a cure.)

Bible Prophecy vs. Eschatology

Dispensationalists concentrate their attention on Bible prophecies at the expense of biblical eschatology. Bible prophecy is not usually about eschatology, i.e., the doctrine of last things. A lot of Christians fail to understand this important point. They love to buy Bible prophecy books, yet they are not really interested in eschatology. They may think they are, but they aren't.

How can a book be about Bible prophecy but not be about eschatology? Easy. For example, a book on the subject of Old Testament prophecies regarding the coming of Jesus the Messiah can certainly be about prophecy yet not be about eschatology. "Yes, yes," you may be thinking, "but what about a book on New Testament prophecy? Surely it has to be about the future. There was nothing of prophetic significance that took place in between the New Testament authors and today." But there was: *the fall of Jerusalem to the Roman army in A.D. 70.* That historic event was clearly prophesied by Jesus (Luke 21:20-24), yet it took place long ago. It took place after the New Testament writings were finished but long before you or I appeared on the scene.

The fact is, the vast majority of prophecies in the New Testament refer to this crucial event, the event which publicly identified the transition from the Old Covenant to the New Covenant, and which also marked the triumph of rabbinic Judaism over priestly Judaism, Pharisee over Sadducee,[11] and the syna-

---

10. Gary North, *Political Polytheism: The Myth of Pluralism* (Tyler, Texas: Institute for Christian Economics, 1989), Part 3.

11. The Sadducee sect of Judaism disappeared, since it had been associated with the priests who officiated at the temple. Herbert Danby, whose English translation of the Mishnah is still considered authoritative by the scholarly world, both Jew and gentile, commented on the undisputed triumph of the Pharisees after the fall of

gogue system over the temple. So central was the destruction of the temple to the future of both Christianity and Judaism that Jesus linked it symbolically to His death and resurrection:

> Then answered the Jews and said unto him, What sign shewest thou unto us, seeing that thou doest these things? Jesus answered and said unto them, Destroy this temple, and in three days I will raise it up. Then said the Jews, Forty and six years was this temple in building, and wilt thou rear it up in three days? But he spake of the temple of his body (John 2:18-21).

Dating The Book of Revelation

"But," you may be thinking to yourself, "John wrote the Book of Revelation (the Apocalypse) in A.D. 96. Everyone agrees on this. Thus, John could not have been prophesying events associated with the fall of Jerusalem, an event that had taken place a quarter of a century earlier." This is the argument of Dallas Theological Seminary professor Wayne House and Pastor Tommy Ice in their theologically creative but highly precarious revision of traditional dispensationalism.[12] It is also the intellectual strategy taken by best-selling dispensational author Dave Hunt, who writes in his recent defense of Chris-

---

Jerusalem (which lives on as Orthodox Judaism): "Until the destruction of the Second Temple in A.D. 70 they had counted as one only among the schools of thought which played a part in Jewish national and religious life; after the Destruction they took the position, naturally and almost immediately, of sole and undisputed leaders of such Jewish life as survived. Judaism as it has continued since is, if not their creation, at least a faith and a religious institution largely of their fashioning; and the Mishnah is the authoritative record of their labour. Thus it comes about that while Judaism and Christianity alike venerate the Old Testament as canonical Scripture, the Mishnah marks the passage to Judaism as definitely as the New Testament marks the passage to Christianity." Herbert Danby, "Introduction," *The Mishnah* (New York: Oxford University Press, [1933] 1987), p. xiii. The Mishnah is the written version of the Jews' oral tradition, while the rabbis' comments on it are called Gemara. The Talmud contains both Mishnah and Gemara. See also R. Travers Herford, *The Pharisees* (London: George Allen & Unwin, 1924).

12. H. Wayne House and Thomas D. Ice, *Dominion Theology: Blessing or Curse?* (Portland, Oregon: Multnomah, 1988), pp. 249-60.

Fear of Men Produces Paralysis 45

tian cultural surrender to humanism that "the Book of Revelation was written at least 20 years after A.D. 70, most likely about A.D. 96. This one fact destroys this entire theory" about the fall of Jerusalem being the prophesied event that many today call the Great Tribulation.[13] But like so much of what Dave Hunt has written,[14] this "fact" is not a fact. John did not write the Book of Revelation in A.D. 96.

When did John write the Book of Revelation? This technical academic question must be answered accurately if we are ever to make sense of New Testament prophecy. Establishing the date of John's Apocalypse and the events that followed within a few months of this revelation is what Kenneth L. Gentry's book, *The Beast of Revelation*, is all about, as is Dr. Gentry's larger and far more detailed study, *Before Jerusalem Fell: Dating the Book of Revelation*. (Both books were published by the Institute for Christian Economics in 1989). If his thesis is correct, then the Great Tribulation is not ahead of us; it is long behind us. If this event is behind us, then all "futurism" – dispensationalism, most contemporary non-dispensational premillennialism, and the more popular forms of amillennialism – is dead wrong. Anyone who says that "dark days are ahead of the Church because the Man of Sin is surely coming" is a futurist.[15] Thus, Gentry's books are not simply obscure academic exercises. If

---

13. Dave Hunt, *Whatever Happened to Heaven?* (Eugene, Oregon: Harvest House, 1988), p. 249.

14. Gary DeMar and Peter J. Leithart, *The Reduction of Christianity: A Biblical Response to Dave Hunt* (Ft. Worth, Texas: Dominion Press, 1988).

15. The other positions are idealism, the Church historical approach, and preterism. The first view does not try to tie the prophecies to any particular post-New Testament event. The prophecies are seen as merely principles. Church historicism teaches that the Book of Revelation describes the course of history. This was the common view of the Reformation, in which all Protestant groups identified the Papacy as the Antichrist. (This was the only universally agreed-upon specifically Protestant doctrine that united all Protestant groups.) The preterists are those who believe that most Bible prophecies had been fulfilled by the time Jerusalem fell, or at least by the time the Roman Empire was Christianized. This is my view, Gentry's, and Chilton's.

futurists prove incapable of refuting these books, they will have surrendered their intellectual position. Since 1989 they have remained silent.

Silence in the Face of Criticism Is Suicidal

It is my opinion that they will prove incapable of refuting Gentry's evidence. It is my opinion that dispensationalists will not even try; they will instead adopt the traditional academic strategy that dispensational seminary professors have used for over half a century to deal with any book that challenges their system: "Let's keep quiet and pray that nobody in our camp finds out about this, especially our brighter students."

As I mentioned in the Preface, the best example of this keep-quiet-and-hope strategy is the unwillingness of any dispensational scholar to challenge postmillennialist Oswald T. Allis' comprehensive critique of dispensationalism, *Prophecy and the Church* (1945) for two decades.[16] Charles C. Ryrie's brief, popularly written, and intellectually undistinguished attempt to refute a carefully selected handful of Allis' arguments appeared in 1965: *Dispensationalism Today*.[17] The fact that this slim volume is still the primary defense of traditional (Dallas Seminary) dispensationalism, despite the fact that it has never been revised, testifies to the **head-in-the-sand strategy** of the dispensationalist academic world to its Bible-believing critics. This dearth of intellectual defenses is especially noticeable today, given the fact of Dr. Ryrie's unexpected and somewhat acrimonious departure from the Dallas Seminary faculty over a decade ago. Another example is their silence regarding William Everett Bell's 1967 New York University doctoral dissertation, "A Critical Evaluation of the Pretribulation Rapture Doctrine in Christian Eschatology," which has been reprinted by Bell. Major books deserve full-scale refutations in books, not brief, negative

---

16. Phillipsburg, New Jersey: Presbyterian & Reformed.
17. Chicago: Moody Press.

book reviews in an in-house, small-circulation journal. Any philosophical, theological, or ideological system that is not defended intellectually and publicly by its academic spokesmen, decade after decade, despite a growing mountain of cogent criticisms, is close to the end of its influence. Its brighter, younger recruits will drift away or else be recruited by the critics. Eventually, the defending institutions will drift theologically, as once-traditional dispensational Talbot Theological Seminary did after 1986 and as Grace Theological Seminary is drifting today (or so it appears: see Chapter 13). A defensive mentality, a "form a circle with the wagons" mentality, cannot be sustained forever. *If a movement does not move forward, it either stagnates or moves backward culturally.* If a movement adopts a view of time which says that cultural progress is the product of its rivals' efforts, that only "upward" movement (death) and "inward" movement (mysticism) are truly significant, then that movement has drunk the eschatological equivalent of "Rev." Jim Jones' Kool-Aid. This analytic principle applies equally well to the New Age mystic's quest for inner escape or the dispensationalist's Rapture fever. This is why dispensationalism is dying.

Bible-believing Christians need an alternative.[18]

Last Days vs. End Times

The last days are different from the end times. The last days refer to the last days of Old Covenant Israel; they are in the past. Still confused? So are millions of other Christians. The confusion stems from the fact that Christians have jumped to the conclusion – a wholly erroneous conclusion – that the "last days" spoken of in the New Testament refer to the last days of the Church (or to the misleadingly identified "Church Age"). This conclusion is not warranted by the various biblical texts. *The last days spoken of in the New Testament were eschatological last*

---

18. Gary North, *Unconditional Surrender: God's Program for Victory* (3rd ed.; Tyler, Texas: Institute for Christian Economics, 1988).

days only for national Israel, not for the New Covenant Church. The "last days" were in fact the early days of the Church of Jesus Christ. They inaugurated the New Covenant era.

How do we know this? How do we know that we are not now living in the Church's last days? Because the New Testament was written in the last days of Israel, which came to a close over 1,900 years ago. The New Testament clearly says so. The author of the Epistle to the Hebrews specifically identified his own era as the "last days." He wrote that God "Hath *in these last days* spoken unto us by his Son, whom he hath appointed heir of all things, by whom also he made the worlds" (Heb. 1:2). He was quite clear: he and his contemporaries were living in the last days. He did not suffer from Rapture fever.

The Destruction of the Temple

We need to ask this obvious question: The last days of what? The answer is clear: *the last days of the Old Covenant, including national Israel*. The New Testament writers were living in *the last days of animal sacrifices in the temple*. This is the primary message of the Epistle to the Hebrews: the coming of a better sacrifice, a once-and-for-all sacrifice, Jesus Christ. We read: "And for this cause he is the mediator of the new testament, that by means of death, for the redemption of the transgressions that were under the first testament, they which are called might receive the promise of eternal inheritance. For where a testament is, there must also of necessity be the death of the testator" (Heb. 9:15-16). The inescapable concomitant of Jesus' sacrifice at Calvary was His annulment of the Old Covenant's sacrificial system, *which took place at the end of the Old Covenant's world*:

> And almost all things are by the law purged with blood; and without shedding of blood is no remission. It was therefore necessary that the patterns of things in the heavens should be purified with these; but the heavenly things themselves with better sacrifices than these. For Christ is not entered into the

holy places made with hands, which are the figures of the true; but into heaven itself, now to appear in the presence of God for us: Nor yet that he should offer himself often, as the high priest entereth into the holy place every year with blood of others; For then must he often have suffered since the foundation of the world: but now once **in the end of the world** hath he appeared to put away sin by the sacrifice of himself. And as it is appointed unto men once to die, but after this the judgment: So Christ was once offered to bear the sins of many; and unto them that look for him shall he appear the second time without sin unto salvation. For the law having a shadow of good things to come, and not the very image of the things, can never with those sacrifices which they offered year by year continually make the comers thereunto perfect. For then would they not have ceased to be offered? Because that the worshippers once purged should have had no more conscience of sins. But in those sacrifices there is a remembrance again made of sins every year. For it is not possible that the blood of bulls and of goats should take away sins. Wherefore when he cometh into the world, he saith, Sacrifice and offering thou wouldest not, but a body hast thou prepared me: In burnt offerings and sacrifices for sin thou hast had no pleasure (Heb. 9:22-10:6; emphasis added).

Notice the key phrase: "in the end of the world." In the original Greek, it reads: "completion of the ages." This phrase must be taken literally, but its literal frame of reference was the fall of Jerusalem and the annulment of the temple's sacrificial system. The author was therefore prophesying the imminent end of national Israel as God's covenant people.[19]

The leaders of national Israel had refused to believe Jesus. Subsequently, they refused to believe the message of the apos-

---

19. Romans 11 teaches that Israel as a separate corporate people will be converted to Christ at some point in the future. On this point, one denied by virtually all amillennial commentators, see the postmillennial commentaries by Robert Haldane, Charles Hodge, and John Murray. Nevertheless, the Jews will regain their status as a covenant people only through adoption into the Church, just as all sinners do. They will not be treated by God differently from any other covenanted people.

tles. They did not admit to themselves the truth of what the New Testament message announced, namely, that *God has no permanent pleasure in burnt animal offerings.* This had been the message of the Old Covenant, too, and their religious predecessors had paid no attention: "For I desired mercy, and not sacrifice; and the knowledge of God more than burnt offerings" (Hos. 6:6). The New Testament authors declared that God would soon bring an end to these futile and misleading animal sacrifices, *never to be restored.*[20] They understood that they were living in the last days of the Old Covenant era, and they warned their readers of this fact. This, in fact, is the primary message of the Book of Revelation.[21]

So, the New Testament authors did write about prophecy, but most (though not all) of their prophetic messages dealt with the immediate fate and future of national Israel. Thus, when they wrote prophetically, they wrote primarily about *Israel's near-term eschatology* (last days), not the Church's long-term

---

20. Traditional dispensationalism teaches that the temple will be rebuilt and animal sacrifices will be restored for a thousand years, even though only as a "memorial," as C. I. Scofield says in his reference note on Ezekiel 43:19. *The Scofield Reference Bible* (New York: Oxford University Press, 1909), p. 890. The embarrassment of the *New Scofield Bible's* revision committee is apparent in the note that this prophecy of restored sacrifices can be explained either in terms of the "memorial" thesis (which they strategically refuse to identify as Scofield's original view) or as figurative – a startling suggestion from theologians who proclaim that dispensationalism's principle of interpretation is "literal whenever possible" (i.e., "literal whenever convenient"). *The New Scofield Bible* (New York: Oxford University Press, 1967), p. 888. If the temple is to be rebuilt for use during the New Testament's millennium – a dispensational doctrine which the revision committee did not dare to challenge – then for what other purpose would the temple be used except for offering animal sacrifices? As a tourist attraction? Thus, if the rebuilt temple of Ezekiel 43 is a prophecy referring to a New Testament era millennium rather than to the rebuilt temple of Nehemiah's day, itself a prophetic symbol of worship in the worldwide Church – which is my view – then the re-establishment of animal sacrifices cannot sensibly be regarded as figurative. But the theological implications of this re-established animal sacrifice system were too embarrassing for the Scofield revision committee to handle forthrightly. They fudged.

21. David Chilton, *The Days of Vengeance: An Exposition of the Book of Revelation* (Ft. Worth: Dominion Press, 1987).

eschatology (end times). They were writing prophetic warnings to people of their own era regarding crises that were almost upon them, not crises of Christians and Jews living at least 1,900 years later.

Let me ask an obvious question, which futurists never publicly ask: If your church were in the early stages of a life-and-death crisis – the public execution of the church's founder – and he gave you a warning regarding problems that would face Christians two thousand years from now, would you regard his warning as timely, fully rational, and relevant to your immediate needs? Would you regard this warning as being of crucial importance to your daily walk before God or the life of the local church? No? Neither would I. *Neither would Jesus' listeners.* Therefore, I conclude that the immediacy of the disciples' concern was the reason why Jesus warned them of the coming tribulation of national Israel: "Now learn a parable of the fig tree; When his branch is yet tender, and putteth forth leaves, ye know that summer is nigh: So likewise ye, when ye shall see all these things, know that it is near, even at the doors. Verily I say unto you, This generation shall not pass, till all these things be fulfilled" (Matt. 24:32-34).

Another question: If that hypothetical warning from the founder referred to events that will be seen by "this generation," would you instinctively conclude – as all dispensational expositors of this verse have concluded and must conclude, given their need for a coherent system of interpretation – that the phrase "this generation" refers to some generation living at least 1,950 years later? No? Then why not take Jesus' words literally? "Verily I say unto you, This generation shall not pass, till all these things be fulfilled."

All of these things *were* fulfilled: in A.D. 70.

But What About the Beast?

Well, what about the Beast? If my thesis is correct – that the phrase "the last days" refers to the last days of Old Covenant

Israel and the destruction of the temple in A.D. 70 – then who was the Beast? After all, if New Testament prophecies regarding the Beast were not fulfilled during the lifetime of John, but refer to some individual still in the Church's future, there would seem to be no reason to believe that the other prophecies regarding "the last days" were also fulfilled in his day. These prophecies must be taken as a unit. It is clear that the Beast is a figure who is said to be alive in the last days. This is why it is imperative that we discover who the Beast is or was. If he has not yet appeared, then the last days must also be ahead of us, unless we have actually entered into them. If he has already appeared, then the last days are over.

Gentry's studies prove beyond much doubt that the prophesied Beast was in fact the emperor Nero. (So, for that matter, does David Chilton's commentary on the Book of Revelation, *The Days of Vengeance*).[22] Gentry's books are not filled with prophecies about brain-implanted computer chips, tatoos with identification numbers, cobra helicopters, nuclear war, and New Age conspiracies. This is why most fundamentalists are not interested in his books. Customers of most Christian bookstores too often prefer to be excited by the misinformation provided by a string of paperback false prophecies than to be comforted by the knowledge that the so-called Great Tribulation is long behind us, and that it was Israel's tribulation, not the Church's. (For biblical proof, see David Chilton's book, *The Great Tribulation*.)[23] They want thrills and chills, not accurate Bible exposition; they want a string of "secret insights," not historical knowledge. Like legions of imaginative children sitting in front of the family radio back in the 1930's and 1940's who faithfully bought their Ovaltine, tore off the wrapper, and sent it in to receive an official "Little Orphan Annie secret decoder," funda-

---

22. David Chilton, *The Days of Vengeance: An Exposition of the Book of Revelation* (Ft. Worth, Texas: Dominion Press, 1987).

23. David Chilton, *The Great Tribulation* (Ft. Worth, Texas: Dominion Press, 1987).

mentalist Christians are repeatedly lured by the tempting promise that they can be "the first ones on their block" to be "on the inside" – to be the early recipients of the "inside dope." And that is exactly what they have been sold, decade after decade.

Nine-year-old children were not totally deceived in 1938. They knew the difference between real life and make-believe. Make-believe was thrilling; it was fun; it was inexpensive; but it was not real. The decoded make-believe secrets turned out to provide only fleeting excitement, but at least they could drink the Ovaltine. Furthermore, children eventually grow up, grow tired of Ovaltine, and stop ordering secret decoders.

When will Christians grow up? When will they grow tired of an endless stream of the paperback equivalent of secret decoders? When will they be able to say of themselves as Paul said of himself: "When I was a child, I spake as a child, I understood as a child, I thought as a child: but when I became a man, I put away childish things" (I Cor. 13:11)?

False Prophecies for Fun and Profit

Those Christians who believe that we are drawing close to the last days are continually trying to identify both the Beast and the Antichrist. This game of "find the Beast and identify the Antichrist" has become the adult Christians' version of the child's game of pin the tail on the donkey. Every few years, the participants place blindfolds over their eyes, turn around six times, and march toward the wall. Sometimes they march out the door and over a cliff, as was the case with Edgar C. Whisenant, whose best-selling two-part book announced in the summer of 1988 that Jesus would surely appear to rapture His Church during Rosh Hashanah week in mid-September. Half the book was called *On Borrowed Time*. The other was more aptly titled, *88 Reasons why the Rapture is in 1988*. I can think of one key argument why his book's thesis was incorrect: no Rapture so far, and it is now February, 1993. So much for all 88 arguments. The anti-Christian world got another great laugh at the expense of millions of fundamentalists who had bought and read his two-part book. The story of Mr. Whisenant's book was front-page news briefly around the U.S. Mr. Whisenant is now ancient history, one more forgotten laughingstock who brought reproach to the Church of Jesus Christ while he gained his brief moment of fame. But replacements will surely follow.

This is the whole problem. The victims self-consciously forget the last self-proclaimed expert in Bible prophecy whose predictions did not come to pass. They never learn to recognize the next false prophet because they refuse to admit to themselves that they had been suckered by the last one. Thus, this sucker's game has been going on throughout the twentieth century, generation after generation, a pathetic story chronicled superbly by Dwight Wilson in his well-documented book, *Armageddon Now!*, a book that was not regularly assigned to students at Dallas Seminary, I can assure you.[24] Again and again, some prominent world political figure has been identified as either the Beast or the Antichrist: Lenin, Mussolini, Hitler, Stalin, and even Henry Kissinger.[25] (It was President Reagan's good fortune that he was a conservative so beloved by fundamentalists, given the remarkable structure of his name: Ronald [6] Wilson [6] Reagan [6].)

Salem Kirban: Master of Pre-1983 Hype

The back cover promotional copy of former best-selling author Salem Kirban's self-published book, *The Rise of Anti-Christ*, is representative of this paperback prophetic literature. Published in 1978, it boldly announced:

---

24. Dwight Wilson, *Armageddon Now!: The Premillennial Response to Russia and Israel Since 1917* (Tyler, Texas: Institute for Christian Economics, [1977] 1991).

25. Salem Kirban, *Kissinger: Man of Peace?* (Huntington Valley, Pennsylvania: Salem Kirban Inc., 1974). As you might expect, this book is no longer in print. It sometimes appears in local library book sales for a dollar or less. If you spot it, buy it. It is a collector's item.

**We are already living in the
AGE OF ANTICHRIST!**
The world is on the threshold of catastrophe. Scientific advances are really scientific tragedies that will spell chaos, confusion and terror.

**Within the next 5 years...
DESIGN YOUR OWN CHILD**
by going to the "genetic supermarket."
YOUR MIND WILL BE PROGRAMMED
without your knowing it!

**Within the next 10 years...
YOUR BRAIN WILL BE CONTROLLED**
by outside sources!
YOUR MEMORY WILL BE TRANSFERRED
into a live embryo.

And so on. None of this has happened, of course. My favorite is this one: "HEAD TRANSPLANTS will become a reality." I wonder who will be the first two volunteers? Who will get what? Kirban's book is to Bible exposition what the *National Enquirer* is to journalism. The trouble is, the *National Enquirer* sells 7 million copies each week; it is by far America's largest-circulation newspaper. Sensationalism sells!

If we take Mr. Kirban's words literally – as literally as he expects us to take the Bible – we are forced to conclude: "This man simply did not know what he was talking about when he wrote those predictions." But he sold a lot of books in the 1970's – 30 different titles on prophecy by 1978 alone, the back cover informs us, plus a huge study Bible, plus a comic book. By 1980, the total number of Mr. Kirban's book titles had soared to 35, according to back cover copy on *Countdown to Rapture* (published originally in 1977). He concluded on page 188 of this book:

"Based on these observations, it is my considered opinion, that the time clock is now at
11:59
When is that Midnight hour . . . the hour of the Rapture? I do not know!"

Kirban wisely avoided the mistake of putting a date on the Rapture – the mistake Mr. Whisenant made – but his book was sufficiently explicit. Given the fact that the supposed "clock of prophecy" reached 11:56 in 1976, when the world's population passed 4 billion people (p. 45), and then reached 11:59 in only one year with the peace accord between Israel and Egypt in 1977 (p. 175), you get the general picture. Only "one minute" to go in 1977! The Rapture will be soon! This is the constant appeal of Rapture fever.

Once again, however, pre-tribulational dispensationalism's notoriously unreliable "clock of prophecy" stopped without warning.[26] The years passed by. No Beast. No Antichrist. Few book sales. Scrap the topic! Try something else. Why not books on nutrition? Presto: Salem Kirban's *How Juices Restore Health Naturally* (1980). Oh, well. Better a glass of fresh carrot juice than another book on the imminent appearance of Jesus or the Antichrist. Few people suffer from carrot juice fever.

Nevertheless, a stopped "clock of prophecy" is always good news for the next wave of pop-dispensational authors: more chances to write new books about the Beast, 666, and the Antichrist. There are always more opportunities for a revival – a revival of book royalties. After all, a sucker is born every minute, even when the "clock of prophecy" has again ceased ticking. The next generation of false prophets can always draw another few inches along the baseline of their reprinted 1936

---

26. Technically speaking, pretrib dispensationalism requires that the clock of prophecy not begin again until the Rapture. But this kind of low-key view of prophecy sells few books. Thus, the dispensationalism known to most buyers of prophecy books is the dispensationalism of the ticking clock, however erratically it may tick.

edition prophecy charts. They can buy some new springs for a rusted prophetic clock. These stopped clocks are a glut on the market about every ten years. Any fledgling prophecy expert can pick one up cheap. Clean it, install new springs, wind it, make a few modifications in a discarded prophecy chart, and you're in business! Example: as soon as Salem Kirban retired, Constance Cumbey appeared.[27]

The main problem with this never-ending stream of utterly false but sensational interpretations of Bible prophecy is that sincere Christian readers are grievously misled by authors who seem to speak authoritatively in the name of the Bible. These writers write authoritatively about topics that they know little or nothing about, or who misrepresent whatever they do know about. It takes time for each prophecy fad to fade. Emotionally vulnerable Christians are warned repeatedly in the name of the Bible that inescapable cataclysmic events are imminent – "signs of the times" – yet these inevitable events never take place as predicted. This goes on decade after decade, generation after generation, although the self-appointed prophets keep changing. Followers keep coming. Nonsense keeps flowing.

---

27. I give little credence to the rumor that "Constance E. Cumbey" is the pen name adopted by Mr. Kirban in 1983. I also have real doubts about the rumor that the woman who claimed to be Mrs. Cumbey was in fact a professional actress hired by Mr. Kirban to make occasional public appearances. Nevertheless, it is remarkable that Mr. Kirban's name appeared on no new prophecy books after 1982, the year before Mrs. Cumbey's *Hidden Dangers of the Rainbow* appeared. Could this be more than a coincidence? It is also strange that "Mrs. Cumbey" seems to have disappeared from public view ever since the second book with her name on it failed to make it into Christian bookstores. Is it possible that "Mrs. Cumbey" was fired by Mr. Kirban when the book royalties faded to a trickle and there was no further demand for her public appearances? I realize that all this may sound a bit implausible to most people, but perhaps not to someone who has accepted the thesis of "Mrs. Cumbey's" *A Planned Deception: The Staging of a New Age "Messiah"* (East Detroit, Michigan: Pointe, 1985). If a "Messiah" can be staged, so can a previously unknown lady researcher from Detroit. The "Messiah" has not yet appeared, and "Constance Cumbey" has now disappeared. Messiahs apparently come and go without much warning – indeed, without ever even appearing in public; so do those who expose them, although this takes a bit longer.

Question: If the pre-tribulation Rapture can come "at any moment," then how can there be any fulfilled prophecies to write about that take place in between the New Testament documents and the future Rapture? How can there be any "prophetic signs of the times"? How can anyone who believes in the "any moment coming" of Jesus also believe some self-declared prophecy expert who announces that specific Bible prophecies are being fulfilled in our day? If any event is said to be a fulfilled Bible prophecy today – an event that absolutely had to take place, as all true Bible prophecies obviously must – then the Rapture surely was not an "any moment Rapture" prior to the fulfillment of the allegedly fulfilled prophecy. Some prophesied event therefore had to happen before the Rapture could occur. This, obviously, is a denial of the doctrine of the "any moment coming" of Christ. This fact does not seem to deter any particular decade's reigning paperback prophets or their gullible disciples.

The Paralysis Factor

Once a particular prophecy expert's predictions begin to be perceived as being embarrassingly inaccurate, another expert appears with a new set of prophecies. Christians who become temporary followers of these false prophets become ominously similar to the misled women described by Paul: "For of this sort are they which creep into houses, and lead captive silly women laden with sins, led away with divers lusts, Ever learning, and never able to come to the knowledge of the truth" (II Tim. 3:6-7). Eventually, these frantic (or thrill-seeking) victims become unsure about what they should believe concerning the future. Everything sounds so terrifying. Christians become persuaded that personal forces beyond their control or the Church's control – evil, demonic forces – are about to overwhelm all remaining traces of righteousness. How, after all, can the average Christian protect himself against mind control and memory transfer, let alone head transplants, assuming such things are both technically and culturally possible and imminent? The fact that such things are not technically possible in the time period claimed for them never seems to occur to the buyers of paperback prophecy books.

A steady stream of this sort of material tends to reduce the ability of Christians to reason coherently or make effective long-term decisions. *Sensationalism becomes addictive.* Sensationalism combined with culture-retreating pietism paralyzed the fundamentalist movement until, in the late 1970's, fundamentalism at last began to change. That transformation is nowhere near complete, but it surely has begun. (See Chapter 11.) Fundamentalists are at last beginning to re-think their eschatology. They are less subject to uncontrolled spasms produced by Rapture fever. The back cover promotional copy on *Whatever Happened to Heaven?* reveals that Dave Hunt is aware of the fact that his version of pop-dispensationalism, like Hal Lindsey's, is fading rapidly. (Mr. Lindsey largely disappeared from public view about the time he married wife number three. Gone are the days of his guest appearances – and everyone else's – on "The Jim and Tammy Show." He does have a radio show and a local television show in southern California.) Hunt's promotional copy announces: "Today, a growing number of Christians are exchanging the hope for the rapture for a new hope . . . that Christians can clean up society. . . ." The promise – unfulfilled, I might add – of the back cover is that this book will show old fashioned dispensationalists "how we lost that hope [the Rapture] and how it can be regained." The success of his books proves that there are still buyers of the old literature who love to be thrilled by new tales of the Beast. This means, of course, that they do not want to hear about the biblical account of the Beast of Revelation. They much prefer fantasy.

Conclusion

Fear paralyzes people if they see no escape, or if their hoped-for escape is seen by them as a miraculous deliverance by forces utterly beyond their control. Also, a short-run perspective inevitably impoverishes people. The fundamentalist world until the late 1970's had been "immobilized for Jesus" by its all-pervasive dismissal of the "inevitably grim" pre-Rapture future. Despairing Christians have believed with all their hearts that anything they could do to improve this world would inevitably be swallowed up by the work of the Beast and the Antichrist. They asked themselves: Why work, save, and postpone the present enjoyments of this world in order to build up a capital base that will be inherited by your enemies?

It is time for a resurrection: the resurrection of Christian hope. It is time for a parallel resurrection: the resurrection of comprehensive Christian service in every area of life. This means that it is time for Christian dominion. It is time to stop asking ourselves, "What ever happened to heaven?" and start asking: "What ever happened to the Great Commission and the kingdom of God?"[28] Heaven is for dead men in Christ; earth is for living men in Christ. Our responsibility for this world ends only at the point of our physical death or our complete physical and mental incapacitation. Let those fundamentalists whose primary goal in life is to escape earthly responsibility in the present and surely in the future – and also to "get out of life alive" at the Rapture – bury their talents in ceaseless speculations regarding heaven. The rest of us should concentrate on the goal of building the kingdom of God through covenantal faithfulness to God's law.[29] We should begin to take seriously God's promise to the righteous man: "His soul shall dwell at ease; and his seed shall inherit the earth" (Psa. 25:13).

---

28. Kenneth L. Gentry, Jr., *The Greatness of the Great Commission: The Christian Enterprise in a Fallen World* (Tyler, Texas: Institute for Christian Economics, 1990).

29. Greg L. Bahnsen, *By This Standard: The Authority of God's Law Today* (Tyler, Texas: Institute for Christian Economics, 1985).

3

PESSIMISM PRODUCES PARALYSIS

And all the children of Israel murmured against Moses and against Aaron: and the whole congregation said unto them, Would God that we had died in the land of Egypt! or would God we had died in this wilderness! And wherefore hath the LORD *brought us unto this land, to fall by the sword, that our wives and our children should be a prey? were it not better for us to return into Egypt? And they said one to another, Let us make a captain, and let us return into Egypt (Num. 14:2-4).*

The origin of the idea of progress was exclusively Western; in fact, it was originally a Christian idea. Only with the widespread acceptance of the biblical concept of linear time did men begin to believe that there could be earthly progress. They began to act in terms of a view of life that says that whatever a man does lives after him, and that future generations will be different to some degree because he lived, worked, and died exactly when he did.

Nevertheless, linear history is not, in and of itself, progressive history. Something more was needed: the idea of compound growth, or *positive feedback*. It is not simply that history is linear; it is that it is also *progressive*. Such a view of history rests squarely on Deuteronomy 28:1-14. It also rests on the notion of *covenantal reinforcement*, as described in Deuteronomy 8:18:

> But thou shalt remember the LORD thy God: for it is he that giveth thee power to get wealth, that he may establish his covenant which he sware unto thy fathers, as it is this day.

This is positive feedback: covenantal faithfulness brings external blessings from God, which in turn are supposed to reinforce people's confidence in the covenant, leading them to greater faithfulness, bringing them added blessings, and so forth. It was the postmillennial optimism of early Calvinism and English Puritanism that first introduced this worldview of culture-wide, compounding, covenantal growth to Western civilization.[1] The vision of Deuteronomy 28:1-14 captivated the English Puritans: the external cultural blessings that inevitably accompany covenantal faithfulness.

The development of the Calvinistic and Puritan doctrine of both spiritual and cultural progress reshaped the West. For the first time in human history, men were given a full-blown idea of progress, which was above all a doctrine of ethical progress. This vision was secularized by the *philosophes* of the Enlightenment, but that secularized version of progress is rapidly fading from the humanist West.[2] Belief in the universality of entropy (meaning inevitable decay) is only one of the causes of this growing pessimism, but it is a powerful one.

In the twentieth century, "pessimillennialism" – a term coined by Nigel Lee to describe both premillennialism and amillennialism – have been the dominant eschatologies. Those who hold such views have self-consciously rejected the idea of visible, institutional, social progress. They insist that the Bible does not teach such a hope with respect to the world prior to Christ's personal, physical return in judgment.

---

1. *The Journal of Christian Reconstruction*, VI (Summer 1979): "Symposium on Puritanism and Progress."

2. Robert A. Nisbet, *History of the Idea of Progress* (New York: Basic Books, 1980), ch. 9.

"The Church Cannot Change the World!"

I realize that there are premillennialists who will take offense at this statement. They will cite their obligations under Luke 19:13: "Occupy till I come." But the leaders of the *traditional* premillennial movement are quite self-conscious about their eschatology, and we need to take them seriously as spokesmen. For example, John Walvoord, author of many books on eschatology, and the long-time president of Dallas Theological Seminary, the premier dispensational academic institution, has not minced any words in this regard. In an interview with *Christianity Today* (Feb. 6, 1987), Kenneth Kantzer asked:

> *Kantzer:* **For all of you who are not postmils, is it worth your efforts to improve the physical, social, and political situation on earth?**
>
> *Walvoord:* The answer is yes and no. We know that our efforts to make society Christianized is [sic] futile because the Bible doesn't teach it. On the other hand, the Bible certainly doesn't teach that we should be indifferent to injustice and famine and to all sorts of things that are wrong in our current civilization. Even though we know our efforts aren't going to bring a utopia, we should do what we can to have honest government and moral laws. It's very difficult from Scripture to advocate massive social improvement efforts, because certainly Paul didn't start any, and neither did Peter. They assumed that civilization as a whole is hopeless and subject to God's judgment (pp. 5-I, 6-I).

Who said anything about expecting utopia? Only the pessimists, who use the word in order to ridicule people who preach that Christians are not foreordained to be losers in history. Why is civilization more hopeless than the soul of any sinner? The gospel saves sinners, after all. Why should we expect no major social improvements in society? Jesus said, "All power is given unto me in heaven and in earth" (Matt. 28:18). When He delegated power to His Church – power manifested in miraculous healings and the casting out of demons – Christ transferred power to His followers. Why shouldn't we expect widespread social and institutional healing in history?

The Power of Christ in History

Where is the earthly manifestation of this power? Dispensationalist Dale Hunt is adamant: only in the hearts of believers and (maybe) inside the walls of a local church or local rescue mission. As he says, in response to an advertisement for my Biblical Blueprints Series: "The Bible doesn't teach us to build society but instructs us to preach the gospel, for one's citizenship is in heaven (Col. 3:2)."[3] (It seems to me that he could have strengthened his case that we are citizens of only one "country" by citing a modern translation of Philippians 3:20.) Christ's gospel is supposedly a gospel of the heart *only*. Jesus supposedly saves hearts *only*; somehow, His gospel is not powerful enough to restore to biblical standards the institutions that He designed for mankind's benefit, but which have been corrupted by sin. Hunt's view of the gospel is this: *Jesus can somehow save sinners without having their salvation affect the world around them.* This, in fact, is the heart, mind, and soul of the pessimillennialists' "gospel": "Heal souls, not institutions."

Hunt separates the preaching of the gospel from society. He separates heavenly citizenship from earthly citizenship. In short, he would rewrite the Great Commission: "All power is given unto me in heaven and none in earth." (So, for that matter, would the amillennialist.) Christ's earthly power can only be manifested when He returns physically to set up a top-down bureaucratic kingdom in which Christians will be responsible for following the direct orders of Christ, issued to meet specific historical circumstances. The premillennialist has so little faith in the power of the Bible's perfect revelation, empowered by

---

3. Dale Hunt, *CIT Bulletin* (Feb. 1987), fourth page.

the Holy Spirit, to shape the thoughts and actions of Christians, that he believes that *Jesus must return bodily and personally issue millions of orders per day, telling everyone exactly what to do, case by case, crisis by crisis*. (And Jethro thought the line in front of Moses' tent was too long! See Exodus 18.) If this is not what dispensationalists expect, then they should spell out in detail exactly how Jesus will rule during the future millennium. They have so far refused to do this for over 160 years.

Thus, premillennialists deny the progressive maturation of Christians and Christianity in history. The millennium ruled by Christ, Hunt says, will be a world in which "Justice will be meted out swiftly."[4] Jesus will treat men as fathers treat five-year-old children: instant punishment, no time for reflection and repentance. Christians today are given time to think through their actions, to reflect upon their past sins, and to make restitution before God judges them. Today, they are treated by God as responsible adults. Not in the millennium! *The Church will go from maturity to immaturity when Christ returns in power*. And even with the testimony of the perfect visible rule of Jesus on earth for a thousand years, Satan will still thwart Christ and Christ's Church, for at Satan's release, he will deceive almost the whole world, leading them to rebel against "Christ and all the saints in Jerusalem."[5]

The Failure of the Gospel in History?

In short, the plan of God points only to the defeat of His Church in history, according to dispensationalism. Satan got the upper hand in Eden, and only the raw power of God in final judgment at the end of history can wipe out the kingdom of Satan and restore the creation to wholeness. *The gospel in history is doomed to cultural failure*. In premillennialism and amillen-

---

4. Dave Hunt, *Beyond Seduction: A Return to Biblical Christianity* (Eugene, Oregon: Harvest House, 1987), p. 250.

5. *Idem.*

nialism, we see the underlying theology of the power religion: the issues of history will be settled in Christ's favor only through a final *physical* confrontation between God and Satan. The history of the Church is therefore irrelevant: the conflict of the ages will be settled apart from the gospel, ethics, and the dominion covenant issued to Adam (Gen. 1:26-28), Noah (Gen. 9:1-17), and the Church (Matt. 28:18-20). The conflict of the ages will be settled in a kind of cosmic arm wrestling match between God and Satan. The Church is nothing more than a vulnerable bystander.

But we all know who will win in a war based on power. We know that God has more power than Satan. Satan knows, too. What Christians need to believe, now and throughout eternity, is that the authority which comes to Christians as God's reward to His people in response to their righteousness under Christ and biblical law is greater than the power granted by Satan to his followers for their rebellion against God. Yet premillennialism and amillennialism deny this fundamental truth. They preach that the power granted to Satan's human followers in history is greater than the power granted by God to His people in history. They preach *historic defeat for the Church of Jesus Christ*.

Institutional Defeat?

The social and intellectual problem for the consistent premillennialist or amillennialist is *motivation*. He has raised the institutional white flag to the devil. He has already mentally surrendered this world to Satan. Walvoord, as a consistent premillennial dispensationalist, assures us: "We know that our efforts to make society Christianized [are] futile because the Bible doesn't teach it." He deliberately ignores the Old Testament prophets. He does not want Christians to preach prophetically, for the prophets called Israel back to obedience to biblical law, and *dispensationalism rejects biblical law*. Walvoord calls only for a vague, undefined "moral law" to promote an equally vague "honest government." Without specifics, this is meaningless rhetoric. It is the theology of the rescue mission: sober them up, and then send them to Church until they die or Jesus comes again. This is the "Christian as a nice neighbor" version of what should be "salt and light" theology: "Save individuals, but not societies." We return to *Christianity Today* (Feb. 6, 1987):

> *Kantzer:* **Are we saying here that the Christian community, whether premil, postmil, or amil, must work both with individuals as well as seek to improve the structures of society? In other words, is there nothing within the millennial views that would prevent a believer from trying to improve society?**
>
> *Walvoord:* Well, the Bible says explicitly to do good to all men, especially those of faith. In other words, the Bible does give us broad commands to do good to the general public (p. 6-I).

Broad commands are worthless without specifics. *A call to "do good" is ethically meaningless without Bible-based standards of good.* A Communist or a New Age evolutionist could agree with Walvoord's statement, since it contains no specifics. In response, Prof. John J. Davis of Gordon-Conwell Theological Seminary, a postmillennialist, replied:

> But generally speaking, the premillennialist is more oriented toward helping those who have been hurt by the system than by addressing the systematic evil, while the postmillennialist believes the system can be sanctified. That's the basic difference with regard to our relationship to society (pp. 6-I, 7-I).

The Ultimate Form of Pessimism

When dispensationalists are called pessimists by postmillennialists – as we postmillennialists unquestionably do call them – they react negatively. This is evidence of my contention that *everyone recognizes the inhibiting effects of pessimism.* People do not like being called pessimists. Walvoord is no exception. But his defense is most revealing:

> **Walvoord:** Well, I personally object to the idea that premillennialism is pessimistic. We are simply realistic in believing that man cannot change the world. Only God can (p. 11-I).

"Man cannot change the world." What does this mean? That man is a robot? That God does everything, for good and evil? Walvoord obviously does not mean this. So, exactly what does he mean? That men collectively can do evil but not good? Then what effect does the gospel have in history? If he does not want to make this preposterous conclusion, then he must mean that men acting apart from God's will and God's law cannot improve the world, long-term. If God is willing to put up with the victory of evil, then there is nothing we Christians can do about it except try to get out of the way of victorious sinners if we possibly can, while handing out gospel tracts on street corners and running rescue missions. The question is: *Is* God really willing to put up with the triumph of sinners over His Church in history? Yes, say premillennialists and amillennialists. No, say postmillennialists. This is the heart of the two-way argument.

What Walvoord is *implying but not saying* is that the postmillennialists' doctrine of the *historical* power of regeneration, the *historical* power of the Holy Spirit, the *historical* power of biblical law, and the *continuing validity* of God's dominion covenant with man (Gen. 1:26-28) is theologically erroneous, and perhaps even borderline heretical. But this, of course, is precisely the reason we postmillennialists refer to premillennialists as pessimistic. They implicitly hold the reverse doctrinal viewpoints: the historical *lack* of power of regeneration, the historical *lack* of power of the Holy Spirit, the historical *lack* of power of biblical law, and the *present suspension* of God's dominion covenant with man. (Carl McIntyre's premillennial Bible Presbyterian Church in 1970 went on record officially as condemning the doctrine of the cultural mandate of Genesis 1:28.)[6]

Walvoord says that only God can change the world. My, what an insight! *Who does he think postmillennialists believe will change the world for the better?* Of course God must change the world. Given the depravity of man, He is the only One who can. But how does He do this? Through demons? No. Through fallen men who are on the side of demons in their rebellion against God? No. So, what is God's historic means of making the world better? *Through the preaching of the gospel.* This is what postmillennialists have always taught. *But the comprehensive success of the gospel in history is what premillennialists have always denied.* They do not believe in comprehensive redemption.[7] They categorically deny that the gospel of Christ will ever change most men's hearts at any future point in history. The gospel in this view is a means primarily of *condemning gospel-rejecting people to hell*, not a program leading to the victory of the Church in history. The gospel cannot transform the world, they insist. Yet they resent being called pessimists.

Pessimism regarding the transforming power of the gospel of Jesus Christ in history is what *defines* pessimism. There is no pessimism in the history of man that is more pessimistic than this eschatological pessimism regarding the power of the gospel in history. The universal destruction of man by nuclear war – a myth, by the way[8] – is downright optimistic compared to pessimism with regard to the power of the gospel in history. It testifies that the incorrigible human heart is more powerful than God in history, that Satan's defeat of Adam in the garden

---

6. Resolution No. 13, reprinted in R. J. Rushdoony, *The Institutes of Biblical Law* (Nutley, New Jersey: Craig Press, 1973), pp. 723-24.

7. Gary North, *Is the World Running Down? Crisis in the Christian Worldview* (Tyler, Texas: Institute for Christian Economics, 1988), Appendix C: "Comprehensive Redemption: A Theology for Social Action."

8. Arthur Robinson and Gary North, *Fighting Chance: Ten Feet to Survival* (Ft. Worth, Texas: American Bureau of Economic Research, 1986).

is more powerful in history than Christ's defeat of Satan at Calvary. There is no pessimism greater than Dave Hunt's statement, which is representative of all premillennialism (and amillennialism, for that matter): even the millennial reign of Christ physically on earth will end when the vast majority of people will rebel against Him, converge upon Jerusalem, and try to destroy the faithful people inside the city: "Converging from all over the world to war against Christ and the saints at Jerusalem, these rebels will finally have to be banished from God's presence forever (Revelation 20:7-10). The millennial reign of Christ upon earth, rather than being the kingdom of God, will in fact be the final proof of the incorrigible nature of the human heart."[9] (Why these rebellious human idiots will bother to attack Jerusalem, a city which Hunt believes will be filled with millions of resurrected, death-proof Christians who returned to rule with Christ at the beginning of the millennium, is beyond me. I will let premillennialists worry about this. I have already provided a postmillennial answer as to what Revelation 20:7-10 means, including who rebels and why, in my book, *Dominion and Common Grace*,[10] which was written specifically to deal with this exegetical problem.)

Hunt goes on (and on, and on): "A perfect Edenic environment where all ecological, economic, sociological, and political problems are solved fails to perfect mankind. So much for the theories of psychology and sociology and utopian dreams."[11] Here is the key word used again and again by premillennialists to dismiss postmillennialism: *utopia*. ("Utopia": *ou* = no, *topos* = place.) In short, they regard as totally mythological the idea that God's word, God's Spirit, and God's Church can change the hearts of *most* people sometime in the future. They *assume*

---

9. Dave Hunt, *Beyond Seduction*, p. 250.
10. Gary North, *Dominion and Common Grace: The Biblical Basis of Progress* (Tyler, Texas: Institute for Christian Economics, 1987).
11. Hunt, *Beyond Seduction*, p. 251.

(without any clear biblical support) that Revelation 20:7-10 describes a final rebellion in which *most people on earth rebel*, despite the fact that only one-third of the angels ("stars") rebelled with Satan, and only one-third of the earth is symbolically brought under God's wrath in the Book of Revelation's judgment passages (Rev. 8:7-12; 9:15, 18).

Over and over, premillennialists accuse postmillennialists of having too much confidence in man. This is really astounding, when you think about it, because all the primary defenders of modern postmillennialism have been Calvinists, and usually followers of Van Til. Normally, nobody accuses Calvinists of having too elevated a view of man. Calvinists proclaim the doctrine of man's total depravity and his inability to respond in faith to the gospel apart from God's predestinating irresistible grace to force conversions.

Postmillennialists are not arguing for confidence in "mankind as such." They are only arguing for the increasing long-term influence in history of *regenerate, covenantally faithful* people compared to *unregenerate, covenantally rebellious people*. What the amillennialists and premillennialists argue is the opposite: the steadily increasing long-term authority in history of unregenerate, covenantally rebellious people compared to the long-term authority of regenerate, covenantally faithful people. It is not "confidence in man" that is the basis of postmillennial optimism; it is *confidence in the covenantal faithfulness of God* in rewarding covenant-keepers in history (Deut. 28:1-14) and punishing covenant-breakers in history (Deut. 28:15-68).[12]

Scofield and Evolutionism

It is annoying, to say the least, to read Walvoord's attack on postmillennialism as an ally of evolutionary liberalism:

---

12. Ray R. Sutton, *That You May Prosper: Dominion By Covenant* (rev. ed.; Tyler, Texas: Institute for Christian Economics, 1992), ch. 4.

During the last part of the nineteenth century, evolution emerged as an explanation for why things were getting better. In those days, prophecy conferences included postmils, amils, and premils, but it became a battle between the premil view and the evolutionary view that seemed to fit postmillennialism. So premillennialism became a battle between fundamentalism and liberalism. I'm afraid the postmillennial position is still closely associated with evolution and liberalism (*CT*, 2/6/87, p. 8-I).

Here is the man who was president for thirty years of a seminary that has never offered a course defending the six-literal-day creation. He says that postmillennialism favors evolutionism, yet it was R. J. Rushdoony, a postmillennialist, who got Morris and Whitcomb's *Genesis Flood* into print through Presbyterian & Reformed Publishers after dispensationalist Moody Press made it clear to the authors that Moody's editors rejected their literal-day view of the Genesis week.[13] The intellectual leaders of postmillennialism in the United States are all six-literal-day creationists. Is Dallas Seminary's faculty? No.

Dispensational premillennialists are hardly consistent defenders of this literal view of Genesis 1, given the fact that C. I. Scofield taught the "gap theory" in the notes of his famous reference Bible. This theory proposes two separate creations by God, the one described in Genesis 1:1, and then another preceding Genesis 1:2. (The "gap" refers to the supposed time gap between the two creations, although the word is more properly applied to the *gap of revelation* that this hypothesis inserts in between Genesis 1:1 and 1:2.) In between the two creations, there was enough time to absorb all the geological ages that the humanists can throw at us. (How the formless and void re-created world of Genesis 1:2 left geological traces of countless ages, with all those detailed fossil forms embedded in the rocks,

---

13. Henry M. Morris, *History of Modern Creationism* (San Diego, California: Master Book Pubs., 1984), p. 154.

is a bit of a problem, of course.) Scofield speaks of the "dateless past" as holding enough time to allow all geological eras.[14]

This "gap theory" had been developed in the early nineteenth century as a way to enable Bible-believing Christians to accept the findings of uniformitarian geology without giving up their faith in a literal Bible. Henry Morris, Duane Gish, and most other Scientific Creationists have long recognized the deadly threat that this compromising theory poses to biblical creationism.[15] It had been the acceptance by Christians of the ages-long time scheme of the pre-Darwin geologists that led to Darwinism in the first place, and made it far easier for Darwinism to be accepted by Christians.[16]

A Stolen Worldview

Christianity is the source of the idea of progress in the history of mankind. Other groups have stolen this vision and have reworked it along anti-Christian lines, from the Enlightenment[17] to the Social Gospel movement, but this does not mean that postmillennial optimism is the cause of the thefts. And it surely does not mean that eschatological pessimism is in any way an effective shield against humanism, New Age philosophy, or socialism.

What is even more galling is that dispensationalist author Dave Hunt has tried to link the Christian Reconstruction movement with the New Age movement, simply because Christian Reconstructionists, as dominion theologians, proclaim the legitimacy of social action along biblical lines. He writes: "Closely related in belief are several other groups: the Reconstructionists

---

14. C. I. Scofield, *Scofield Reference Bible* (New York: Oxford University Press, [1909] 1917), p. 3n.

15. Morris, *History of Modern Creation*, pp. 41, 58-61, 92.

16. Gary North, *The Dominion Covenant: Genesis* (2nd ed.; Tyler, Texas: Institute for Christian Economics, 1987), Appendix C: "Cosmologies in Conflict: Creation vs. Evolution."

17. Robert A. Nisbet, "The Year 2000 and All That," *Commentary* (June 1968).

such as Gary North et al, as well as Christian socialists such as Jim Wallis (of *Sojourners*), Tom Sine et al whose major focus is upon cleaning up the earth ecologically, politically, economically, sociologically etc. They imagine that the main function of the Church is to restore the Edenic state – hardly helpful, since Eden is where sin began. Many groups are beginning to work together who disagree on some points but share with the New Agers a desire to clean up the earth and establish the kingdom."[18] Hunt's view is clear: *historical optimism regarding the positive cultural effects of the gospel is innately demonic; optimism regarding the gospel's cultural effects is inherently New Age philosophy.* Anyone who wonders why dispensationalism has been culturally impotent need search no farther than the writings of Dave Hunt. He believes with all his heart that *Jesus is a loser in history,* for His Church has been predestined by God to lose.

Christian Reconstructionists teach that there will be a future era in which the gospel heals the souls of men, and these healed people will then work to subdue the earth to the glory of God. This optimism about visible manifestations of God's kingdom on earth, he says, is what the New Age movement is all about.

On the contrary, what the New Age movement is all about is the defeat of Christianity in history. The key New Age doctrines are these: (1) the self-transcendence of man into a higher being (through "higher consciousness" techniques, or drugs, or power), and (2) the law of reincarnation (karma). Christian Reconstruction reaffirms the doctrine of the absolute Creator-creature distinction, following the lead of Cornelius Van Til. Christian Reconstruction also preaches the doctrine of final judgment at the end of history and God's preliminary sanctions in history. What Christian Reconstruction denies is what Hunt affirms as inevitable and what the New Agers hope for above all: *the defeat of Christianity in history.*

---

18. Dave Hunt, *CIB Bulletin* (Feb. 1987), front page.

Conclusion

Christianity is the religion of historic optimism. The power of Christ in history is made manifest through the preaching of the gospel of redemption. As the gospel takes root in society after society, the covenantal blessings of God will begin to transform the earth. This is a long-term process. It has already taken almost 2,000 years, and it may take a thousand more. It may take even longer. But the progressive sanctification of Christians leads to the progressive sanctification of the institutional Church. The "salt and light" gospel of comprehensive redemption eventually serves as the leaven of righteousness that increasingly limits the power of Satan's human disciples. We never will see perfection, for sin will be in the world until the final judgment, but neither will we see the earthly triumph of Satan. His victory over Adam was overcome by Christ's victory at Calvary. The resurrection is our model, not the Fall of man in Eden.

Walvoord is the dean of dispensational theologians. He made it clear in his *Christianity Today* interview that he does not believe in the possibility of comprehensive redemption in Church history. He calls his view "realism." I call it pessimism. It is this pessimism that has justified the retreat of fundamentalists from the preaching of Christ's comprehensive gospel: *the replacement of evil by good in every area of life.* It has led to the triumph of humanism by default, with Christians' tax money financing this triumph. It has led to the paralysis of dispensationalism: emotional, intellectual, and institutional. It has led to Rapture fever: the "blessed hope" for a people without earthly hope.

4

DISPENSATIONALISM REMOVES EARTHLY HOPE

> *A Psalm of David. The* LORD *is my shepherd; I shall not want. He maketh me to lie down in green pastures: he leadeth me beside the still waters. He restoreth my soul: he leadeth me in the paths of righteousness for his name's sake. Yea, though I walk through the valley of the shadow of death, I will fear no evil: for thou art with me; thy rod and thy staff they comfort me. Thou preparest a table before me in the presence of mine enemies: thou anointest my head with oil; my cup runneth over. Surely goodness and mercy shall follow me all the days of my life: and I will dwell in the house of the* LORD *for ever (Psa. 23:1-6).*

One of the great evils of dispensationalism is that it self-consciously strips from Christians the Old Testament's many comforts offered by God to His people. Dispensationalists regard the 23rd psalm as the equivalent of Santa Claus: a comforting story fit for children but not for adults. There are many dispensational local churches that refuse to recite any of the psalms. There are even some local assemblies that refuse to recite the Lord's Prayer, consigning it to the "pre-crucifixion Jewish dispensation." They refuse to acknowledge the lawful inheritance of the Church in history:

What man is he that feareth the LORD? him shall he teach in the way that he shall choose. His soul shall dwell at ease; and his seed shall inherit the earth. The secret of the LORD is with them that fear him; and he will shew them his covenant. Mine eyes are ever toward the LORD; for he shall pluck my feet out of the net (Psa. 25:12-15).

For evildoers shall be cut off: but those that wait upon the LORD, they shall inherit the earth (Psa. 37:9).

For such as be blessed of him shall inherit the earth; and they that be cursed of him shall be cut off (Psa. 37:22).

Blessed are the meek: for they shall inherit the earth (Matt. 5:5).

Just Around the Corner!

If the Rapture is just around the corner, then the Beast and the Antichrist are in our midst already, preparing to take advantage of every opportunity to deceive, persecute, and tyrannize the world generally and Christians in particular. This would mean that all attempts by Christians to improve this world through the preaching of the gospel and obedience to God's Word are doomed. There would be insufficient time to reclaim anything from the jaws of inevitable eschatological defeat. This is precisely what dispensationalists believe, as I hope to demonstrate in this subsection.

Dave Hunt assures us that the cultural defeat of the Church of Jesus Christ is inevitable. Our task is to escape this world, not change it. Those who teach otherwise, he says, "mistakenly believe that the church is in this world to eliminate evil, when in fact it is only here as God's instrument of restraint. It is not our job to transform this world but to call out of it those who will respond to the gospel."[1] In short, he views the Church's

---

1. Dave Hunt, *Whatever Happened to Heaven?* (Eugene, Oregon: Harvest House, 1988), pp. 268-69.

work in this world in terms of his view of the Church's only hope: *escape from the trials and tribulations of life*. We are to call men out of this world, spiritually speaking, so that Jesus will come back in the clouds and call His Church out of this world, literally speaking.[2]

His view is exactly the same as that of House and Ice, who make it plain that Christians are working the "night shift" in this world. (And we all know how far removed from the seats of influence all "night shift" people are!) They write: "The dawn is the Second Coming of Christ, which is why he is called the 'morning star' (2 Peter 1:19). Our job on the 'night shift' is clarified by Paul in Ephesians 5:1-14 when he says we are to expose evil (bring it to light), not conquer it. . . ."[3]

The Right Hand of Glory

This anti-dominion perspective conveniently ignores the "passage of passages" that dispensationalist authors do their best to avoid referring to, the Old Testament passage which is cited more times in the New Testament than any other, Psalm 110. What few Church historians have recognized is that it was also the Church fathers' most cited passage in the century after the fall of Jerusalem.[4] (Dispensationalists keep citing unnamed early Church fathers in general for support of their thesis that the early Church fathers were all premillennialists – an assertion disproved by one of their own disciples.)[5] Psalm 110 may

---

2. For a Bible-based explanation of what "this world" means, see Greg L. Bahnsen, "The Person, Work, and Present Status of Satan," *Journal of Christian Reconstruction*, I (Winter 1974), pp. 20-30. See the extract I provide in my book, *Is the World Running Down? Crisis in the Christian Worldview* (Tyler, Texas: Institute for Christian Economics, 1988), pp. 220-22.

3. H. Wayne House and Thomas D. Ice, *Dominion Theology: Blessing or Curse?* (Portland, Oregon: Multnomah Press, 1988), p. 172.

4. David Hay, *Glory at the Right Hand* (Nashville, Tennessee: Abingdon, 1973).

5. In a 1977 Dallas Seminary Th.M. thesis, Alan Patrick Boyd concluded that the early Church fathers were both amillennial and premillennial, and he rejected then-Dallas professor Charles Ryrie's claim that the early Church fathers were all premil-

Dispensationalism Removes Earthly Hope 79

be the dispensationalists' least favorite Bible passage, for good reason.

> The LORD said unto my Lord, Sit thou at my right hand, until I make thine enemies thy footstool. The LORD shall send the rod of thy strength out of Zion: rule thou in the midst of thine enemies (Psa. 110:1-2).

This passage makes it clear that a legitimate goal of God's people is the extension in history and on earth of God's kingdom, to rule in the midst of our spiritual enemies and opponents. But more to the point, the Lord speaks to Jesus Christ and informs Him that He will sit at God's right hand until His enemies are conquered. Obviously, God's throne is in heaven. This is where Jesus will remain until He comes again in final judgment. *Jesus sits tight while His people extend His rule.*

This is also what is taught by the New Testament's major eschatological passage, I Corinthians 15. It provides the context of the fulfillment of Psalm 110. It speaks of the resurrection of every person's body at the last judgment. Jesus' body was resurrected first in time in order to demonstrate to the world that the bodily resurrection is real. (This is why liberals hate the doctrine of the bodily resurrection of Christ, and why they will go to such lengths in order to deny it.)[6] This passage tells us when all the rest of us will experience this bodily resurrection. What it describes has to be the final judgment.

> For as in Adam all die, even so in Christ shall all be made alive. But every man in his own order: Christ the firstfruits; afterward

---

lennialists. Boyd, "A Dispensational Premillennial Analysis of the Eschatology of the Post-Apostolic Fathers (Until the Death of Justin Martyr)." Gary DeMar summarizes Boyd's findings in his book, *The Debate Over Christian Reconstruction* (Ft. Worth, Texas: Dominion Press, 1988), pp. 96-98, 180n.

6. A notorious example of such literature is Hugh J. Schonfield, *The Passover Plot: New Light on the History of Jesus* (New York: Bantam, [1966] 1971). It had gone through seven hardback printings and 14 paperback printings by 1971.

they that are Christ's at his coming. Then cometh the end, when he shall have delivered up the kingdom to God, even the Father; when he shall have put down all rule and all authority and power. For he must reign, till he hath put all enemies under his feet. The last enemy that shall be destroyed is death (I Cor. 15:22-26).

Jesus reigns until God the Father has put all enemies under Jesus' feet. But Jesus reigns from heaven; if this were not true, then how on earth could He be seated at the right hand of God, as Psalm 110 requires? *Any suggestion that Jesus will rule physically on earth in history (meaning before the final judgment), away from His place at God's right hand, is also a suggestion that the right hand of glory is not all that glorious.* Yet this is exactly what premillennialists say must and will happen in history. This is premillennialism's distinctive doctrine.

Representative Presence

What premillennialism inevitably denies is that Jesus Christ reigns in history through His earthly followers, and *only* through them, just as Satan rules his kingdom in history through his earthly followers, and *only* through them. Satan never will appear physically in history to command his troops, and neither will Jesus Christ. Satan does not have to reign from some city in order for him to exercise power; neither does Jesus Christ. Are we to believe that Satan's kingdom is not a true kingdom just because he is not present physically? Yet Dave Hunt, exposer of cults and New Age conspiracies, denouncer of satanism everywhere, nevertheless insists: "There can be no kingdom without the king being present. . . ."[7] He refuses to understand what Jesus taught from the beginning: *Jesus Christ is covenantally present with His people in their weekly worship services and especially during the Lord's Supper.*[8] Jesus exer-

---

7. Hunt, *Whatever Happened to Heaven?*, p. 259.
8. Dave Hunt is quite self-conscious about his rejection of any view of the Lord's

cises covenantal judgment in the midst of the congregation during the Lord's Supper, which is why *self-judgment* in advance is required.

> Wherefore whosoever shall eat this bread, and drink this cup of the Lord, unworthily, shall be guilty of the body and blood of the Lord. But let a man examine himself, and so let him eat of that bread, and drink of that cup. For he that eateth and drinketh unworthily, eateth and drinketh damnation to himself, not discerning the Lord's body. For this cause many are weak and sickly among you, and many sleep. For if we would judge ourselves, we should not be judged. But when we are judged, we are chastened of the Lord, that we should not be condemned with the world. Wherefore, my brethren, when ye come together to eat, tarry one for another (I Cor. 11:27-33).

I suspect that it is dispensationalism's lack of emphasis on the sacrament of Holy Communion that has led them to adopt the strange belief that Satan's kingdom rule is real even though he is not physically present on earth, yet Jesus' kingdom reign cannot become real until He is physically present on earth. In each case, the two supernatural rulers rule *representatively*. In neither case does the Bible teach that the supernatural ruler needs to be bodily present with his people in order for him to exercise dominion through them.

Obvious, isn't it? But when have you heard a sermon or read a book that mentions this?

No Earthly Hope

If the Church is just about out of time, as dispensational authors keep insisting, decade after decade, then what legitimate hope can Christians have that they can leave the world a

---

Supper that involves anything more than a memorial: *ibid*, p. 302.

better place than they found it? None, says Lehman Strauss in Dallas Seminary's journal, *Bibliotheca Sacra*:

> We are witnessing in this twentieth century the collapse of civilization. It is obvious that we are advancing toward the end of the age. Science can offer no hope for the future blessing and security of humanity, but instead it has produced devastating and deadly results which threaten to lead us toward a new dark age. The frightful uprisings among races, the almost unbelievable conquests of Communism, and the growing antireligious philosophy throughout the world, all spell out the fact that doom is certain. I can see no bright prospects, through the efforts of man, for the earth and its inhabitants.[9]

This same pessimism regarding Christians' ability to improve society through the preaching of the gospel has been affirmed by John Walvoord, for three decades the president of Dallas Seminary: "Well, I personally object to the idea that premillennialism is pessimistic. We are simply realistic in believing that man cannot change the world. Only God can."[10] But why can't God change it through His servants, just as Moses changed the world, and as the apostles changed it? The apostles' enemies announced regarding them: "These that have turned the world upside down are come hither also" (Acts 17:6b). No one has ever announced this about dispensationalists!

A Question of Responsibility

This utter pessimism concerning the earthly future of the institutional Church and Christian civilization is what lies behind the traditional premillennialists' lack of any systematic social theory or recommended social policies. They believe that it is a waste of their time thinking about such "theoretical"

---

9. Lehman Strauss, "Our Only Hope," *Bibliotheca Sacra*, Vol. 120 (April/June 1963), p. 154.

10. *Christianity Today* (Feb. 6, 1987), p. 11-I.

matters, since they believe that the Christians will never be in a position to implement them, even if they exist. The fact is, because they self-consciously reject the idea that Old Testament laws are in any way morally or legally binding on Christians and non-Christians alike, *dispensationalists have no place to go in order to discover Bible-mandated social policies.* Tommy Ice admitted in a debate with me and Gary DeMar: "Premillennialists have always been involved in the present world. And basically, they have picked up on the ethical positions of their contemporaries."[11] They have had nothing to add because (1) they have no hope in the future, and (2) they reject biblical law.

Dispensationalists have *no earthly hope in the Church's future*. This means that dispensational theology lures God's people out of society. The dispensationalist has no concept of positive social change and positive social transformation because he has no concept of ethical cause and effect in history. He explicitly denies the continuing authority of Deuteronomy 28:1-14. He even denies the continuing authority of the Ten Commandments, as former Dallas Seminary professor S. Lewis Johnson did in 1963:

> At the heart of the problem of legalism is pride, a pride that refuses to admit spiritual bankruptcy. That is why the doctrines of grace stir up so much animosity. Donald Grey Barnhouse, a giant of a man in free grace, wrote: "It was a tragic hour when the Reformation churches wrote the Ten Commandments into their creeds and catechisms and sought to bring Gentile believers into bondage to Jewish law, which was never intended either for the Gentile nations or for the church."[12] He was right, too.[13]

---

11. April 12, 1988; cited by Gary DeMar, *The Debate Over Christian Reconstruction*, p. 185. Audio tapes of the debate are available for $10 from the Institute for Christian Economics. The debate was Dave Hunt and Tommy Ice vs. Gary North and Gary DeMar.

12. Citing Barnhouse, *God's Freedom*, p. 134.

13. S. Lewis Johnson, "The Paralysis of Legalism," *Bibliotheca Sacra*, Vol. 120 (April/June 1963), p. 109.

Legitimizing Cultural Retreat

Because he has no faith in the long-term efforts of Christians to transform this world through obedience to God, the consistent dispensationalist retreats from the hard conflicts of society that rage around him, just as the Russian Orthodox Church did during the Russian Revolution of 1917. The existence of this dispensationalist attitude of retreat is openly admitted by dispensational pastor David Schnittger:

> North and other postmillennial Christian Reconstructionists label those who hold the pretribulational rapture position pietists and cultural retreatists. One reason these criticisms are so painful is because I find them to be substantially true. Many in our camp have an all-pervasive negativism regarding the course of society and the impotence of God's people to do anything about it. They will heartily affirm that **Satan is Alive and Well on Planet Earth,** and that this must indeed be **The Terminal Generation;** therefore, any attempt to influence society is ultimately hopeless. They adopt the pietistic platitude: *"You don't polish brass on a sinking ship."* Many pessimistic pretribbers cling to the humanists' version of religious freedom; namely Christian social and political impotence, self-imposed, as drowning men cling to a life preserver.[14]

Removing Illegitimate Fears

David Chilton shows in *The Great Tribulation* that Christians' fears regarding some inevitable Great Tribulation for the Church are not grounded in Scripture. Kenneth Gentry shows in his books on Bible prophecy that the Beast of Revelation is not lurking around the corner. Neither is the Rapture. Thus, Christians can have legitimate hope in the positive earthly outcome of their prayers and labors. Their sacrifices today will make a difference in the long run. There is *continuity* between

---

14. David Schnittger, *Christian Reconstruction from a Pretribulational Perspective* (Oklahoma City: Southwest Radio Church, 1986), p. 7.

Dispensationalism Removes Earthly Hope 85

their efforts today and the long-term expansion of God's civilization in history ("civilization" is just another word for "kingdom"). Jesus' words are true: there will be no eschatological discontinuity, no cataclysmic disruption, no *Rapture* in between today and Christ's second coming at the final judgment:

> Another parable put he forth unto them, saying, The kingdom of heaven is likened unto a man which sowed good seed in his field: But while men slept, his enemy came and sowed tares among the wheat, and went his way. But when the blade was sprung up, and brought forth fruit, then appeared the tares also. So the servants of the householder came and said unto him, Sir, didst not thou sow good seed in thy field? from whence then hath it tares? He said unto them, An enemy hath done this. The servants said unto him, Wilt thou then that we go and gather them up? But he said, Nay; lest while ye gather up the tares, ye root up also the wheat with them. Let both grow together until the harvest: and in the time of harvest I will say to the reapers, Gather ye together first the tares, and bind them in bundles to burn them: but gather the wheat into my barn (Matt. 13:24-30).

The apostles did not understand the meaning of this parable. Neither do dispensationalists:

> Then Jesus sent the multitude away, and went into the house: and his disciples came unto him, saying, Declare unto us the parable of the tares of the field. He answered and said unto them, He that soweth the good seed is the Son of man; **The field is the world**; the good seed are the children of the kingdom; but the tares are the children of the wicked one; The enemy that sowed them is the devil; **the harvest is the end of the world**; and the reapers are the angels. As therefore **the tares are gathered and burned in the fire; so shall it be in the end of this world**. The Son of man shall send forth his angels, and they shall gather out of his kingdom all things that offend, and them which do iniquity; And shall cast them into a furnace of fire: there shall be wailing and gnashing of teeth. Then shall the righteous shine

forth as the sun in the kingdom of their Father. Who hath ears to hear, let him hear (Matt. 13:36-43; emphasis added).

Dispensationalists refuse to hear.

This book presents a message of moral responsibility. Every message of true hope inevitably is also a message of moral responsibility. In God's world, there is no hope without moral responsibility, no offer of victory without the threat of persecution, no offer of heaven without the threat of hell. Deny this, and you deny the gospel. He who has ears to hear, let him hear.

A Question of Time

Why would a Christian economics institute publish a book on the Beast of Revelation and another on the dating of the Book of Revelation? Because a crucial aspect of all economics, all economic growth, is time perspective. Those individuals and societies that are future-oriented save more money, enjoy lower interest rates, and benefit from more rapid economic growth. A short-run view of the future is the mark of the gambler, the person in poverty, and the underdeveloped society. Those who think in terms of generations and plan for the future see their heirs prosper; those who think in terms of the needs and desires in the present cannot successfully compete over the long haul with those who are willing to forego present consumption for the sake of future growth.

Furthermore, dispensationalists insist, the Beast is coming, and so is the Antichrist. That horror is just around the corner. The Great Tribulation is imminent. Nothing can stop it. Nothing will resist its onslaught. Nothing we leave behind as Christians will be able to change things for the next generation. It is all hopeless. All we can legitimately hope for, we are told, is our escape into the heavens at the Rapture.

It is no wonder that American Christians have been short-run thinkers in this century. They see failure and defeat in the immediate future, relieved only (if at all) by the Rapture of the Church into heaven. This is Dave Hunt's message. He sees no earthly hope for the Church apart from the imminent return of Christ.

But such a view of the future has inescapable practical implications, although more and more self-professed dispensationalists who have become Christian activists, and who have therefore also become operational and psychological postmillennialists, prefer to believe that these implications are not really inescapable. If the "Church Age" is just about out of time, why should any sensible Christian attend college? Why go to the expense of graduate school? Why become a professional? Why start a Christian university or a new business? Why do anything for the kingdom of God that involves a capital commitment greater than door-to-door evangelism? Why even build a new church?

Here, admittedly, all dispensational pastors become embarrassingly inconsistent. They want big church buildings. Perhaps they can justify this "worldly orientation" by building it with a mountain of long-term debt, just as Dallas Seminary financed its expansion of the 1970's. They are tempted to view the Rapture as a personal and institutional means of escape from bill-collection agencies. A person who really believes in the imminent return of Christ asks himself: Why avoid personal or corporate debt if Christians are about to be raptured out of repayment? Why not adopt the outlook of "eat, drink, and be merry, for tomorrow we will be rescued by God's helicopter escape"?

The Helicopter Man

Dave Hunt does not want to become known as "Helicopter Hunt," but that really is who he is. His worldview is the fundamentalists' worldview during the past century, and especially since the Scopes "Monkey Trial" of 1925,[15] but its popularity

---

15. George Marsden, *Fundamentalism and American Culture: The Shaping of Twenti-*

is fading fast. No wonder. Many Christians today are sick and tired of riding in the back of humanism's bus. They are fed up with being regarded as third-class citizens, irrelevant to the modern world. They are beginning to perceive that their shortened view of time is what has helped to make them culturally irrelevant.

The older generation of American fundamentalists is still being thrilled and chilled in fits of Rapture fever, but not so much the younger generation. Younger fundamentalists are now beginning to recognize a long-ignored biblical truth: *the future of this world belongs to the Church of Jesus Christ if His people remain faithful to His word.* They are beginning to understand Jesus' words of victory in Matthew 28: "And Jesus came and spake unto them, saying, All power is given unto me in heaven and in earth. Go ye therefore, and teach all nations, baptizing them in the name of the Father, and of the Son, and of the Holy Ghost. Teaching them to observe all things whatsoever I have commanded you: and, lo, I am with you alway, even unto the end of the world. Amen" (vv. 18-20). They have at last begun to take seriously the promised victory of the Church's Great Commission rather than the past horror of Israel's Great Tribulation. They are steadily abandoning that older eschatology of corporate defeat and heavenly rescue.

In short, Christians are at long last beginning to view Jesus Christ as the Lord of all history and the head of His progressively triumphant Church rather than as "Captain Jesus and His angels."

The Same Argument the Liberals Use

By interpreting Jesus' promise that He would soon return in power and judgment against Israel as if it were a promise of His second coming at the Rapture, dispensationalists are caught in a dilemma. They teach that Paul and the apostles taught the

---

eth-Century Evangelicalism, 1870-1925 (New York: Oxford University Press, 1980).

early Church, in Dave Hunt's words, to "watch and wait for His imminent return,"[16] yet Jesus has delayed returning physically for over 1,950 years. *How can we escape the conclusion that the apostles misinformed the early Church*, a clearly heretical notion, and an argument that liberal theologians have used against Bible-believing Christians repeatedly in this century? But there is no way out of this intellectual dilemma if you do not distinguish between Christ's coming in judgment against Israel in A.D. 70 and His physical return in final judgment at the end of time.

Contrary to Dave Hunt, with respect to the physical return of Jesus in judgment, the early Church was told just the opposite: do *not* stand around watching and waiting. "And while they looked steadfastly toward heaven as he went up, behold, two men stood by them in white apparel; Which also said, Ye men of Galilee, why stand ye gazing up into heaven? this same Jesus, which is taken up from you into heaven, shall so come in like manner as ye have seen him go into heaven. Then returned they unto Jerusalem from the mount called Olivet, which is from Jerusalem a sabbath day's journey" (Acts 1:10-12).

Conclusion

Those who prefer figuratively to stand around looking into the sky are then tempted to conclude, as Dave Hunt concludes, that the Church today, by abandoning pre-tribulational dispensationalism – as if more than a comparative handful of Christians in the Church's history had ever believed in the pre-tribulational Rapture doctrine, invented as recently as 1830[17] – has "succumbed once again to the unbiblical hope that, by exerting godly influence upon government, society can be trans-

---

16. Hunt, *Whatever Happened to Heaven?*, p. 55.

17. Dave MacPherson, *The Unbelievable Pre-Trib Origin* (Kansas City, Missouri: Heart of America Bible Society, 1973); *The Great Rapture Hoax* (Fletcher, North Carolina: New Puritan Library, 1983).

formed."[18] It is time, he says, for Christians to give up "the false dream of Christianizing secular culture. . . ."[19]

In short, let the world go to hell in a handbasket on this side of the millennium. Christians living today supposedly will escape this supposedly burning building because we all have been issued free tickets on God's helicopter escape.

This escape never comes. The supposedly imminent Rapture has now been delayed for almost two millennia. The Bible-believing fundamentalist considers this delay and grows increasingly frantic and therefore increasingly vulnerable to crackpots.

He worries: Could the theological liberals be correct? Were the apostles confused about God's timing? Did they give false information about the imminent Rapture to their readers?

Rather than conclude this, dispensational commentators have played exegetical games with Jesus' clear statement regarding the tribulation that would face the early Church: "Verily I say unto you, This generation shall not pass, till all these things have been fulfiilled" (Matt. 24:24). The Great Tribulation took place in A.D. 70: the fall of Jerusalem and the destruction of the temple, just as He warned (Luke 21:20-22). It is finished.

Dispensationalists are culturally paralyzed by their belief in a future Great Tribulation. They want to escape both personal and corporate responsibility. They are willing to believe anything and anyone who promises them an excuse for continuing to do almost nothing positive culturally and intellectually. This is why they readily accept the idea of today's ticking prophetic clock, even though this belief necessarily denies the traditional dispensational doctrine of the any-moment Rapture. They care little about the utterly scrambled condition of their movement's theology. They care only about an imminent escape from long-term responsibility: the Rapture. *Rapture fever destroys men's ability to reason theologically.* It weakens God's Church.

---

18. Hunt, *Whatever Happened to Heaven?*, p. [8].
19. *Idem.*

5

A COMMITMENT TO CULTURAL IRRELEVANCE

Behold, I have taught you statutes and judgments, even as the LORD my God commanded me, that ye should do so in the land whither ye go to possess it. Keep therefore and do them; for this is your wisdom and your understanding in the sight of the nations, which shall hear all these statutes, and say, Surely this great nation is a wise and understanding people. For what nation is there so great, who hath God so nigh unto them, as the LORD our God is in all things that we call upon him for? And what nation is there so great, that hath statutes and judgments so righteous as all this law, which I set before you this day? (Deut. 4:5-8).

God told Moses that Israel's obedience to God's laws would stand as a testimony to the nations. The nation of Israel would become a beacon to the world. *There is an unbreakable connection between national obedience and world evangelism.* Jesus appealed to this same idea when He described the Church as a city on a hill (Matt. 5:14). But this connection between corporate obedience, God's corporate blessings, and world evangelism is denied by dispensationalists. "That was for Israel, not for the Church." But what about Jesus' words about the city on a hill? "That was before the crucifixion. That was for Israel, too: the kingdom of heaven, not the kingdom of God. That was not for the Church." Then what is for the Church, ethically speaking?

They never say. In over 160 years, no dispensationalist author has had a book published dealing with the details of New Testament social ethics.

The result, in the words of dispensationalist author Tommy Ice, is that "Premillennialists have always been involved in the present world. And basically, they have picked up on the ethical positions of their contemporaries."[1] The question is: How reliable are the ethical positions of their contemporaries?

The Two-Storey World of Humanism

In the early writings of premillennialist Francis Schaeffer, we read of modern philosophy's two-storey[2] universe. The bottom storey is one of reason, science, predictable cause and effect, i.e., Immanuel Kant's *phenomenal* realm. This view of the universe leads inevitably to despair, for to the extent that this realm is dominant, man is seen to be nothing more than a freedomless cog in a vast impersonal machine.

In order to escape the pessimistic implications of this lower-storey worldview, humanists have proposed an escape hatch: a correlative upper-storey universe. The upper storey is supposedly one of humanistic "freedom": faith, feeling, emotion, personality, randomness, religion, non-cognitive reality, i.e., Kant's *noumenal* realm. It also supposedly provides meaning for man, but only non-cognitive ("irrational") meaning. It is meaning which is meaningless in rational ("lower storey") terms. There is no known point of contact or doorway between these two realms, yet modern man needs such a doorway to hold his world and his psyche together. This is why the modern world is in the midst of a monumental crisis, Schaeffer argued.

---

1. Debate between Dave Hunt and Tommy Ice vs. Gary DeMar and Gary North. Cited by DeMar, *The Debate Over Christian Reconstruction* (Ft. Worth, Texas: Dominion Press, 1988), p. 185.

2. I use "storey" to identify layers of a building; I use "story" to identify tales.

Schaeffer got the core of this idea from his professor of apologetics at Westminster Theological Seminary, Cornelius Van Til, although you would not suspect this by reading any of Schaeffer's footnotes. Van Til argued throughout his long career that all non-Christian philosophy from the Greeks to the present is dualistic: a war between the totally rational and the totally irrational. Creating a memorable analogy, Van Til said that the irrationalist and the rationalist are like a pair of washerwomen who support themselves by taking in each other's laundry. The intellectual problems created by each school of thought are unresolvable in terms of its own presuppositions, and so the defenders of each system seek temporary refuge in the very different but equally unresolvable problems of the rival school.

Why do they do this? Because non-Christian man prefers to believe anything except the God of the Bible, who issues His covenant law and holds all men responsible for obeying it, on pain of eternal judgment. They would prefer to dwell in an incoherent dualistic universe of their own devising rather than in God's universe, dependent on His grace.

The Two-Storey World of Orthodox Christianity

The New Testament teaches that there are two realms of existence in this world: the eternal and the temporal. Each of these realms is itself divided: life vs. death. Jesus said: "He that believeth on the Son hath everlasting life: and he that believeth not the Son shall not see life; but the wrath of God abideth on him" (John 3:36). The person who in history rejects Jesus Christ as Lord and Savior is *already dead*. He shall not see life, either in this world or the next.

These two realms – time and eternity – are linked together by the sovereign God of the Bible, who created all things. They are connected by the sovereignty of God and His covenant: a judicial covenant.[3] It is Jesus Christ, as God the Creator, who binds all things together; it is Jesus Christ

> Who is the image of the invisible God, the firstborn of every creature: For by him were all things created, that are in heaven, and that are in earth, visible and invisible, whether they be thrones, or dominions, or principalities, or powers: all things were created by him, and for him: And he is before all things, and by him all things consist. And he is the head of the body, the church: who is the beginning, the firstborn from the dead; that in all things he might have the preeminence. For it pleased the Father that in him should all fulness dwell; And, having made peace through the blood of his cross, by him to reconcile all things unto himself; by him, I say, whether they be things in earth, or things in heaven (Col. 1:15-20).

Thus, the kingdom of God encompasses all the creation. It alone is the source of unity. The two realms – time and eternity – are united under God's covenant. Men participate in this unified kingdom either as covenant-keepers or covenant-breakers. Heaven is linked to earth by God's law, which is why Jesus taught His people to pray: "Thy kingdom come. Thy will be done in earth, as it is in heaven" (Matt. 6:10). The progressive manifestation of the kingdom of God on earth – "thy kingdom come" – is seen in the progressive subduing of the world in terms of God's revealed law: "thy will be done." Thus, the link between heaven and earth is God's covenant: *faithfulness* (through Jesus Christ, empowered by the Holy Spirit) to God's covenant law. The link between hell and earth is also God's covenant: *rebellion* against God's covenant law.

This covenantal and therefore *legal* link between heaven and earth is explicitly denied by modern fundamentalism. Fundamentalism denies the continuing authority of God's law. Thus,

---

3. Ray R. Sutton, *That You May Prosper: Dominion By Covenant* (2nd ed.; Tyler, Texas: Institute for Christian Economics, 1992).

A Commitment to Cultural Irrelevance

fundamentalism faces the same dilemma that humanism faces: a radical break between the upper storey and the lower storey.

The Two-Storey World of Fundamentalism

Fundamentalism's lower storey is the world of work, economics, professional training, art, institutions, authority, and power, i.e., the "secular" realm. This realm is governed not in terms of the Bible but in terms of supposedly universal "neutral reason" and natural law. (So far, this is basically the thirteenth-century worldview of Thomas Aquinas and medieval scholastic philosophers.) The Bible supposedly does not speak directly to this realm, we are assured by both the fundamentalists ("We're under grace, not law!") and the secular humanists ("This is a pluralistic nation!"). Thus, there is no theological or judicial basis for Christians to claim that they are entitled to set forth uniquely biblical principles of social order. Above all, Christians are not supposed to seek to persuade voters to elect political rulers who will enforce biblical laws or principles. This means that rulers must not be identifiably Christian in their social and political outlook. Christians are allowed to vote and exercise civil authority only insofar as they cease to be explicitly biblical in their orientation. In short, only *operational humanists* should be allowed to rule. This is political pluralism, the reigning political gospel in our age – in an era which believes that only politics is gospel.[4]

Crumbs from Humanism's Table

This view of the world – "the world under autonomous man's law" – leads Christians to an inescapable pessimism regarding the Church's present and its earthly future, for this view asserts that Christians will always be under the humanists'

---

4. Gary North, *Political Polytheism: The Myth of Pluralism* (Tyler, Texas: Institute for Christian Economics, 1989).

table, eating the crumbs that may occasionally fall from that table. This view of the relationship between the saved and the lost in history is the reverse of what the Bible teaches: "Then came she and worshipped him, saying, Lord, help me. But he answered and said, It is not meet to take the children's bread, and to cast it to dogs. And she said, Truth, Lord: yet the dogs eat of the crumbs which fall from their masters' table. Then Jesus answered and said unto her, O woman, great is thy faith: be it unto thee even as thou wilt. And her daughter was made whole from that very hour" (Matt. 15:25-28). Because modern fundamentalism has reversed the biblical worldview in this regard, it promotes a despair similar to that which is promoted by the humanists' view of the lower-storey world of science and technology. It destroys freedom under God.

The Upper Storey

To escape this inherent despair, fundamentalists have turned to their own version of the humanists' escape hatch: an upper-storey universe. This upper storey is the world of faith, expectation, and hope: the heavenly realm. It is a hope in heaven – a world above and beyond this world of Christian powerlessness and defeat. With respect to this world, there is a preliminary way of escape: the Christian family and the local church. In other words, Christians find solace in the time that remains after the work day is over and on weekends. This world of *temporary rest and recreation* – a realm of exclusively individual healing – does not and cannot heal the State or society in general. God's healing is limited to individual souls, families, and churches. Why? We are never told precisely; it just is.[5]

---

5. A growing number of Christians now contend that God's healing can work in education, too. This has split churches all over the nation. The idea that Christians need to start their own private schools, pulling their children out of the humanistic, tax-supported, officially "neutral" public schools, is regarded as a heresy by most Christians, who continue to tithe their children to the Moloch State.

A Commitment to Cultural Irrelevance

Fundamentalists believe that the individual Christian must live in both realms during his stay on earth, but he is not supposed to take the first realm very seriously – the realm of a person's job. This is why fundamentalists have invented the phrase, "full-time Christian service": it contrasts the world of faith where ministers and missionaries work vs. the world where the rest of us work. This distinction is very similar to the monastic outlook of Roman Catholicism, which distinguishes between the "secular clergy" – parish priests who work with common people in their common affairs – and the "regular clergy," meaning the monks who have retreated from the normal hustle and bustle of life (the "rat race"). Yet your average fundamentalist would be shocked to learn that he is thinking as a Roman Catholic thinks. He would probably deny it. But he has to think this way, for he has adopted the Roman Catholic (scholastic) doctrine of law: "natural law" for the lower storey, and God's revelation for the upper storey.

A Culturally Impotent Gospel

Fundamentalists believe that Christians are not supposed to devote very much time, money, and effort to transforming the "secular" world. We are assured that it cannot be transformed, according to Bible prophecy, until Jesus comes physically seven years after the Rapture to set up His One World State with headquarters in Jerusalem. Anything that Christians do today to build a better world will be destroyed during the seven-year tribulation period.[6] John Walvoord, former president of Dallas

---

6. In 1962, I was told by a dispensational college's president that the Stewart brothers, who financed the creation of formerly dispensationalist Biola College (then called the Bible Institute of Los Angeles), and who also financed the publication and distribution of the tracts that became known as *The Fundamentals*, shipped crates of Bibles to Israel to be hidden in caves there, so that Jews could find them during the Great Tribulation. I was told years later by an amillennial pastor that Arabs later used pages in these Bibles for cigarette paper, which may just be a "sour grapes" amillennial apocryphal legend. The point is this: Why waste money on Bibles to be hidden in caves? Answer: because of a specific eschatology.

Theological Seminary, insists: "Well, I personally object to the idea that premillennialism is pessimistic. We are simply realistic in believing that man cannot change the world. Only God can."[7] "Realism" sounds a lot better than "pessimism," but the psychological results are the same: retreat from cultural involvement. As Christians, we must be content with whatever the humanists who control the "lower realm" are willing to dish out to us, just so long as they leave us alone on Sunday.

The first president of Grace Theological Seminary, Alva J. McClain, wrote a five-and-a-half-page essay on "A Premillennial Philosophy of History" for Dallas Seminary's *Bibliotheca Sacra* in 1956. This essay should be read by every dispensationalist, not to learn what this view of history is, which the essay never says, but to learn that a major theologian of the movement did not bother to describe it. McClain rejected postmillennialism, although he did admit that "Classical postmillennialism had plenty of defects, but it did make a serious attempt to deal with human history."[8] He then dismissed – in one paragraph per error – modern liberalism, neo-orthodoxy, amillennialism (Louis Berkhof), and all those who think "there will never be such a 'Golden Age' upon earth in history. . . ."[9] (The "golden age" was a pagan Greek concept.) This left exactly half a page for a thorough discussion of the premillennial view of history. He never said what this is. He simply concluded, "The premillennial philosophy of history makes sense. It lays a Biblical and rational basis for a truly optimistic view of human history."[10]

McClain refused even to mention the key historical issue for those living prior to the Rapture: What is the basis of *our* optimism regarding the long-term future of our earthly efforts? Clearly, dispensationalists have none. The results of our efforts,

---

7. *Christianity Today* (Feb. 6, 1987), p. 11-I.
8. McClain, *Bibliotheca Sacra, op. cit.*, p. 112.
9. *Ibid.*, p. 115.
10. *Ibid.*, p. 116.

A Commitment to Cultural Irrelevance 99

dispensationalists would have to say if they had the courage to discuss such things in public, will be swallowed up during the Great Tribulation after the Rapture. This is a self-consciously pessimistic view of the future of the Church, and it has resulted in cultural paralysis whenever it has been widely believed by Christians; therefore, the intellectual leaders of dispensationalism refuse to discuss it forthrightly. It is just too embarrassing. *They deliberately adopt the language of postmillennial optimism to disguise a thoroughgoing pessimism.* They keep pointing to the glorious era of the millennium in order to defend their use of optimistic language, never bothering to point out that the seven years that precede it will destroy the results of gospel preaching during the entire Church Age. After all, every Christian will have been removed from the earth at the Rapture (an explicit denial of the historical continuity predicted in Christ's parable of the wheat and tares: Matthew 13:20, 38-40). McClain's essay is representative of what has passed for world-and-life scholarship within dispensationalism since 1830: non-existent.

While McClain may have fooled those who read *Bibliotheca Sacra* regularly, the troops in the pews have not been fooled. Dave Hunt is willing to say publicly what dispensationalism means, and without any apologies. Dispensational theology obviously teaches the defeat of all the Church's cultural efforts before the Rapture, since the millennium itself will be a cultural defeat for God, even with Jesus reigning here on earth in His perfect body.

> In fact, dominion – taking dominion and setting up the kingdom for Christ – is an *impossibility*, even for God. The millennial reign of Christ, far from being the kingdom, is actually the final proof of the incorrigible nature of the human heart, because Christ Himself can't do what these people say they are going to do....[11]

---

11. Hunt, "Dominion and the Cross," Tape 2 of *Dominion: The Word and New World Order* (1987), published by Omega Letter, Ontario, Canada. See his similar

Here we have it without any sugar-coating: there is no connection between the upper storey of God's spiritual kingdom and the lower storey of human history, not even during the millennium. The two storey-world of fundamentalism is so radically divided that even God Himself cannot bind the two together. That is an impossibility, says Hunt. In the best-selling writings of Dave Hunt, the legacy of Scofield has come to fruition: a cultural rose which is all thorns and no blooms. The seminary professors can protest that this is not the "real" dispensationalism, but this complaint assumes that the movement's scholars have produced a coherent alternative to pop-dispensationalism. They haven't.

Dispensationalists say that Christians *in principle* are impotent to change things in the "lower storey," and to attempt to do so would be a waste of our scarce capital, especially time. While the few academic leaders of dispensationalism have been too embarrassed to admit what is obviously a consistent cultural conclusion of their view of history, the popularizers have not hesitated, especially in response to criticisms of the Reconstructionists. Consider the words of dispensationalist tabloid newspaper publisher Peter Lalonde. A friend of his wanted Christians to begin to work to change the "secular world." Lalonde cited in response J. Vernon McGee's classic phrase on polishing brass on a sinking ship:

> It's a question, "Do you polish brass on a sinking ship?" And if they're working on setting up new institutions, instead of going out and winning the lost for Christ, then they're wasting the most valuable time on the planet earth right now, and that is the serious problem in his thinking.[12]

---

statement in his book, *Beyond Seduction*: "The millennial reign of Christ upon earth, rather than being the kingdom of God, will in fact be the final proof of the incorrigible nature of the human heart." *Beyond Seduction: A Return to Biblical Christianity* (Eugene, Oregon: Harvest House, 1987), p. 250.

12. "Dominion: A Dangerous New Theology," Tape 1 of *Dominion: The Word and*

Because this attitude toward social change has prevailed within American fundamentalism since at least 1925, those who attempt to dwell only in the "lower storey" – non-Christians – have had few reasons to take fundamentalism very seriously. American Christians have been in self-conscious cultural retreat from historic reality and cultural responsibility for most of the twentieth century.[13] Meanwhile, as non-Christians have become steadily more consistent with their own worldview, they have begun to recognize more clearly who their enemies really are: Christians who proclaim the God of the Bible, i.e., the God of final judgment. Thus, we are now seeing an escalation of the inherent, inevitable conflict between covenant-keepers and covenant-breakers in the United States.

The Great Escape Hatch

Modern premillennial fundamentalism proclaims that there is only one biblical solution to this escalating conflict: the Rapture. The Rapture of the saints is said to come in history, not at the end of history, as postmillennialists and amillennialists insist. The Rapture serves them psychologically as the hoped-for Great Escape Hatch. This is the "hope of historical hopes" for Bible-believing fundamentalists, as Dave Hunt insists in his 1988 book, *Whatever Happened to Heaven?*

The theological world of fundamentalism is a two-storey world, and those who lived psychologically in that upper storey were content, up until about 1975, to let the humanists run things in the lower storey. But the Rapture has been delayed again and again, and those who have been running things "downstairs" are getting pushy in their monopolistic control over education, politics, the media, and just about everything else. Fundamentalists are at long last getting sick and tired of

---

New World Order.
13. Douglas W. Frank, *Less Than Conquerors: How Evangelicals Entered the Twentieth Century* (Grand Rapids, Michigan: Eerdmans, 1986).

being pushed around. They want to have a greater voice in running affairs the lower storey. But the older version of fundamentalism teaches that this is a false hope, both morally and prophetically, while the secular humanists still argue that the Christians have no authority, no moral right, to exercise such authority. After all, we are told by both fundamentalists and secular humanists, this is a pluralist nation. (*Pluralism* means that Christians have no legal rights except to pay taxes to institutions controlled by humanists.)

So, we find that fundamentalism is splitting apart psychologically. The "lower storey" activists are tired of listening to the escapism of the "upper storey" pietists. As the activists grow increasingly impatient with the arguments of the passivists, they begin to abandon the theology that undergirds passivism: original Scofieldism. Fundamentalism in general now has only two legitimate hopes: the imminent Great Escape of the Rapture or the long-term overturning of the older two-storey fundamentalist theology. Either Scofieldism's promise must come true, and very soon, or else it will be abandoned.

What about the former hope, i.e., the Rapture? It is fading fast among Christian activists. Dispensationalists have been repeatedly frustrated by the public announcement of, and subsequent delay of, the Rapture. A lot of them have now begun to lose interest in that much-abused doctrine. For at least a decade, we have not heard sermons by television evangelists about the imminent Rapture. Since 1979, the dispensationalist dam has begun to leak. The pent-up lake of frustrated Christian social concern and social relevance is now pouring through holes in the dam. When it finally breaks, as hole-ridden dams must, the world of dispensationalism will be swept away.

The Death of Dispensational Theology

If dispensational theology were still strong and healthy, it might be able to delay the looming transformation of the dispensational movement. But it is not healthy. Theologically

A Commitment to Cultural Irrelevance 103

speaking, meaning *as a coherent system*, dispensational theology is dead. Its brain wave signal has gone flat. It has now assumed room temperature. RIP. It was not killed by its theological opponents. Its defenders killed it by a thousand qualifications. They revised it into oblivion.[14] Like a man peeling an onion, dispensational theologians kept slicing away the system's embarrassing visible layers until there was nothing left. The last remaining layer was removed by H. Wayne House and Thomas Ice in their 1988 book, *Dominion Theology: Blessing or Curse?*

As an intellectual system, dispensationalism never had much of a life. From the beginning, its theological critics had the better arguments, from George Bush in the 1840's to Oswald T. Allis' classic study, *Prophecy and the Church*, published in 1945. But the critics never had many followers. Furthermore, the critics were trained theologians, and dispensationalists have never paid much attention to trained theologians. Besides, there were not very many critics. Because dispensationalists had no self-consciously scholarly theology to defend and no institutions of somewhat higher learning until well into the twentieth century, their critics thought that they could safely ignore the dispensational movement. They always aimed their published analyses at the academic Christian community. They thought they could call a halt to the rapid spread of dispensationalism through an appeal to the Scriptures and an appeal to the scholarly Christian community. They were wrong. Theirs was a strategic error; popular mass movements are not directly affected by such narrow intellectual challenges. Indirectly over time, yes, but not directly. Few people adopt or abandon their theological views by reading heavily footnoted and carefully argued scholarly books. Thus, the appeal of dispensational theology was not undermined by its theological opponents; instead, it collapsed of its own weight. Like a former athlete who dies of a heart attack at age 52 from obesity and lack of exercise, so did

---

14. See Chapter 8.

dispensational theology depart from this earthly vale of tears. Dispensational theologians got out of shape, and were totally unprepared for the killer marathon of 1988: the 40th anniversary of the creation of the State of Israel, and the year of Edgar Whisenant.

The Heart, Mind, and Soul of Dispensationalism

The strength of dispensationalism was never its formal theological argumentation, but rather its ethical and motivational conclusions, namely, that Christians have almost no influence in this world, will never have much influence, and most important, are not morally responsible before God for exercising lawful authority in this so-called "Church Age." The dispensational system was adopted by people who wanted to escape from the burdens of cultural responsibility. This retreatist mentality has been freely admitted by Thomas Ice's former associate, David Schnittger. (I quoted this in the previous chapter, but it bears repeating.)

> North and other postmillennial Christian Reconstructionists label those who hold the pretribulational rapture position pietists and cultural retreatists. One reason these criticisms are so painful is because I find them to be substantially true. Many in our camp have an all-pervasive negativism regarding the course of society and the impotence of God's people to do anything about it. They will heartily affirm that **Satan is Alive and Well on Planet Earth**, and that this must indeed be **The Terminal Generation**; therefore, any attempt to influence society is ultimately hopeless. They adopt the pietistic platitude: *"You don't polish brass on a sinking ship."* Many pessimistic pretribbers cling to the humanists' version of religious freedom; namely Christian social and political impotence, self-imposed, as drowning men cling to a life preserver.[15]

---

15. David Schnittger, *Christian Reconstruction from a Pretribulational Perspective* (Oklahoma City: Southwest Radio Church, 1986), p. 7.

To justify this otherwise embarrassing motivation – cultural withdrawal – fundamentalist Christians adopted the doctrine of the pre-tribulation Rapture, the Church's hoped-for Escape Hatch on the world's sinking ship. The invention of the doctrine of the pre-tribulation Rapture in 1830 by either J. N. Darby (the traditional dispensational view) or by a young Scottish girl during a series of trances (Dave MacPherson's revisionist view) was the key element in the triumph of dispensationalism. It has therefore been the steady decline of interest in this doctrine during the 1980's that has publicly marked the demise of the dispensational system. Dave Hunt wrote *Whatever Happened to Heaven?* in 1988, but this is not what he really was asking. What his book asks rhetorically is this: *What Ever Happened to Fundamentalists' Confidence in the Doctrine of the Pre-Tribulation Rapture?* (Heaven has been close by all along; the pre-tribulation Rapture hasn't.)

Hoping to Get Out of Life Alive

The appeal of this doctrine was very great for over a century because it offered Christians a false hope: to be able to go to heaven without first going to the grave. Traditional dispensationalists want to become modern Elijahs: not as he lived his life, which was painful, risky, and highly confrontational with the religious and political authorities (I Ki. 18), but as he ended his life, when God's chariot carried him to heaven (II Ki. 2). Fundamentalists regard the critics of dispensationalism as enemies of "the blessed hope," namely, the hope in life after life. They fully understand what the postmillennialist is telling them: "You are going to die!" For over a century, dispensationalism's recruits in the pews refused to listen to such criticism. They traded their God-given heritage of Christian cultural relevance – which requires generations of godly service and compound growth in every area of life – for a false hope: getting out of life alive. It was a bad bargain. It was a mess of pottage in exchange for the birthright.

The culmination and epitaph of the dispensational system can be seen on one short bookshelf: the collected paperback writings of "serial polygamist" Hal Lindsey and accountant Dave Hunt, plus a pile of unread copies of Edgar C. Whisenant's two-in-one book, *On Borrowed Time* and *88 Reasons Why the Rapture Is in 1988* (1988), which predicted that the Rapture would take place in September of 1988. (It also appeared under other titles.) Mr. Whisenant claims that it sold over a million copies in 1988. I have also seen the figure of over four million copies. In any case, a lot of copies were distributed.

That these authors best represent dispensationalism in our day is denied (always in private conversation) by the faculty and students of Dallas Theological Seminary, but the embarrassed critics have ignored the obvious: the dispensational movement is inherently a paperback book movement, a pop-theology movement, and always has been. It does not thrive on scholarship; it thrives on sensational predictions that never come true. Anyone who doubts this need only read Dwight Wilson's book, *Armageddon Now!*[16]

1988-1991

The year 1988 was the year of the public demise of dispensational theology: no Rapture. The Church is still here despite the 40th year of "the generation of the fig tree," i.e., the State of Israel. Whisenant's book appeared in July, confidently prophesying the Rapture for September, 1988.[17] Dave Hunt's *Whatever Happened to Heaven?* also appeared.

Then, in October, came the book by House and Ice, *Dominion Theology: Blessing or Curse?* It was a hardback dispensational

---

16. Dwight Wilson, *Armageddon Now!: The Premillenarian Response to Russia and Israel Since 1917* (Tyler, Texas: Institute for Christian Economics, [1977] 1991).

17. Later, he said it would be by January of 1989. Then he updated it to September of 1989. By then, his victimized former disciples were not listening to him any more.

A Commitment to Cultural Irrelevance

book. It also appeared on the surface to be a scholarly book. Therefore, it sank without a trace; fundamentalist readers are not interested in scholarly books. *House Divided* buried that ill-conceived effort, and in so doing, buried the last vestiges of dispensational theology.[18]

In 1989 the Berlin Wall came down. In 1990, Iraq invaded Kuwait, and Dallas Seminary professor Charles Dyer rushed into print with his paperback sensation, *The Rise of Babylon: Sign of the End Times*. Not to be outdone, John Walvoord resurrected his 1974 potboiler, *Armageddon, Oil, and the Middle East Crisis*. Book sales soared, only to crash in flames in February, 1991, when the U.S. military smashed Iraq's army. Later that year, the attempted *coup* by hard-line Soviet bureaucrats failed to dislodge Boris Yeltsin, but it did ruin Gorbachev's career. So much for Robert Faid's 1988 potboiler, *Gorbachev! Has the Real Antichrist Come?*

This feeding frenzy of "ticking clock" prophecy books cooled after the Soviet Union began falling apart. Israel's predicted invader from the north no longer has any viable candidates. The State of Israel no longer faces any nation that conceivably can assemble an army of millions. The paperback experts in Bible prophecy again look like fools and charlatans. The dispensational movement has once again been publicly embarrassed by its book royalty-seeking representatives. The world howls in derisive laughter, for good reason. The paperback prophecy experts conveniently forget about Nathan's accusation against David: ". . . by this deed thou hast given great occasion to the enemies of the LORD to blaspheme. . ." (II Sam. 12:14). They, too, have given great cause to the many enemies of God to ridicule Christianity. But, unlike David, who repented of his sin, these people keep repeating theirs, updating nonsense.

---

18. Greg L. Bahnsen and Kenneth L. Gentry, Jr., *House Divided: The Break-Up of Dispensational Theology* (Tyler, Texas: Institute for Christian Economics, 1989).

In the March 18, 1991, issue of *Newsweek*, after the war with Iraq had ended, the magazine's Kenneth Woodward, who writes the "Religion" section, wrote this:

> And Walvoord, at 80, expects the rapture to occur in his own lifetime. So many people will be suddenly missing, he muses, "I wish I could be around to see how the media explain it."

Dr. Walvoord will go to his reward in the same way that all Christians have gone since the days of Christ: by way of death. But he does not want to believe this. Neither do millions of his dispensationalist peers. They prefer to embarrass the Church of Jesus Christ, decade after decade, by their crackpot prophecies rather than face the reality of their own mortality.

The Quiet Defection of the Seminaries

What few dispensationalists in the pews realize is that even Dallas Seminary no longer emphasizes dispensational theology to the degree that it once did. Ever since its accreditation in the mid-1970's, it has emphasized such topics as Christian counselling far more than 1950's dispensationalism. The departure of Charles Ryrie from the Dallas faculty was symbolic of this shift in emphasis. So was the departure of Dr. House.

In the late 1980's, Talbot Theological Seminary in La Mirada, California, abandoned traditional dispensationalism and adopted some undefined new variant. For the sake of alumni donations, however, neither seminary discusses these changes openly. Within a few years, the shake-up hit Grace Theological Seminary. First, John C. Whitcomb was fired in 1990, three months before his scheduled retirement. In December, 1992, Grace sent out a letter announcing a complete restructuring of the seminary. It abandoned its Th.D. and Th.M. programs.

The problem is, dispensational seminaries keep such inside information bottled up, concealed above all from their donors. They refuse to tell their financial supporters what is going on.

They expect old donors to finance a new theology. They have adopted a *strategy of silence* with their donors – the same strategy they have long used with respect to their published critics.

Conclusion

God has given His people a great degree of responsibility in the New Testament era. We are required to proclaim His gospel of comprehensive redemption.[19] We are to work to fulfill the Great Commission, which involves far more than preaching a world-rejecting gospel of personal escape into the clouds.[20] Through the Church, Christ's body, the combined efforts of Christians through the ages can and will combine to produce the visible transformation of a sin-governed world: not attaining perfection, but rolling back the effects of sin in every area of life. This is the true meaning of progress.

Fundamentalist Christians reject this God-given assignment in history: the cost of progress seems too high to them. They have adopted a view of Bible prophecy that rationalizes and baptizes their flight from responsibility. They invent fairy tales for children and call them the old-time religion. Stories invented in 1830 are seriously presented by seminary professors as the historic legacy of the Church, despite the existence of evidence to the contrary presented by their own students.[21]

It is time for grown-up Christians to put away such fairy tales and accept their God-given responsibilities. Sadly, they resist. They still hope for deliverance: getting out of life alive at the terrible price of leaving no legacy to the future.

---

19. Gary North, *Is the World Running Down? Crisis in the Christian Worldview* (Tyler, Texas: Institute for Christian Economics, 1988), Appendix C: "Comprehensive Redemption: A Theology for Social Action."

20. Kenneth L. Gentry, Jr., *The Greatness of the Great Commission: The Christian Enterprise in a Fallen World* (Tyler, Texas: Institute for Christian Economics, 1990).

21. Alan Patrick Boyd, "A Dispensational Premillennial Analysis of the Eschatology of the Post-Apostolic Fathers (Until the Death of Justin Martyr)," Th.M. thesis, Dallas Theological Seminary, 1977.

6

A GHETTO ESCHATOLOGY

And they send unto him certain of the Pharisees and of the Herodians, to catch him in his words. And when they were come, they say unto him, Master, we know that thou art true, and carest for no man: for thou regardest not the person of men, but teachest the way of God in truth: Is it lawful to give tribute to Caesar, or not? Shall we give, or shall we not give? But he, knowing their hypocrisy, said unto them, Why tempt ye me? bring me a penny [denarion], that I may see it. And they brought it. And he saith unto them, Whose is this image and superscription? And they said unto him, Caesar's. And Jesus answering said unto them, Render to Caesar the things that are Caesar's, and to God the things that are God's. And they marvelled at him (Mark 12:13-17).

There are few passages in Scripture that are quoted more enthusiastically by pietists, statists, and humanists than this one: "Render to Caesar the things that are Caesar's, and to God the things that are God's." Why? Because this passage initially seems to separate the kingdom of God from the kingdom of Caesar, thereby granting *autonomous authority* to Caesar.

Once Caesar has received this supposed grant of authority, however, he and his disciples seek to expand that kingdom. Step by step, law by law, tax by tax, intrusion by intrusion, the messianic kingdom of the State grows at the expense of the messianic kingdom of God. No judicial barrier to Caesar's kingdom is acknowledged as sacrosanct by Caesar's worshippers; no realm of autonomy from Caesar is acknowledged except the conscience, and only if conscience never utters an audible word of protest. Every barrier to Caesar's kingdom is regarded as subject to future revision. The foreign policy of the messianic State is clear: "What's Caesar's is Caesar's, and what's God's is negotiable."

But why should Christian pietists cite this passage with equal enthusiasm? Because it is perceived as relieving them from any personal responsibility to resist the relentless expansion of Caesar's kingdom. They follow the lead of the statists and humanists: Caesar's kingdom is defined as everything external, while God's kingdom is exclusively internal. Conscience must always remain internal. It must never be allowed to display its presence by public acts of resistance. This view of civil law justifies life in the Christian ghetto, far from the seats of influence. Yet Jesus said to His disciples: "And I appoint unto you a kingdom, as my Father hath appointed unto me; That ye may eat and drink at my table in my kingdom, and sit on thrones judging the twelve tribes of Israel" (Luke 22:29-30). Ghetto-dwelling Christians resent this degree of responsibility.

Whose Coin Is This?

Jesus was being challenged by Pharisees who wanted to compromise Him publicly. They asked Him about paying taxes to Rome. If He told them that this payment was warranted, the people would abandon Him. If He told them that such taxes were not warranted, the Romans would arrest Him. This looked like a perfect trap. It wasn't.

He asked them to bring Him a coin. When they did this, He sprung their trap on them. The coin was a Roman *denarius*, a silver imperial coin used for paying taxes, according to numismatist-theologian Ethelbert Stauffer.[1] Tiberius Caesar's picture

---

1. Ethelbert Stauffer, *Christ and the Caesars* (Philadelphia: Westminster Press,

was on one side, with an announcement in Latin, which in the Greek provinces was translated as "Emperor Tiberius august Son of the august God." On the reverse was an image of Tiberius' mother seated on a throne of the gods, with the words "Pontifix Maximus," meaning high priest. Stauffer writes: "The coin, in brief, is a symbol both of power and of the cult."[2]

If the Pharisees possessed such a coin, or even handled it, they were implicitly acknowledging that Caesar had lawful authority over them. Coinage then (as now) was a mark of State sovereignty. It was Julius Caesar who had first placed his own picture on Roman coins, and this was seen as an assertion of divinity. He was then assassinated. In 132-35 A.D., during Bar Kochba's rebellion, the Jewish revolutionary leader had the imperial *denarii* collected, the faces beaten flat by hammers and replaced by pictures of Hebrew Temple vessels.[3]

The Pharisees had either polluted themselves ritually by using a coin with Caesar's image on it or else were acknowledging that they were under sovereign authority, and therefore compelled to use such a coin. The coin symbolized both the power and the benefits of Roman rule. It therefore symbolized the historical condition of Israel in Jesus' day: under God's judgment.

What Does God Own?

The Jews knew very well what God owns: everything. "For every beast of the forest is mine, and the cattle upon a thousand hills" (Psa. 50:10). When Jesus told them to render unto Caesar the things that were Caesar's, He could not possibly have meant that Caesar possessed an autonomous kingdom with autonomous claims on men's obedience or assets. He meant only that Caesar was a lawful monarch whose coins

---

1955), p. 123.
   2. *Ibid.*, p. 125.
   3. *Ibid.*, p. 126.

A Ghetto Eschatology

testified publicly to the Jews' position of political subordination to Rome. To deny this fact in public would have constituted an act of rebellion. The Pharisees, who served as civil agents of the Roman state, knew this all too well. They kept prudently silent.

By speaking of things belonging to Caesar, Jesus was affirming the existence of legitimate political power in history. God delegates political power to specific men to manage as stewards, just as He delegates ownership of property to specific individuals and families. As the ultimate sovereign Owner, God is at the top of a hierarchy. Power is delegated to men. It is never held autonomously by men. By telling men to render to Caesar what belonged to Caesar, *Jesus was identifying Caesar as a ruler under God: the recipient of delegated power*. Jesus was denying the supposed right of Caesar to command worship as a god.

Jesus' answer drove home the economic point: *ownership and authority are never autonomous*. They are always delegated by God. This hierarchical pattern of ownership is basic to economics, politics, and all government. A sovereign God delegates limited power to His subordinates. The existence of a hierarchy of authority therefore leads to the question that constitutions and courts must answer: Where are the God-established covenantal boundaries of power separating State, Church, family, and individuals?

More to the point, where are we given *authoritative answers* to these questions regarding judicial boundaries, in nature or in the Bible? This is what the pietists prefer not to discuss. This question raises the issue of the biblical legitimacy of natural law theory, the implicit alternative system to biblical law in Christian political theory. The obvious answer – obvious to everyone except millions upon millions of humanist-educated Christians – is that the Bible is the place where we must begin our search for these boundaries. But to say this is to reject the judicial foundations of natural law theory and its corollary, political pluralism. American pietists resent any such challenge. They much prefer to abandon at least three-fourths of the Bible, and so they have.

Then what is to prevent Caesar from demanding three-fourths of whatever Christians own or produce? Mere tradition? The threat of a tax revolt? Well, then, Caesar will remain content – this year – to take only 40% of his servants' income: twice what Pharaoh extracted from the Egyptians (Gen. 47:26), which was twice what Samuel identified as political tyranny (I Sam. 8:15, 17). Caesar knows that his pietistic Christian servants will not quote the Old Testament at him. They have abandoned it.

They have also abandoned earthly hope. They have devised eschatologies of inevitable failure – ghetto eschatologies – that match their ghetto political theory.

A Letter from the Fundamentalist Ghetto

In my ICE cover letter of January, 1992, I began with this statement:

> The decline of Christian scholarship in this century has been disgraceful. What began as an erosion of scholarship in the late sixteenth century has become a collapse today. Things are so bad that in the field of history the humanists are generally producing better works of scholarship on Christianity's role in history than Christians are.

I went on to report on the availability of a CD-ROM version of Migne's Latin Church Fathers, which I recommended for purchase by every Christian college (*not*, it needs to be said, every Christian individual). Then I made a prediction: "I doubt that a dozen will buy it, even if they all hear about it. So abysmal is the level of Christian education today that there are no students and few faculty members who can read Latin well, let alone understand the theology of the Church fathers and assess its development through the centuries." Why did I say this? Be-

A Ghetto Eschatology

cause of my understanding of pietist theology and its effects on the modern Church.

> We have closed off ourselves from the history of the Church because we have abandoned faith in the future of the Church. We are present-oriented. Therefore, according to political scientist Edward Banfield, *we are lower class*. Banfield defines as upper-class person as future-oriented. It is not how much money a person has, but rather what his view of the future is, which determines his class position. By this definition, the modern Church is lower class.

> I have heard Christian parents ask the rhetorical question: "What good is Latin, anyway?" In short: "What good is accurate knowledge of the past?" To a present-oriented person who would be content with his place in life with a steady job but not a true calling before God, not much. To a present-oriented church whose pastor would be happy to have a congregation filled with such people, not much. This is the problem we face today.

In late January, I received a letter from the leader of an Oklahoma parachurch ministry. He got onto the ICE mailing list in January. (So far, he has ordered no books.) Legally, I can name him and limit my extracts to 10% of his letter. I can also quote it in full, but not name him. I have decided to do the latter, since I feel certain that nobody in my circles has ever heard of him or his ministry, and his letter is just too choice to exclude a single word.

As you read it, think to yourself: "If future-orientation is upper class, then what is this?" Think also: "If he is right about how to fund missions, then why should Christians ever build a college, or even attend a college?" Here is the entire text of his letter, which was printed out on a cheap dot-matrix printer. (Nothing like a dot-matrix printer to identify yourself as an under-funded, one-man operation!) This letter is, I assure you, a rigorously consistent application of the pietistic, premillennial theology of modern fundamentalism.

* * * * * * * * * *

Enclosed is a short paper on a "Christians politics". A true follower of Christ will lay down the fleshly ambitions that the world offers and work for eternal things instead. I have yet to see true evangelism taking place amongst the reconstructionists. It concerns me to see a great degree of compromise in proclaiming the gospel, amongst the kingdom now teachers. I wonder if you claim allegiance with the prosperity teachers, the charismatics and ecumenicalism we see all around us today? I noticed your latest offer of the Church Fathers on CD-ROM for $60,000. Couldn't this sum be better spent on missionaries? The Bible (sola scriptura) is or should be sufficient for us. Each of us will stand before God someday and account for our time, money and what we did with the truth and light we possess!

What happened to Abraham Kuyper's Holland? What was the result of Constantine's "conversion"? Is the Roman Catholic Church the mother church or the mother of harlots? Do you condone the political allies of "christians" with Moonies as we've seen in the American Freedom Coalition? Were the Declaration of Independence signers Master Masons by coincidence? Is America getting better or worse?

Evil men and seducers shall wax worse and worse, deceiving, and being deceived. 2 Timothy 3:13. I believe we are seeing this before our very eyes. Even the elect are being deceived. Satan wishes men to be diverted from the great commission, that of seeing individuals of all nations following Him, being baptized and discipled for His kingdom. The more time spent on earthly pursuits, i.e. politics, studying vain subjects, social

A Ghetto Eschatology

actions and filling our brains with more useless knowledge, the less time there will be to do His work He left for us to do.

I don't doubt that you have more knowledge than most men in the Western Hemisphere. You must be brilliant to have written the volumes and millions of words in your books. The crux is that with greater knowledge comes greater responsibility.

* * * * * * * * * *

He also included a poem, which by taking the first letter of each stanza, we get the following: OUR POLITICS ARE IN HEAVEN. It includes this stanza:

> Each Christian who thus VOTES NOT, testifies
> Exactly where his place of power lies.

He then assured me: "If preachers and teachers were subject to the Word of God as to the Christian's new heavenly relationship, as being no longer of this evil world, they would let the world take care of its own politics and cease reasoning about it."

I understand his point. Why bother to vote in a pluralist society if the Church of Jesus Christ is doomed to defeat anyway? Voting would be pointless, except as a holding action. Our citizenship is in heaven, and *only* in heaven, he says. While the Bible teaches a doctrine of dual citizenship – heaven and earth, eternity and time – pietists reject this doctrine. Consistent pietists are like the Amish: they do not get involved in "gentile" politics.

His view of politics is the only view that is consistent with premillennialism. (It is also the only view that is consistent with amillennialism.) It rests explicitly on a specific view of the future of the gospel: the predestined impossibility of world transformation – including politics, but not limited to politics – through faithful preaching and honest, Christ-honoring living.

It is the view promoted by Dave Hunt. Dave Hunt is consistent. So is his debate partner, Tommy Ice.[4]

Those inconsistent premillennialists who are political activists resent it when I say this, but I keep getting letters like this one. While it is becoming more acceptable for premillennialists to get involved in politics, the system militates against such commitments. This premillennial pietist is consistent: Christians should direct their resources into missions, narrowly defined, that is, pietistically defined. What Kenneth Gentry calls *The Greatness of the Great Commission* is ignored.[5]

A Crucial Shift in Dispensational Rhetoric

What is significant is this: in the last fifteen years, *the leaders of American fundamentalism have ceased to talk like Dave Hunt*, a fact that Mr. Hunt has publicly deplored. They are no longer consistent regarding premillennialism and social activism. Not that they believe in biblical law, of course. But they do believe in conservative social and political action. (See Chapter 11.)

Paralleling this shift toward activism has been the quiet abandonment of dispensational theology. As of early 1993, the only easily available book still defending the details of dispensationalism was a reprint of Charles Ryrie's 1965 book, *Dispensationalism Today*. It ought to be called, *Dispensationalism Yesterday*.

Dispensational eschatology is dying because fundamentalist activism and outrage at humanism are growing. Ghetto eschatology is no longer popular with Christians who are trying to move out of the psychological ghetto and into positions of influence. To put it bluntly, you don't run for President on a dispensational ticket. You run in order to win.

---

4. Gary DeMar, *The Debate Over Christian Reconstruction* (Ft. Worth, Texas: Dominion Press, 1988).

5. Kenneth L. Gentry, Jr., *The Greatness of the Great Commission: The Christian Enterprise in a Fallen World* (Tyler, Texas: Institute for Christian Economics, 1990).

A Ghetto Eschatology

When Christians seek to make permanent, meaningful, Bible-based changes in the world outside the local Christian ghetto, they become *operational postmillennialists*. This is why there are so few Christians involved in social action who are willing to spell out the details of their officially held premillennial or amillennial views. They do not even try to explain in print how such views can be reconciled with activism. *They have abandoned such views psychologically*, except for those few who are willing to become kamikazes for Christ. As I have said for years, once a Protestant evangelical starts thinking "activism," he begins to shed his pessimillennial eschatology, whether pre-mil or a-mil. It just sort of drops away, like a snake's skin.

The question of mitivation cannot be ignored in the realm of politics. People rarely commit very much to holding actions; they commit only to what they regard as a strategy for victory.

The Dominion Covenant

In the worldview of a committed premillennialist, *history is irrelevant*. The Church is culturally irrelevant to history, and history is irrelevant to the Church. When you live in an eschatological ghetto theologically, you are always tempted to create a fantasy world mentally. You begin to imagine that you live in a hermetically sealed-off world in which you and your fellow ghetto residents are isolated from the cultural world around you. Like the lunatic locked safely in a padded cell, it makes no difference to you if your neighbors in the next cell are adulterers or not, are drunks or not, are decent people or not. Just so long as someone outside your padded cell continues to pay someone to feed you, clothe you, house you, and heal your bodily pains, nothing outside your little world makes any difference.

God has given Christians an assignment in history:

And God said, Let us make man in our image, after our likeness: and let them have dominion over the fish of the sea, and over the fowl of the air, and over the cattle, and over all the earth, and over every creeping thing that creepeth upon the earth. So God created man in his own image, in the image of God created he him; male and female created he them. And God blessed them, and God said unto them, Be fruitful, and multiply, and replenish the earth, and subdue it: and have dominion over the fish of the sea, and over the fowl of the air, and over every living thing that moveth upon the earth (Gen. 1:26-28).

God promises His people a great inheritance in history:

> His soul shall dwell at ease; and his seed shall inherit the earth (Psa. 25:13).

> For evildoers shall be cut off: but those that wait upon the LORD, they shall inherit the earth (Psa. 37:9).

> But the meek shall inherit the earth; and shall delight themselves in the abundance of peace (Psa. 37:11).

> Blessed are the meek: for they shall inherit the earth (Matt. 5:5).

Jesus fed the multitudes and healed the sick. Then He told the apostles: "Verily, verily, I say unto you, He that believeth on me, the works that I do shall he do also; and greater works than these shall he do; because I go unto my Father. And whatsoever ye shall ask in my name, that will I do, that the Father may be glorified in the Son. If ye shall ask any thing in my name, I will do it. If ye love me, keep my commandments. And I will pray the Father, and he shall give you another Comforter, that he may abide with you for ever (John 14:12-16).

Ah, yes: the *commandments*. The law of God. You know: *the Old Testament*. When we turn to the Old Testament, we find lots and lots of examples of covenant-based social betterment. We find whole passages that promise social betterment in response to covenantal faithfulness, passages such as Leviticus 26:3-13 and Deuteronomy 28:1-14. This means that *Christians must*

A Ghetto Eschatology 121

preach God's covenant lawsuit to nations as well as individuals: a covenant lawsuit in history that includes both law and sanctions. Problem: premillennialists deny the historical validity of God's sanctions in New Covenant history. They also have a tendency to deny the continuing validity of God's Old Covenant case law applications of the Ten Commandments. They are, in short, *antinomians*. They reject the specific sanctions that God has always required His covenant people to preach to the lost. Premillennialists no longer believe that God raises up Jonahs to preach God's covenant lawsuit: a message warning of the coming destruction of any covenant-breaking society that persists in its evil ways. They no longer believe that God brings negative sanctions in history against covenant-breaking societies.

The pessimillennialist, whether premillennial or amillennial, wants Christians to believe that God no longer backs up His own covenant with action. In fact, God supposedly has allowed Satan to impose the terms of his covenant: covenant-breakers get steadily richer and more powerful, while covenant-keepers are consigned by covenant-breakers to living in ghettos in between persecutions. The pessimillennialist is content with life in his ghetto because he believes that the only alternatives in history are life in the Gulag archipelago or literal execution.

Does Eschatology Matter?

People frequently ask me, "Does it really make much difference what eschatology a Christian holds?" My answer: "It depends on what the particular Christian wants to do with his life." So far, at least, eschatology has been a major factor in sorting out the published leaders from literate followers in what has become known as the Christian Reconstruction movement. This is the more academically oriented branch of the dominion theology movement. There are numerous defenders of dominion theology who maintain publicly that they are still premillennialists, although we have yet to see a book by one of these premillennialists that states clearly just exactly how God's call to

Christians to rebuild the world in terms of God's kingdom principles (a code phrase for "biblical law" in fundamentalist circles) is possible to sustain institutionally in a world that is inevitably going to reject Christ's gospel this side of the physical return of Christ to set up an earthly millennium. Such a book is clearly needed. It must be an apologetic – "This we believe!" – but not apologetic: "It's a shame that we Christians are inevitably going to fail, but here goes!"

Suicide Squads

Try recruiting people into a full-scale suicide squad in a war that the recruiters insist is already lost. The postmillennialist asserts openly that such an appeal will fail to recruit very many self-sacrificing people over the long haul. Dave Hunt asserts this, too. The postmillennialist thinks that it is far easier to recruit people who believe that the war is lost into a movement that self-consciously stresses personal retreat from the political and social conflicts of life, and which denies that Christians as Christians have any responsibility to change the world. So does Dave Hunt.

Anyone who believes that the world will inevitably drift into greater and greater sin, and that Christians will enjoy progressively less influence historically, is a highly unlikely candidate for a lifetime of study – probably self-financed study – to discover how Bible principles (Old Testament law) could and should be applied in history in a specific academic field which is also a real-world field. Their unwillingness to pay the price to find out what God expects His people to do has left the evangelical Church without relevant answers, hampering its evangelism.

Lalonde and Hunt vs. Premillennialist Activism

Anyone with such a view of the world's future would have to be a kind of masochist to drain away time and money on such a personal scale in order to produce a life's work of guaranteed antiquarianism. In a sense, such an effort would be immoral. It would be a misallocation of a Christian's limited resources. Consistent dispensationalist newsletter writer Peter Lalonde has accused Christians of near-immoral behavior for concentrating on such real-world solutions to real-world problems. Such efforts to transform the world are all futile, he says, and therefore they are a waste of God's gifts to Christians. I cited him in the previous chapter: "It's a question, 'Do you polish brass on a sinking ship?' And if they're working on setting up new institutions, instead of going out and winning the lost for Christ, then they're wasting the most valuable time on the planet of earth right now, and that is the serious problem. . . ."[6]

Premillennial political activists need to respond to Lalonde if they are determined to defend premillennialism. But they refuse. Premillennialists refuse to admit the obvious: *premillennialism undermines Christian activism*. But it is easier to ignore theology than provide answers: the strategy of silence.

Self-Fulfilling Prophecies

Eschatology counts, especially in personal motivation. Eschatology leads to self-fulfilling institutional prophecies. The pessimillennialist believes that the world is progressively controlled by Satan and those ethically covenanted to Satan. Thus, he is tempted to regard as historically futile the development of exclusively and explicitly biblical "blueprints" that should be used by Christians to replace the present humanist social order.[7] He does not wish to waste resources on futile projects.

With so few pessimillennial authors devoting themselves to such detailed intellectual work, the intellectual leadership of

---

6. Peter Lalonde, "Dominion: A Dangerous New Theology," Tape One of *Dominion: The Word And New World Order* (Ontario, Canada: Omega-Letter, 1987), 3 tapes.

7. See the multi-volume set, the Biblical Blueprints Series, published by Dominion Press, P. O. Box 7999, Tyler, Texas 75711.

such practical efforts necessarily and steadily falls by default to theonomic (God's law) postmillennialists. Simultaneously, postmillennialist scholars, because they do believe that such comprehensive social transformation is not only possible but inevitable, work hard to achieve dominion in history.

Pessimillennialists self-consciously preach the progressive future failure of the gospel and therefore the inability or unwillingness of the Holy Spirit to transform the world positively in terms of kingdom standards. Dave Hunt goes so far as to say that God Himself is incapable of establishing His kingdom on earth: "In fact, dominion – taking dominion and setting up the kingdom for Christ – is an impossibility, even for God. The millennial reign of Christ, far from being the kingdom, is actually the final proof of the incorrigible nature of the human heart, because Christ Himself can't do what these people say they are going to do. . . ."[8]

Whether premillennialist scholars like it or not, Dave Hunt has become the spokesman for premillennial social philosophy in this decade. He is the best-selling premillennialist author. Silence by premillennialist leaders regarding Hunt's books and his kingdom-denying conclusion is an admission that he in fact speaks for premillennialism today. Traditional kingdom-affirming premillennialists lose theologically to Hunt by default.

And once they lose theological leadership to Hunt, they lose intellectual leadership to the Christian Reconstructionists.

Intellectual Leadership: Losing by Default

This does not mean that non-postmillennialists will never produce works in the field of applied Christian theology. Dutch amillennialists have done so. Premillennialists have done so, especially in the field of natural science.[9] Nevertheless, it is not

---

8. Dave Hunt, Tape Two, "Dominion and the Cross," in *Dominion: The Word And New World Order*.

9. Almost always, however, from the point of view of historic pessimism: an

an accident that as of 1993, all of the major academic works in the Christian Reconstruction movement have been written by postmillennialists. I am speaking here of books written from the perspective of a Christian theology of positive cultural transformation, in contrast to merely negative Christian academic criticism.[10] I mean books that really do propose specific, Bible-mandated ways to reconstruct today's humanism-dominated society.

It is also not an accident that the bulk of the premillennial leaders and their organizations that directed the formation of the New Christian Right in 1979 and 1980 have disappeared from the political scene, just as I predicted in 1982.[11] Most people are highly unlikely to stay in the front lines of Christian social and political reform without the psychological support of a consistent theology of social and political reform. The humanist news media sharks will grind them down relentlessly on the altogether relevant question of theocracy, and premillennialist leaders' timid supporters will cease sending them money if they say publicly that they believe in theocracy. So the leaders either waffle or grow suspiciously silent. Neither waffling nor silence changes society or gathers the troops together for a full-scale confrontation. Christian political leaders need biblical law (which dispensationalism denies) and a positive eschatology (which premillennialism denies). Christian media leaders are presently terrified of both.

Christian Reconstructionists therefore have won the intellectual leadership of Christian activists by default. Like Harry Truman, we can stand the heat, so we stay in the kitchen.

---

improper use of the second law of thermodynamics, or "entropy." See Gary North, *Is the World Running Down? Crisis in the Christian Worldview* (Tyler, Texas: Institute for Christian Economics, 1988).

10. I have in mind here the negative critical works of premillennialist Francis Schaeffer and Dutch tradition amillennialists Herman Dooyeweerd and Cornelius Van Til. I also have in mind Herbert Schlossberg's *Idols for Destruction*.

11. Gary North, "The Intellectual Schizophrenia of the New Christian Right," *Christianity and Civilization*, 1 (1982). See also Chapter 11, below.

Eschatology unquestionably matters in the life of a Christian scholar who regards his life's work as anything more important than going through a series of academically acceptable intellectual exercises. Postmillennialism is an important motivation to those scholars who are self-consciously dedicated to long-term Christian Reconstruction. I devote ten hours a week, fifty weeks per year, to writing my economic commentary on the Bible. Anyone who holds a different eschatology is unlikely to sit down for ten hours or more per week, for thirty or forty years, to discover exactly what the Bible teaches about a real-world subject, and how its principles might be applied by people in the New Testament era. *I win by their default.*

Time is on the Reconstructionists' side, not the side of our many critics. I believe that Christians have plenty of time to work toward the transformation of this world, so I work long and hard to publish the intellectual foundations of this transformation. In contrast, pessimillennialists believe that Jesus is coming soon. They waste little time on such "utopian" intellectual projects. I see hope in long-term scholarship; pessimillennialists see little hope in long-term anything.

Time is also on our side in another sense. Christian Reconstructionist authors have built up a large body of published materials. The more we write, the more difficult it is for anti-Reconstruction scholars to refute us: too much material to refute easily. We can also respond to them within thirty days: newsletters. To put it bluntly, we Reconstructionists have mailing lists, non-profit foundations with some money in the bank, and at least a small and dedicated market of book buyers.

Christian Reconstruction in general is winning the war of ideas through our critics' default. They have not done their academic homework. Literate Christians recognize this.

Our Christian critics really do believe that they can fight something (a growing body of Reconstructionist literature) with nothing (snide remarks, an occasional book review in some unread academic periodical, unpublished grumbling, and above all, the silent treatment: the academic blackout). They are incorrect. You cannot beat something with nothing. When the long-awaited Christian revival hits, our views will sweep the field, both academically and politically, simply because nobody else will be on the field. We can surely beat nothing with something. Our heavy investment today will pay off in the future.

This chapter should not be regarded as a denial that premillennialists and amillennialists can produce academic works that are useful for Christian reconstruction. What I am arguing is that any call by pessimillennialists to reconstruct society along Christian lines must always be accompanied by this warning in fine print: "Warning: this call to Christian Reconstruction can never be achieved in Church history." Full-time historical defeatists such as Dave Hunt have built their careers telling their dispensational followers – millions of them, if book sales are indicative of anything – that all such efforts to improve society are futile, that to argue otherwise is psychologically inconsistent for a premillennialist, and that those people who argue otherwise are either New Agers or dupes of the New Agers.

Conclusion

Eschatology matters. If you commit yourself to any version of pessimillennialism, you will spend your life in a psychological ghetto. If every Christian were to do this, the messianic State would expand without resistance until it threatened to swallow the Church.

Modern dispensationalism rests on a view of history that proclaims the future as lost to Christians during this, the so-called Church Age. The Great Tribulation after the Rapture will destroy the work of the Church that has been built up prior to the Rapture. That is, the legacy of Christ to His Church is doomed to total destruction when the Jews of the Great Tribulation era are confronted with the alliance against them led by the Antichrist and the Beast. The inheritance of the ages is incapable of being passed down by Christians to their spiritual heirs because of two future discontinuities: the Rapture and the Great Tribulation. No matter how good our work as Christians may be, it is doomed.

This view of the future has produced a ghetto mentality, a "form a circle with the wagons" mentality. It has placed a premium on cultural and intellectual defenses against the external world. It has also placed barriers against a systematic cultural and intellectual offense against the external world. Humanism's victory prior to the bodily return of Christ is inevitable, we are assured; any other view is dismissed as "utopian."

This outlook has created an incentive for Christians to narrow their definition of personal responsibility to the local church, the family, and perhaps the lower levels of education. Above the high school level, Christians become openly dependent on one variety or another of humanism to provide the form and content of education. Christian colleges require their faculty members to earn Ph.D. degrees from accredited universities, knowing full well that no accredited Christian evangelical university grants a Ph.D. This mentality lives on the academic and intellectual crumbs that fall from the humanists' tables. For over a century, evangelical Christians have been content to live with this state of affairs. They see no alternative. *They conform to this world because they acknowledge no hope for this world.* Unlike the Amish, who recognize their limits as ghetto residents and who therefore refuse to send their children to school above the eighth grade, fundamentalists send their children, intellectually unprepared, through the gauntlet of humanistic education, usually beginning in kindergarten. The Amish lose few of their children to the world outside their ghetto; in contrast, fundamentalists have lost millions of theirs.

Those who live in ghettos are at the mercy of the messianic State. They become willing to render everything to Caesar while they wait for the return of Jesus. A minority of Christian activists now recognize the sell-out involved in such a view of the future. They are steadily abandoning dispensationalism.

7

HOUSE OF SEVEN GARBLES

[In response to Dallas Seminary professor H. Wayne House's book, *Dominion Theology: Blessing or Curse?*, co-authored by Thomas Ice, I wrote this chapter as a newsletter in 1988, which I sent to every faculty member at Dallas Seminary. Within a few months, Dr. House was no longer on the faculty at Dallas. Why he departed, I do not know. I have revised this chapter slightly. The remarkable transformation in Dr. House's thinking since 1988 is indicated by the citation which concludes this chapter. Note: Thomas Ice claims in the book to have been a Reconstructionist. There is no published evidence supporting this claim.]

In 1988, after 15 years of Dallas Seminary's self-imposed strategic silence, one of its professors went into print with a critique of the Christian Reconstruction movement. H. Wayne House offers us *Dominion Theology: Blessing or Curse?*[1] Guess what? He does *not* think that Dominion Theology (which he equates with Christian Reconstruction, probably for the sake of increased book sales) is a blessing.[2]

---

1. Portland, Oregon: Multnomah Press.
2. Dr. Greg Bahnsen reported to me in 1992 that he had a meeting with Professor House after House had departed from Dallas Seminary. Bahnsen reports that Dr. House was quite conciliatory. Dr. House told Bahnsen that he regretted having become involved with the *Dominion Theology* book project. Because of the

Professor House has made at least seven key intellectual errors – garbled interpretations – but far more costly to Dr. House was his decision to allow Tommy Ice to become co-author. Unfortunately for Professor House's academic reputation, he was unsuccessful in controlling Mr. Ice's more intemperate and outlandish statements. What Dr. House failed to perceive is that when an unknown author with no reputation to lose and something nutty to prove persuades a better-known author with academic credentials to team up with him, the professional has lots to lose, while the amateur has everything to gain. House lost; Ice gained – until Bahnsen and Gentry wrote *House Divided* (1989). Then both House and Ice lost. It was a brief moment of glory for Ice, and a continuing embarrassment for House.

Several of the book's chapters are technical, detailed discussions of biblical law. They are pretty slow reading. They are at least judicious and deal directly with the text of the opponent. I have in mind Chapters 5-7 dealing with Greg Bahnsen's *Theonomy in Christian Ethics* (1977). These clearly are chapters written by Professor House. Other chapters rely heavily on footnotes to various Reconstructionist newsletters rather than on extended theological discussions in Reconstructionist books, and are written in a style best described as neo-hysterical. These I believe were written by Tommy Ice. Nevertheless, both men are responsible for *Dominion Theology: Blessing or Curse?*[3]

---

changes that have taken place in House's thinking, not to mention his employment, ever since Bahnsen and Gentry replied in 1989, I have no reason to doubt Dr. Bahnsen's account of the meeting.

3. I wrote in 1988 that their exegetical house of cards would topple publicly in the spring of 1989. Dr. House had scheduled a debate with Greg Bahnsen at the Simon Greenleaf School of Law in Orange County, California. Dr. House had declined the opportunity to debate Ray Sutton at this meeting, after Sutton accepted House's tactically unwise challenge to debate him. Sutton is an ex-dispensationalist and a Dallas Seminary graduate who knew every weak spot in House's system. Dr. Sutton outlined his *resurrected and now-universal New Covenant* line of attack in his private phone conversations with Professor House, who then apparently decided that debating Bahnsen was safer. Out of the frying pan and into the fire! House backed out of the debate by refusing to allow Bahnsen to cross-examine him in a rebuttal.

A Fig Tree Grows in Dallas

Dominion Theology gives away entire departments of the dispensational store in its attempt to refute Reconstructionism, at a time when dispensationalism is already sitting on mostly empty shelves. Readers need to be aware of the historical setting of this book. Here is what they have not been told.

In the mid-1970's, Dallas Seminary sought and received academic accreditation for the first time. The school added psychology and counselling courses. It then reduced the Greek and Hebrew language requirements that had been the standard at Dallas for half a century.

The school began to lose its best and brightest faculty members. S. Lewis Johnson left. Bruce Waltke left, the school's preeminent Old Testament scholar. Even worse, Waltke subsequently became a Reformed amillennial Calvinist and now teaches at Westminster Seminary in Philadelphia – a devastating intellectual blow to Dallas, since Dallas had relied on Waltke's presence on the faculty as a way to tell the world that its theological position is defendable exegetically.[4] Ed Blum left. Charles Ryrie left (or was fired). Then Dallas fired three of its men in 1987 for holding charismatic doctrines. One by one, the exodus has continued. A lot of very cautious faculty members remain. They have chosen not to rock the boat by exposing their theological flanks in public debate. Until now.

The old guard of John Walvoord and J. Dwight Pentecost grew even older and retired. Only Robert Lightner remains to defend the good old cause, but he does not write scholarly

---

4. Waltke left Westminster in 1990, just after he contributed a chapter to the ill-fated *Theonomy: A Reformed Critique*, edited by William S. Barker and W. Robert Godfrey (Grand Rapids, Michigan: Zondervan Academie, 1990). For responses, see *Theonomy: An Informed Response*, edited by Gary North (Tyler, Texas: Institute for Christian Economics, 1991); Greg L. Bahnsen, *No Other Standard: Theonomy and Its Critics* (Tyler, Texas: Institute for Christian Economics, 1991); Gary North, *Westminster's Confession: The Abandonment of Van Til's Legacy* (Tyler, Texas: Institute for Christian Economics, 1991).

books. In fact, until House's book appeared, Dallas Seminary's recent faculty members were known mainly for their unwillingness to write books on dispensational themes. They have avoided the whole topic like a plague – or like a topic that could get them fired if they slipped up. They know that if they initiate an attack, they will then be called upon to defend themselves, *and they all know that they cannot successfully defend themselves by using the broken shield of Scofield's rickety, patched-up system.* This is House's dilemma; he must now defend himself. It was a risk-free deal for Tommy Ice; not for Wayne House.

A quiet revolution has been going on at Dallas Seminary. Dallas has quietly abandoned "the true and ancient faith, as delivered by Lewis Sperry Chafer." The outline of the "new, improved" dispensational faith, as tentatively offered by Professor Craig Blaising in 1988, is as yet unclear in its details. [He co-edited the 1993 book, *Dispensationalism, Israel and the Church.* This book is narrow in its focus. What is lacking is a comprehensive presentation of the new dispensationalism.]

Obviously, *the holders of this reworked version of the faith are skating on thin career ice.* If they go too far, they will lose their jobs, and where do you go to teach seminary as a "not quite dispensationalist"? Yet they know that they can no longer defend the dispensational faith, even in its revised, 1967, *New Scofield Reference Bible* version. Dallas Seminary's theological position has become increasingly murky as its student body has grown to 1,700.

Don Quixote Rides Again!

Into this scene rode Tommy Ice and his faithful, cautious, and somewhat hesitant partner, Wayne House, like Don Quixote and Sancho Panza, with Ice seated shakily on the aging Rosinante of the *Scofield Reference Bible* notes. These two chivalrous warriors have engaged in a series of fierce battles against a squad of stick men, mostly of their own creation, labeled "Rushdoony," "North," "Bahnsen," "Chilton," and "Jordan."

And let me assure you, these stick men have been soundly defeated in 460 pages of poorly typeset and improperly proofread pages.

But one name is strangely absent: "Sutton." Not even his stick figure representative is allowed onto the battlefield by Ice and House. The only reference to Sutton's five-point covenant model is conveniently hidden in the book's bibliography. There was a reason for this strategy. Even dressing up a stick man in Sutton's covenant model is too risky, for to discuss this explicit covenant model points to *the threatening link between the Old Testament covenant order and the New Testament covenant order* – a link which, if true, would demolish dispensational theology. (And it *is* true.) Ice and House have seen this looming danger, and have judiciously avoided it as much as humanly possible. Out of a total of 798 footnotes in their book, there is a grand total of five references to Sutton's book on the covenant, *That You May Prosper* (1987).

You can always spot the weak points in a man's presentation by locating the handful of inescapable topics that he nonetheless refuses to discuss. Dr. House and Mr. Ice have identified the topic which they do not want to discuss: the five-point covenant model. It structures the first five books of the Bible, meaning the Pentateuch (see North, *The Dominion Covenant: Genesis*, 1987 edition, Introduction), the Ten Commandments (see North, *The Sinai Strategy*, Preface), Deuteronomy (see Sutton, *That You May Prosper*), the Book of Revelation (see Chilton, *The Days of Vengeance*), and much, much more.

The five-point supposed Reconstructionist outline on page 17 has points two and five reversed, making it appear as though it is not quite Sutton's model. There is one short paragraph on page 347 that mentions that I have said that Sutton's model is the crucial structuring device for Reconstructionist thought, but they do not even outline it for the benefit of their readers. They know that Chilton adopted this model to structure his commentary on the Book of Revelation, *The Days of*

Vengeance (1987), yet in chapter after chapter devoted to their attempted refutation of Chilton, this absolutely central fact is never even mentioned. They know that seven of the ten volumes in the Biblical Blueprint Series[5] adopt Sutton's five-point covenant model as their structure. Not a word of this is mentioned, either. You need not bother straining your eyes in search of any reference to Sutton's newsletter, *Covenant Renewal*. There are dozens of references to newsletters that I even forgot that I wrote, but nary a mention of the one newsletter that is the foundation of what we in the "Tyler camp" are doing. This silence is deafening. It is clearly deliberate.

There is another topic which they self-consciously refuse to discuss: *the work of the Holy Spirit in New Testament times as the empowering factor in Christians' being able to extend dominion through Christ*, who is seated majestically in the heavens at the right hand of God. They admit that we teach this (p. 50), but then they fail to respond. Over a hundred pages later, they devote one sentence to the topic, saying that the Holy Spirit empowered the apostles to preach against sin (p. 152) Social sin? Another unmentionable! *In their view, there are no social sins except murder that can be confidently challenged in the name of God's permanent law.*

Tommy Ice admits in the book's opening paragraph that he was David Schnittger's pastor when the latter wrote his booklet, *Christian Reconstruction from a Pretribulational Perspective*,[6] a document referred to continually in the Reconstructionist book that refutes Dave Hunt, *The Reduction of Christianity*, by Gary DeMar and Peter Leithart.[7] *Schnittger's booklet is a devastating criticism of traditional dispensationalism's systematically world-retreating outlook.* He freely admitted that we Reconstructionists have been correct

---

5. Ft. Worth, Texas: Dominion Press, 1986-87.
6. Oklahoma City: Southwest Radio Church, 1986.
7. Ft. Worth: Dominion Press, 1988. Distributed by Dominion Press, P.O. Box 7999, Tyler, Texas.

in pointing to dispensationalism's retreatism. But Ice and House systematically ignored this crucial dispensational document: it admits far too much. Schnittger's booklet has been flushed down the Dallas Seminary memory hole. "Schnittger? Who's Schnittger?" This is highly suspicious. It is also quite traditional. This has long been Dallas Seminary's approach to apologetics: *refutation by black-out*.

With these warnings in mind, let us survey some of the highlights of *Dominion Theology: Blessing or Curse?* Few Christian books of supposedly high academic caliber have ever been so garbled.

Garble #1: Sutton's Five-Point Covenant Model

The biblical covenant's points are: (1) God's transcendence yet immanence (presence); (2) hierarchy/authority/representation; (3) ethics/law/dominion; (4) oath/sanctions (blessing and cursing); (5) succession/inheritance/continuity. Its acronym is **THEOS**.

What our two authors fail to tell their readers is that *they are both staunch defenders of point one, the absolute predestination of God.* Their Arminian fundamentalist readers really ought to be informed about this. Silence is not golden at this point.

Then comes point two: *hierarchy*. They refuse to discuss how this works in the so-called Church Age. But they forthrightly tell us how it will work during the dispensational millennial age: "Premillennialists plead guilty to the desire to have a 'top-down' kingdom. We eagerly look forward to Jesus Christ's earthly reign" (p. 237). This is in response to my criticism: "The premillennialist has so little faith in the power of the Bible's perfect revelation, empowered by the Holy Spirit, to shape the thoughts of Christians, that Jesus must return and personally issue millions of orders per day telling everyone what to do, case by case, crisis by crisis." I had thought mine was a highly critical observation; they openly confirm the accuracy of my original accusation, and they rejoice in it.

In short, *they place traditional dispensationalism at the forefront of the judicial principle of benevolent totalitarianism.* They believe that Jesus prefers to work as Satan does – through a rigid, top-down bureaucracy – rather than through the bottom-up appeals court hierarchy of Exodus 18 and Matthew 18. They refuse even to mention the humanist world's existing system of bureaucratic, top-down hierarchy, but they forthrightly affirm Satan's bureaucratic vision as the true kingdom standard for the dispensational millennium.

Garble #2: Becoming a Perfect Bureaucrat

Tommy Ice ends his Preface with these words: "My blessed hope, however, continues to be that Christ will soon rapture his Bride, the Church, and that we will return with him in victory to rule and exercise dominion with him for a thousand years upon the earth. Even so, come Lord Jesus!"

Ice knows very well that I upended his partner Dave Hunt on this very point during our April debate, because Hunt was completely ignorant of the fact that the traditional dispensational view of the "raptured saints" during the millennium is that they will *not* return to earth to reign with Jesus. J. Dwight Pentecost says, "Thus the millennial age will be concerned only with men who have been saved but are living in their natural bodies."[8] John Walvoord writes in *The Rapture Question* (revised edition, 1979): "The Scriptures declare emphatically that life on earth in the Millennium relates to a people not translated and not resurrected, a people in their mortal bodies" (p. 86). Well, the Scriptures failed to declare this emphatically enough to register with Tommy Ice, who wants with all his heart to return in bureaucratic power with Jesus in his very own sin-free, death-free body and kick a little donkey!

---

8. Pentecost, "The Relation between Living and Resurrected Saints in The Millennium," *Bibliotheca Sacra*, Vol. 117 (Oct. 1960), p. 341.

As I said of Dave Hunt's view, which is identical to Ice's, "It sounds great, but I think he makes these things up as he goes along." So does Ice. These people rewrite a whole system of eschatology in order to appeal to uninformed laymen in their movement, and then they pretend that this is the original version. This is not what I would call honest dealing with one's overly trusting followers.

Garble #3: The Old Historical Shell Game

In their chapter, "Is Premillennialism a Heresy?" they attack David Chilton for the latter's accusation that premillennialism was first invented by Cerinthus, a second-century heretic. They acknowledge that nobody else in the Reconstructionist camp has sided with Chilton on this, and they quote me in saying that many of the early Church fathers were premillennial. Chilton's gift is exegesis, not historiography, so I will not run to his defense at this point.

What is important to understand is that by spending a chapter defending the early Church origins of premillennialism, the authors are playing a game that has been basic to Dallas Seminary's creaky defense of its faith: *dead silence regarding the 1830 origin of the pre-tribulation Rapture doctrine.* Post-trib dispensationalist Dave MacPherson has inflicted a devastating wound on the pre-trib camp by showing that a teenage Scottish girl named Margaret Macdonald, a disciple of a mystic named Edward Irving, came up with this doctrine during a private "revelation from God."[9] The traditional Dallas Seminary-taught view has always been that John Nelson Darby discovered the doctrine in 1830. *In either case, traditional pre-tribulational dispensationalism cannot trace its origins back to anyone prior to 1830.*

If Mr. MacPherson is categorically wrong, as Mr. Ice insisted that he is in a letter to me, then why hasn't Dallas Seminary's

---

9. MacPherson, *The Unbelievable Pretrib Origin*, *The Great Cover-up*, and *The Great Rapture Hoax*.

Church history professor John Hannah presented the evidence? Why has he been silent about this since 1973? Why hasn't any full-length historical refutation of MacPherson's thesis appeared from the traditional dispensational camp?

The two authors then attack postmillennialism because it was supposedly invented by unitarian Daniel Whitby, who was born in 1638, despite the overwhelming evidence that the New England Puritans of the 1630's were postmillennial, and that they brought the doctrine to North America from England. The authors know about Iain Murray's book, *The Puritan Hope*, in which the Puritan origins of postmillennialism are discussed.[10] They know that as the editor of *The Journal of Christian Reconstruction*, I published an entire issue on "Puritanism and Progress" (Summer, 1979), in which the documentary evidence is presented. They simply ignore all this. They write: "Thus, the system called postmillennialism was born in the early 1700s as a hypothesis" (p. 209) *This is not scholarship; this is self-conscious propaganda and active deception of their unsuspecting and overly trusting readers.* This is a high school debating technique disguised as scholarship. This is not the way that men with academic integrity are supposed to conduct public debate, let alone Christian academics. As I said earlier, Professor House has the most to lose; he had an academic reputation prior to this book.

When Mr. Ice launched this ancient "Whitby" attack in the rebuttal portion of our April 1988 debate, I reminded him that his system was invented in 1830, and that Calvinistic postmillennialism can trace its history at least back to 1630. (Actually, it goes back to John Calvin.) He did not respond to my rebuttal. How could he? But he drags out all the old arguments again, as if he had never attended the debate, as if he were deaf. He *is* deaf. Judicially deaf. *Hearing he will not hear*. (And let it be known: Professor House was also in attendance that evening.)

---

10. Edinburgh: Banner of Truth, 1971.

This shell game has been going on at Dallas for decades. "Keep your eye on the pre-trib, premillennial pea, my friends. See how it goes here, under this 1830 pretribulation Rapture shell. Now, with just a few deft shuffles . . . presto: we now find it under the historic premillennial shell of the early Church! Thus, we can see that C. I. Scofield was a defender of eschatological orthodoxy. Now, take this postmillennial pea. We place it under the seventeenth-century Puritan shell. A few deft shuffles . . . presto: we now find it under Daniel Whitby's eighteenth-century unitarian shell. Thus, we can see that postmillennialism has very questionable ancestry!" Ice and House continue to push around these mostly empty shells. Bad habits picked up in one's youth are difficult to break.

Garble #4: An Inner Kingdom Only

Matthew 13 is filled with parables about God's kingdom in history. Several proclaim the Church's *continuity in history*, also called the *leaven principle* (Matt. 13:33-34): the influence of the gospel continues to transform history without a break until the final judgment. These parables are the most difficult passages in the Bible for premillennialists. The authors cite Grace Seminary's Alva J. McClain, who referred to them as "these difficult parables" (p. 226). They are not difficult for postmillennialists! On the contrary, they are foundational.

To escape the Reconstructionists' accusation that dispensationalism is socially paralyzing, they say: "Dispensationalists agree that it is wrong to limit God to only the spiritual or inner realm. This is why we so strongly believe in a literal kingdom of Christ, which will encompass his rule over every area of life" (p. 247, note 65). They have now given the game away. *The external kingdom is supposedly exclusively millennial, i.e., future.* They say that insofar as we are speaking of the so-called Church Age – the here and now – God *has* limited His kingdom to the inner or spiritual realm. This is what author Dave Hunt says repeatedly in his *Seduction* books.

They then quote favorably Samuel J. Andrews, whose words, if taken literally (the "Dallas hermeneutic"), set forth the foundation for *the rule of the tyrannical Saints* – something the authors accuse us Reconstructionists of promoting. We have seen the results of this sort of premillennialism in the revolutionary "Christian" communist movements of the late Middle Ages.[11] This is what can happen when you combine apocalyptic premillennialism and a theological hostility to revealed biblical law:

> It is as its Head that He rules over [the Church], not as its King; for this latter title is never used of this relation. Nor is His rule over His Church legal and external, like that of an earthly king. . . . The relation between Him, the Head, and the Church, His Body, is a living one, such as nowhere else exists, or can exist; His will is the law, not merely of its action, but of its life. . . . He rules in the Church through the law of common life. . . (p. 235).

Spoken like a true Brother of the Free Spirit! Get out your shotguns and hide your wives and daughters: premillennialists are on the march again. Fortunately, this book tells dispensationalists not to march, but to stand dead still: ". . . God has told us to take up a defensive posture against the enemy . . . stand and resist . . . the sword is for a counterattack . . . stand" (p. 156). This book is a 460-page tract to *stand pat for Jesus*. It is a theological defense of John Milton's line, "They also serve who only stand and wait." Milton had an excuse, however. He was totally blind. Then again, now that I think about it. . . .

Garble #5: Neither Biblical Law Nor Natural Law

The non-Reconstructionist Christian, we are told, "is not under the law as a rule of life; rather we are under the law of Christ" (p. 184). This they call Wisdom. Wisdom "does not

---

11. Norman Cohn, *The Pursuit of the Millennium* (2nd ed.; New York: Harper Torchbook, 1961); and the early modern era: Igor Shafarevich, *The Socialist Phenomenon* (New York: Harper & Row, [1975] 1980), ch. 2.

legislate civil penalties" (p. 186). Civil penalties can be imposed in the name of Christ only during his top-down, international, bureaucratic reign (the millennium). Personal progressive sanctification also has nothing to do with God's law: "Christ has freed us from the law for salvation or sanctification" (p. 185). Therefore, "millennial standards await Christ's victorious return" (p. 148). Until then, we must stand pat for Jesus. No explicitly Christian civil sanctions!

There is only one alternative to biblical law: *natural law*. Yet the authors do not once mention this phrase. Both men regard themselves as followers of Calvinist philosopher Cornelius Van Til; both know that natural law is a Stoic pagan myth; and both reject former Dallas Seminary professor Norman Geisler's natural law neo-scholasticism. So, they just stay silent about alternatives. They hope that no one will raise the obvious question: *By what standard* does any Christian government – Church, State, or family – execute lawful judgment in history? Just wait for Jesus, they reply. We must remain silent until then.

Garble #6: Dispensationalism's Social Relevance Today

Not wanting to seem retreatist and socially irrelevant, the authors hasten to assure the readers: "Our job is to be a faithful witness to those in the darkness of Plato's cave. We are to shine the light of God's word on current issues in order to remove the shroud of darkness cast over this world system by Satan" (p. 155). *How?* Their book denies biblical law. They do not mention natural law. *What Bible-revealed light can dispensationalism shine?*

I know: the same light that Dallas Seminary shined in 1973 after *Roe v. Wade* – a City of Dallas case – legalized abortion. Remember Dallas Seminary's response? "Hear no social evil, see no social evil, speak no word of condemnation."

In a century and a half, there has not been a single published book on dispensational social theory written by a dispensationalist. I wonder why. (No, I really don't.) The dispensational movement gave up its one recent opportunity to say something relevant in the late 1960's. It remained silent, as always. Its heart had died by 1970.

Garble #7: Noah's Covenant is the Church's

Ray Sutton and the "Tyler" Reconstructionists argue that it was with the death and resurrection of Jesus Christ that a *resurrected new covenant* was inaugurated. God's five-point covenant is now universal, the standard for the nations, because the Church and the gospel are now universal (Matt. 21:43; 28:18-20). But Professor House does not want to deal with this possibility, for it conflicts with his foundational theological argument in *Dominion Theology*: the terms of Noah's covenant alone bind Gentiles, while the Mosaic law was only for ancient Israel.

House equates Christ's law for the Church Age with Noah's covenant: "Since a law is given within the context of a covenant, the nations could not be given the Mosaic Law since they are under the Noahic covenant" (p. 130). *Are* is present tense. This is the book's key covenantal thesis. House wants us to believe this because there was only one civil sanction, and only one civil law, in Noah's covenant: execution for murder (Gen. 9:5). If his thesis is true, then everything else about civil government is up for grabs. The Christian would then have almost zero to say judicially about anything. *This in principle turns society over to humanists and other covenant-breakers.*

But it is worse than this. He writes: "The Noahic covenant is perpetual" (p. 127). This implies that *the Mosaic law will not even be adopted during the millennium,* contradicting all previous dispensational theologians. In his attack on Bahnsen's view of a universal Old Covenant law-order internationally, *House has scrapped traditional dispensationalism.* In short, Noah's covenant – devoid of all but one civil law and one sanction – is all that Christians have or will ever have to call society to account.

If you are wondering why dispensationalism is culturally irrelevant, search no farther. When you argue that Noah and the rainbow are more socially relevant than the resurrection of Christ, His giving of the Great Commission, the revealed law of God, and the empowering of Christians by the Holy Spirit, you will remain culturally irrelevant.

Conclusion

Dominion Theology: Blessing or Curse? is 460 pages long. There seem to be errors on at least 410 of these pages. (The rest are indexes and bibliography.) Gary DeMar's book, *The Debate Over Christian Reconstruction*, appeared three weeks before the Ice-House book did, and many of the authors' theological objections to what they call dominion theology were answered in detail there. They were answered in much greater detail in Bahnsen and Gentry's *House Divided*.[12] These answers have not satisfid Rev. Ice, who remains a lonely and even obsessed defender of what he regards as traditional dispensationalism, but Dr. House seems at least willing to let bygones be bygones – the main bygone being his career as a professor.

The dispensational movement waited 15 years until Rev. Ice volunteered to carry its banner into battle against the dreaded Reconstructionists. His friend Sancho did not help much in this ill-conceived and ill-executed task. Ice and House dropped this banner and have substituted a "new, improved" one. They have abandoned traditional dispensationalism in the name of dispensationalism's key conclusion: the continued social irrelevance of Christianity. I can safely say that the dispensational movement is now buried intellectually unless someone else picks up the original banner, tattered though it is, and at least stands with it.

* * * * * * * * * * * *

---

12. Tyler, Texas: Institute for Christian Economics, 1989.

In *The Journal of the Evangelical Theological Society* (March 1992), the lead article was written by Dr. House: "Creation and Redemption: A study of Kingdom Interplay." In that essay he writes the following:

> . . . the work of God in the redemption of man has been known as the mediatorial kingdom. The way in which this rule is carried out is dependent on the nature of the existence in which God places man. For example, the control that God exercises over his creatures (especially humans) in the natural and moral order we call creation relates to social relationships, issues of dominion in the earth, and interaction with other created beings and things (pp. 4-5).

> Moreover, as we Christians spread the good news of Christ to others and share the compassion and love of God to others, the kingdom to come becomes the kingdom on this earth. Heaven gradually comes to earth, though certainly one day this will be so in fullness and glory (p. 11).

This is the postmillennial view. Dr. House has left Rev. Ice high and dry. But Rev. Ice's embarrassing condition is a minor issue. The major issue is this: How does House's essay fit the theology of dispensationalism? Is this one more revision or a subtle abandonment of the system? I ask: How many revisions can the dispensational system bear? I also ask: How many more defections by its leading theologians can the movement stand?

Dispensationalism has faced a major problem since 1945: *very few of its defenders are willing to go into print to answer criticisms, especially those suggested by covenant theologians.* Meanwhile, its published defenders either embarrass the movement by their incompetence or else they start sounding more and more like covenant theologians. One by one, they add their revisions of the traditional dispensational system until almost every major point in the old system is abandoned. They have revised dispensationalism to death, but have offered nothing to replace it.

8

REVISING DISPENSATIONALISM TO DEATH

Dispensationalists should be open to, sensitive to, and ready to entertain any future development of theology based on a proper theological method, giving primary consideration to the ongoing work of interpreting the Scripture. Many dispensationalists are encouraging this, and that is why development can be seen within the system.

Craig A. Blaising (1988)[1]

By the year 2000, Dallas Theological Seminary will no longer be dispensational. [Professional] priorities are elsewhere than the defense of systematic dispensationalism from external criticism.

Thomas D. Ice (1989)[2]

In April of 1988, the year the Rapture did not happen, four decades after the formation of the State of Israel, Rev. Thomas Ice and Dave Hunt debated Gary DeMar and me in a public meeting in a Dallas hotel.[3] In response, DeMar wrote *The Debate Over Christian Reconstruction* (1988). DeMar was already the

---

1. Craig A. Blaising, "Development of Dispensationalism by Contemporary Dispensationalists," *Bibliotheca Sacra* (July-September 1988), p. 255.
2. Interview with Martin Selbrede, *Counsel of Chalcedon* (Dec. 1989).
3. Audiotapes and a videotape of this debate are available from the ICE.

co-author, along with Peter Leithart, of *The Reduction of Christianity* (1988), which was a response to Hunt's *Beyond Seduction* (1987). Also in 1988, then-Dallas Seminary professor H. Wayne House and Rev. Ice wrote *Dominion Theology: Blessing or Curse?* A year later, the Institute for Christian Economics published a rebuttal, *House Divided: The Break-Up of Dispensational Theology*.[4] All of this writing and publishing took place within a period of two years.

House Divided publicly buried an expired theological system. What is even more significant about this burial is that dispensationalism's official defenders have been almost as active in gathering dirt to shovel on the casket as its theonomic critics are.[5]

The Academic Game of Quiet Revising

House and Ice quietly revised the fundamental doctrines of traditional dispensational theology. They no longer believe that the old dispensational theology can be successfully defended, a suspicion obviously shared by Dallas Theological Seminary Professor Craig Blaising, as revealed by the citation which begins this chapter. For example, they (i.e., House) argue that the death penalty is still valid in New Testament times because this was part of Noah's covenant (Gen. 9:5-6) – a pre-Mosaic covenant.[6] This was Calvinist theologian John Murray's argument a generation ago.[7] It is a bit odd to see dispensationalists appealing to traditional covenant theology when defending dispensationalism against theonomy. Professor House in this case has dressed John Murray's covenant theology in Lewis Sperry

---

4. Available from the ICE; $25, hardback.

5. See, for example, John MacArthur, Jr., *The Gospel According to Jesus* (Grand Rapids, Michigan: Zondervan Academie, 1988), which documents the antinomianism of conventional dispensationalism. See Chapter 10, below.

6. House and Ice, *Dominion Theology: Blessing or Curse?* (Portland, Oregon: Multnomah Press, 1988), p. 130.

7. John Murray, *Principles of Conduct: Aspects of Biblical Ethics* (Grand Rapids, Michigan: Eerdmans, 1957), p. 118.

Chafer's clothing. It is not that the dispensational Emperor has no clothes; it is that the few presentable clothes that he has were stolen from his long-term rival's wardrobe.

Ryrie's Tactic

It should also be noted that Charles Ryrie played a similar academic game in *Dispensationalism Today* back in 1965. He used arguments very similar to O. T. Allis' covenant theology to defend traditional dispensationalism against the discontinuity-based attacks by ultradispensationalists (e.g., E. W. Bullinger, C. R. Stam, J. C. O'Hair). I refer here to the devastating and utterly irrefutable (for a Scofield dispensationalist) argument of the ultradispensationalists that Acts 2 (Pentecost) was clearly a fulfillment of Joel 2. Peter specifically referred to the prophecy in Joel 2 in Acts 2:16-20. This means that an Old Testament prophet forecasted the events of Acts 2. This poses a horrendous problem for Scofieldism. Dispensational theology has always taught that the so-called "Church Age" – also called "the great parenthesis" – was completely unknown in the Old Testament and not predicted by any prophet. But Peter said that Pentecost was known to an Old Testament prophet, Joel. The conclusion is inescapable: *the Church could not have begun at Pentecost; it must have started later.* This is exactly what the ultradispensationalists argue – a heretical idea, clearly, but absolutely consistent with the dispensational view of the Church as the great parenthesis.

To escape this problem of radical discontinuity, i.e., New Testament Church vs. Old Testament prophecy, Ryrie appealed to Erich Sauer, but in fact *Sauer's argument rests squarely on the arguments of postmillennial Calvinist O. T. Allis.* The Church was indeed founded at Pentecost; the events of Pentecost were merely transitional. No radical discontinuity should be assumed here, Ryrie insisted. So did Allis.[8] Ryrie also used Stam-type

---

8. Ryrie cites Sauer's argument that the "mystery" of Ephesians 3:1-12 – the

arguments – insisting on a radical discontinuity, Church vs. Israel – against Allis. This theological juggling act was not a successful intellectual defense of traditional dispensationalism; it was nothing less than abject surrender. Ryrie in effect picked up a white flag and identified it as dispensationalism's regimental colors. He publicly gave away the farm.

Theologians inside the dispensational camp apparently recognized what Ryrie had done in the name of defending the traditional system. I think this is the reason why there was no subsequent attempted academic defense of dispensationalism until House and Ice, a generation later, wrote *Dominion Theology*. But they no longer defend original Scofieldism. Neither do their published colleagues at Dallas Seminary. (Professor Robert Lightner still carries the old white flag in the classroom at Dallas, but the Christian book-buying public has never heard of him.)

A "New, Improved" Dispensationalism

Quite frankly, no one is sure just what the "new, improved" dispensational theology looks like. There has been no public presentation of the final version of this revised system, although a book by Robert Saucy of Talbot Seminary is about to be released by Zondervan. The old theological system is bleeding to death, drop by drop, by a thousand qualifications, but nothing has taken its place. There has been an embarrassed silence about this moribund condition for at least two decades. House and Ice have therefore opened a very dangerous can of worms.

House and Ice appeared to be on the offensive in their book, but in fact they were on the defensive. Like a duck gliding rapidly across a lake, everything appears calm on top of the

---

gentiles as fellow-heirs with the Jews in salvation – was not a radically new idea, but only comparatively new, i.e., no radical discontinuity. Ryrie, *Dispensationalism Today* (Chicago: Moody Press, 1965), p. 201. This is of course Allis' argument against all dispensationalism: *Prophecy and the Church* (Philadelphia: Presbyterian & Reformed, 1945), pp. 91-102.

Revising Dispensationalism to Death 149

water, but underneath the surface there is a lot of rapid paddling going on. The fact is, when House and Ice were finished with their attack on Christian Reconstructionism, their targets remained intact – in fact, completely untouched – but House and Ice were out of ammunition. Worse: they had blown up the barrel of their lone remaining canon. That they suspected that this might be the case was indicated by their refusal to allow me and Gary DeMar to see their book's pre-publication manuscript in early 1988, despite the fact that we were scheduled to debate Tommy Ice, who was not a published book author at the time. (A similar lack of confidence burdened Hal Lindsey, who also refused to allow me to read the pre-publication manuscript of *The Road to Holocaust*, despite my repeated written appeals.) People who are confident about their opinions will allow their targeted victims, upon request, to read the attacking manuscripts in advance. (Our responses get into print so rapidly anyway, why bother to play coy?)

Within months of the publication of *Dominion Theology*, Professor House had departed from Dallas Seminary. The reasons were always obscure – rather like Dr. Ryrie's departure earlier in the decade. House was hired by an obscure Baptist college on the West Coast. In 1992, House left that college, too. He is no longer employed by any fundamentalist institution.

Pentecost's Quiet Revision: Leaven and Evil

Dispensationalists can appeal to modern books on eschatology and the millennial kingdom written by McClain and John Walvoord, but the major presentation of their eschatological position is found in *Things to Come* (1958) by Dallas Seminary professor J. Dwight Pentecost. Unknown to most readers, he has significantly revised the book in a key area, and in doing so, he has abandoned the traditional dispensational case for the inevitable defeat of the Church in what the dispensationalists call the "Church Age." In the original edition, he argued for the eventual triumph of unbelief in this, the "Church Age." He wrote that Jesus' parable of the mustard seed (Matt. 13:31-32) points to the expansion of an *evil* tree in history, "a monstrosity. . . . The parable teaches that the enlarged sphere of profession has become inwardly corrupt. This is the characteristic of the age" (p. 147). In his exposition of the parable of the leaven, he argued: "This evidently refers to the work of a false religious system. . . . This figure is used in Scripture to portray that which is evil in character. . ." (p. 148). Summarizing, he wrote: "The mustard seed refers to the perversion of God's purpose in this age, while the leaven refers to a corruption of the divine agency, the Word, through which this purpose is realized" (p. 148). Pentecost's focus here was *ethics*: the progressive triumph of evil through time, during the "Church Age." This could at least serve as the foundation of a dispensational philosophy of history: *the defeat of the saints*. His book did not provide a developed philosophy of history; it provided only a starting point.

Three decades later, he abandoned even this, but very few of his followers are aware of the fact. The 1987 reprint is not a reprint but *a strategically revised edition*. It is nowhere identified as such. Dr. Pentecost had the typesetter carefully superimpose a crucial revised section. The switch is almost undetectable, yet it is a devastating admission for dispensationalism. Here is his revised exposition of Christ's kingdom during the "Church Age." *Mustard Seed*: "This part of the parable stresses the great growth of the kingdom when once it is introduced. The kingdom will grow from an insignificant beginning to great proportions" (p. 147). There is not a word about its ethical corruption. *Leaven*: "When leaven is used in Scripture it frequently connotes evil. . . . Its use in the sacrifices that represent the perfection of the person of Christ (Lev. 2:1-3) shows that it is not always so used. Here the emphasis is not on leaven as though to emphasize its character, but rather that the leaven has been hidden in the meal, thus stressing the way leaven works when once introduced into the meal" (p. 148). In short, *there is now no focus on ethics*: not one word about any evil effects of either the mustard seed or the leaven. Today his focus is on the growth of the kingdom of Christ in history – the *post*millennial focus: "The parable of the mustard and the leaven in meal, then, stress the growth of the new form of the kingdom" (p. 148).

If Christ's kingdom is not being corrupted in our dispensation, then it is either ethically neutral (the kingdom of Christ as ethically neutral?!?) or positive. Pentecost's theological problem is obvious: *there can be no ethical neutrality*. If the necessarily expanding kingdom of Christ is not being steadily undermined by theological and moral perversion, then it must be growing in righteousness. This interpretation is the postmillennial view of the kingdom of God: expansion over time. Matthew 13 is not discussing Satan's kingdom; it is discussing Christ's. Dr. Pentecost has very quietly overthrown the heart and soul of the traditional dispensational system's account of the inevitable progress of evil in this, the "Church Age."[9] Yet no one inside the dispensational camp has been willing to discuss in public the implications of this radical alteration by Pentecost, or explain exactly why it has not, if correct, overthrown the dispensational system. The dispensational system is in transition.[10]

The Dispensational Memory Hole

Decade after decade, dispensational theologians cling to a version of Church history which even their own students know is a series of preposterous falsehoods strung together with classroom polemics. Take, for example, a myth repeated by House and Ice, that the major promoter of postmillennialism was the early eighteenth-century Anglican theologian, Daniel Whitby. Dr. Gentry deals with this in *House Divided*.[11] Now,

---

9. Gary DeMar spotted this shift in early 1992. He looked up Pentecost's section on leaven in the 1987 edition. He found that it was not what Gentry had quoted. He called Gentry, who looked it up in the 1958 edition. The two versions differed.

10. Dr. Gentry writes a monthly newsletter, *Dispensationalism in Transition*, published by the Institute for Christian Economics: P. O. Box 8000, Tyler, TX 75711.

11. Greg L. Bahnsen and Kenneth L. Gentry, Jr., *House Divided: The Break Up of*

anyone with even a brief knowledge of the history of Puritanism knows that there were many postmillennialists in the seventeenth-century Puritan camp, including John Owen. Whitby was born in 1638 and did not write until the early eighteenth century. He is a minor figure in the history of the Church, which is why the dispensationalist polemicists dwell on him as the originator: it makes postmillennialism appear to be a backwater eschatology. Dispensationalists comfort themselves with the thought that "real Bible-believers don't believe in postmillennialism," in the same way that Southern rednecks believe that "real men don't eat quiche." Only dispensational writers have ever proclaimed this Whitby myth, but they have done so generation after generation – *not, however, scholars who teach Church history and who also hold a Ph.D in the field.* Sadly, the Church historians on dispensational campuses are apparently unwilling or psychologically unable to go to their less well-informed colleagues and say, "Look, fellows, this whole story was a myth our founders invented for polemical reasons, and we are making fools of ourselves by continuing to proclaim it." So the Whitby myth goes on, accepted dutifully by generations of C-average students who hate both Church history and systematic theology, but who are "into" local church growth.

Tommy Ice regurgitated this old myth in our debate in 1988; I promptly reminded him of the dating problem with Whitby, and then I reminded him that at least my eschatological system was developed as early as 1600; his was invented in 1830. He had nothing to say in response, but a variation of this same old saw now appears in his book. Why would a man of academic integrity do this? Answer: a man of academic integrity wouldn't.[12]

Dispensational Theology (Tyler, Texas: Institute for Christian Economics, 1989), chaps. 10, 18.

12. On the academic integrity of the two authors, see *House Divided*, Part IV.

Another example: the statement that the early Church fathers were all premillennialists. House and Ice really compound the problem. They say that Daniel Whitby said that the first Nicene council was premillennial.[13] Whitby said exactly the opposite, as Dr. Gentry shows in his chapter in *House Divided* on "The Exposition of the Kingdom." A Th.M. thesis written by a Dallas Seminary student in 1977 took to task Charles Ryrie's statement that the early Church fathers were premillennialists. Not so, the student concluded; there were many amillennialists among them.[14] But do you think any dispensational author is ready to go into print and admit that Ryrie's account is mythical? Not on your life! Yet it was not just Ryrie's account; this myth has been taught by virtually all dispensationalists except those professionally trained in early Church history.

A Movement Without an Official History

What has happened is this: each incoming class of eager seminary students is treated to a rehash of classroom lecture notes – notes that suppress the history of the Church whenever this history comes into conflict with the "received truths" of the dispensationalism of the 1920's through the 1950's. The students are not told of Dave MacPherson's thesis that Margaret Macdonald, a girl about 20 years old, went into trances in 1830 and announced the pre-tribulation doctrine. We are still waiting for Professor John Hannah, a competent and talented Church historian, to go into print and show from original source documents that MacPherson's thesis is nothing but a sham. Strangely, he has decided to remain silent. Or not so strangely, as the case may be.

---

13. House and Ice, *Dominion Theology*, p. 206.
14. Alan Patrick Boyd, A Dispensational Premillennial Analysis of the Eschatology of the Post-Apostolic Fathers (Until the Death of Justin Martyr), unpublished Master's Thesis, Dallas Theological Seminary, May, 1977.

It is worth noting that no Church historian on a dispensational seminary campus has been willing to write a documented, official history of the dispensational movement, for this would involve confronting the embarrassing fact of at least three generations of what had passed for official history before, and what in Stalin's day was called "agitprop." We have in our midst an influential theological and ecclesiastical movement which is now a hundred and sixty years old, yet we still do not have a single, footnoted, carefully researched history of the movement by any professor teaching in a dispensational seminary. What this means is that only anti-dispensationalists and non-dispensationalists have bothered to write the history of the movement. This, to put it mildly, is most peculiar.

I will put it bluntly: *any century-old intellectual-ideological-institutional movement which is incapable of producing its own official history is equally incapable of maintaining itself.* It has lost the war in advance.

I will put it even more bluntly: the reason why dispensationalism has not produced a detailed, documented, publicly accessible history is that *its adherents do not believe that they have a future*. A record of the past, they believe, is hardly worth preserving because the earthly future for Christians will soon be cut short. Premillennialism strikes again!

Unrevised Lecture Notes

Dispensational seminary and Bible college professors (those not teaching Church history) read their worn-out lecture notes to their students – notes copied from their own professors years ago. The myths and outright lies get repeated, incoming class after class. The charade of academic integrity can go on for only as long as these students and graduates refuse to read serious works of scholarship. Understand, most graduates of most seminaries are perfectly content to avoid reading works of scholarship. Those dispensationalists who do read serious books, however, risk experiencing a trauma. They may discover that they had spent three or four years in seminary getting a pack of lies taught to them in the name of historical classroom continuity. Their professors had been equally misinformed by their professors, and so on, right back to the founding of the seminary. Nobody bothers to check the primary source documents, since this might require an updating of his lecture notes.

Dispensational theology is like a large stable that never gets swept out. Nobody wants to go in there with a shovel and broom to remove the accumulated filth, so it just gets deeper and riper. It becomes more obvious to their brighter students that they risk stepping in bad stuff every time they go into a classroom to hear the familiar Party Line. The brighter graduates very often depart from the Party Line. But still the classroom charade goes on. The facts of Church history get dumped down the equivalent of the memory hole in Orwell's *1984*.

This academic practice identifies a dying movement. You cannot legitimately expect to move forward if your students are deliberately misinformed. This is the same crisis facing the Soviet Union and Red China today: ill-informed people make ill-informed decisions. Only those Christian leaders who believe that there is no future, that Jesus is coming again shortly to Rapture them out of their troubles – especially the Augean stables of dispensationalism's unpublished official history – would be so foolish as to refuse to cut their losses, admit the past lies, and do serious historical scholarship in terms of the movement's official theology. Once again, bad eschatology has produced suicidal results.

Black-Outs and Flame-Outs

This is why dispensationalist seminary professors – that is, professors on dispensational seminary campuses who still actually take dispensationalism seriously in their classrooms (a rapidly declining number) – work so hard to keep their students from reading anything that is not on the required reading lists. They know what will happen to the best and the brightest of their students if the students start reading "off campus" books. The familiar defensive measure against this probability (i.e., near certainty) of "corruption" is the creation of a systematic academic black-out, especially the prohibition of debates on campus between the faculty and outside scholars. They know what will happen.

When Dr. Ray Sutton was a student at Dallas Theological Seminary in the mid-1970's, he was told again and again by his professors: "Don't read that book." Almost without exception, the forbidden books were written by Calvinistic authors. (The one major exception: William Everett Bell's 1967 Ph.D. dissertation, "A Critical Examination of the Pretribulation Rapture Doctrine in Christian Eschatology.") Predictably, he went to the library and read these forbidden books. The brighter students always did. By the time he was a senior, Sutton was a Calvinist. So were a lot of his fellow students. When the best response that a movement-oriented faculty member can offer to his movement's academic critics is "Don't read that book," that movement is close to death.

The inability of the Dallas Seminary faculty to provide answers more sophisticated than "Don't read that book!" resulted in 1987 in Sutton's monumental study, *That You May Prosper: Dominion By Covenant*. This book shows that the same biblical covenant model extends from the Old Testament into the New Testament – the ultimate challenge to dispensational theology. That a graduate of Dallas Seminary could produce such a challenge is indicative of the problem facing Dallas Seminary as the last surviving member of what in 1960 were the Big Three dispensational seminaries. And what is Dallas Seminary's public response? Silence. On campus, I suppose it is the old refrain, "Don't read that book."

Dallas Seminary is willing to defend dispensationalism only through threat of dismissal. A student who loses his faith in the system and who admits this publicly is told to leave. So is any faculty member. But the problem with this sort of defense, unless accompanied by a full-scale book-publishing program, is that it affects only those few people who are directly under your control. Also, it cannot defend itself against hiring men who sign a statement which they no longer care to defend in public. This eventually produces a faculty full of time-servers who dabble in biblical scholarship, if at all, only in areas that are academically peripheral to the doubtful distinctives of the institution's mandatory statement of faith. These people bide their time until a quiet transformation of the school becomes institutionally possible. That day came for Talbot. It seems to have come for Grace. It is coming for Dallas. Dispensationalism's torch is burning low. The flame-out approaches.

When it comes, no one who is holding that once-bright torch will admit in public that the original oil is gone. That way, the seminary's naive donors will continue to send in money, despite the fact that they are no longer getting their money's worth. Such is the price of Rapture fever. It eventually blinds all those whom it afflicts.

The Terrible Price of Evasion

Donors who finance a seminary believe they are buying several things. First, they think they are buying a supply of future ministers who will meet the needs of churches. Second, they hope they are financing academic specialists who will promote and defend the particular theological system that the seminary was established to promote and defend. Third, they think they are buying a supply of future scholars who can and will promote and defend the theology.

When a seminary faculty takes money on any other basis, the school should publicly announce any exceptions to these three tasks. Seminaries never do, but they should. Thus, if they are no longer willing to promote the seminary's theology openly and forcefully, they should say so. If they decide that their personal intellectual reputations will be sacrificed if they publicly defend the system, they should say so. They never do, of course, but they should.

The faculties of Talbot Seminary, Grace Seminary, and Dallas Seminary have been unwilling for many decades to reply to O. T. Allis' book, *Prophecy and the Church* (1945). This refusal was entirely self-serving. Allis was the most prominent defender of the integrity of the Old Testament's text in his generation, the author of *The Five Books of Moses* (1943). He could not be dismissed as some crackpot or theological amateur. He was in fact a master theologian. His comprehensive criticism of dispensationalism's eschatology remains the most powerful ever offered. Yet almost half a century later, no dispensational scholar has written a book of equal length and detail to refute Allis. Charles Ryrie's thin book, *Dispensationalism Today* (1965), was devoted only in part to Allis.

Their failure to respond indicates an inability of dispensationalism's academic defenders to defend the system. If they were willing to announce publicly that they are incapable of answering a particular critic, this would be honest, but to do so would be a kind of intellectual suicide. The fact is, a failure to respond is intellectual suicide, but it is death by slow poison in private rather than a quick end to one's misery in public.

When I decided to challenge dispensationalism publicly, beginning with my book, *75 Bible Questions Your Professors Pray You Won't Ask* (1984), I committed myself to respond immediately to any counter-attack. I stand ready to publish a rapid reply to any academic critic who writes a book, and also popular critics who have a large readership. Thus, when Dave Hunt devoted a few pages to Christian Reconstruction in his *Seduction of Christianity* (1987), I hired Gary DeMar and Peter Leithart to write *The Reduction of Christianity* (1988). That book appeared within 12 months of Hunt's effort. I do my best to reduce to a minimum the time elapsed between the criticism and our response. When Hunt and Tommy Ice took on Gary DeMar and me in April of 1988, I had DeMar's *The Debate Over Christian*

Revising Dispensationalism to Death 159

Reconstruction in print before the end of the year. When House and Ice's *Dominion Theology: Blessing or Curse?* was published in the fall of 1988, I had Bahnsen and Gentry's *House Divided* in print within eight months. Anything less constitutes surrender.

When Hal Lindsey had his scurrilous book, *The Road to Holocaust*, published by Bantam Books (hardly a Christian publisher!) in June of 1988, I had DeMar and Leithart's reply in print within 30 days: *The Legacy of Hatred Continues: A Response to Hal Lindsey's **The Road to Holocaust***. This appeared in time for the Christian Booksellers' Association annual meeting in July. I had my representative hand out free copies of this book to dozens of booths, nipping Lindsey's attack in the bud. I caught Lindsey flat-footed; he had egg all over his mustache. He had refused to allow DeMar and me to see his manuscript in advance, and had repeatedly refused to meet with DeMar and me in advance, although we put our requests in writing. He paid no more attention to Matthew 18:15-17 than he has paid to Matthew 5:32. He has never responded or apologized. In 1990, he allowed an uncorrected paperback reprint, with every factual error left intact, including the incorrect names of the men and institutions he was attacking. I regard Lindsey as an intellectual fraud who is more interested in collecting new wives than in correcting past injustices. I am aware of no scholar who takes him seriously. Dallas Seminary has never invited him to lecture on prophecy or eschatology. Nevertheless, we replied to his false accusations to prove they were false.

The point is, when you are being paid to defend a position, you must be ready to reply, point by point, to major published critics. Otherwise, your followers will conclude that you are incapable of replying, either because you are not intellectually competent or else your position cannot be defended. When Westminster Seminary published *Theonomy: A Reformed Critique* in October of 1990, I had my response in print by the following April: *Westminster's Confession*. I followed this with Bahnsen's reply, *No Other Standard*, that summer. Then came the book I edited, *Theonomy: An Informed Response* in December. We replied three books to one within 14 months. I said in print that if the Westminster faculty replied to any of these books, I would publish at least one volume in response, and I would keep replying, volume for volume, until I had the last word. We theonomists have not heard from Westminster Seminary again.

You must also launch an attack on your attackers; defense is never sufficient to win a war for ideas. This is what the defense of the faith requires: a victory. But dispensationalists refuse to acknowledge this fact, *because they believe that the Church's failure in this dispensation is predestined*. They are consistent with their theology. They pretend that by their silence they can defer major problems until the Rapture solves them. They preach a theology of deferral, of intellectual disengagement. *They practice what they preach*. This is suicidal. One by one, their faculty members quietly abandon the original position; one by one, their brightest graduates defect. Eventually, the seminary itself defects, and the existing faculty is fired. This has happened at both Talbot and Grace. Tommy Ice thinks something like this will happen at Dallas by the year 2000.

The fact is, a failure to respond in print is symptomatic of a position that cannot be successfully defended. This is indicative of a dying theology. *It is only a matter of time before the defections erode the future of the movement*. When a seminary's faculty members refuse to defend the school's theology in print, it is only a matter of time before that seminary will depart from the received tradition. A theology that is not worth risking one's reputation to defend is not worth defending when the climate of theological opinion shifts against the older belief.

A paradigm shift is now in progress in dispensationalism. Its systematic cultural irrelevance has become an embarrassment to hundreds of thousands of Christian activists, who, unlike tenured faculty members, are willing to take a public stand against abortion or the public schools. Dallas Seminary's continued silence on *Roe v. Wade* after two decades has condemned the dispensational system. Moral revulsion against the silence of the leaders on the part of laymen who are willing to take risks continues to erode their confidence in dispensational theology and the academic leaders produced by it. Dispensationalist professors today can neither defend their theological system nor defend the right to life. *Dispensationalism today is visibly bankrupt*; theologically, it always has been, but this fact was not publicly visible until after the legalization of abortion. This moral defection by seminary faculties is an extension of their intellectual defection after the publication of Allis' *Prophecy and the Church*. One by one, these seminaries are going bankrupt. Leadership is slipping away from them, as well it should.

Conclusion

I will say it once again, just to be sure that everyone understands: *Dominion Theology: Blessing or Curse?* (1988) was a public admission of the death of dispensationalism. So is the failure of any dispensationalist scholar to respond to *House Divided*. House and Ice provided the first full-scale statement of the dispensational position – by way of refuting theonomy – that we have seen since Ryrie's brief and ineffective 1965 book, *Dispensationalism Today*. That book failed to answer the critics of dispensationalism. *Dominion Theology: Blessing or Curse?* is far worse, from the point of view of Scofieldism: it raised even more explosive questions, yet pretended to have answers to theonomy. *House Divided* disproved this claim within months. No one has challenged *House Divided*, least of all ex-professor House.

I will say it once again: *the theological debate is over*. I said this in 1989, and I am saying it again. Christian Reconstructionism has not yet won the debate with every known theological critic (although we are working on it), but it has won the debate with the dispensationalists. By engaging dispensationalism directly, Dr. Bahnsen and Dr. Gentry brought up to date the brilliant and deliberately long-ignored work of O. T. Allis. Allis inflicted mortal wounds on dispensational theology in 1945. Bahnsen and Gentry merely acted as public coroners. Their autopsy report is now on record. Ladies and gentlemen, the cadaver is surely dead; rigor mortis has set in. It is time to give it a decent Christian burial.

If I am wrong, then it will be easy for the defenders to prove me wrong. All they need to do is *agree with each other* on what dispensationalism is – what its fundamental, "non-negotiable" doctrines are – and then *publish a consistent systematic theology*. It must be an extension of the original dispensational system. It must answer O. T. Allis, Ray Sutton, Greg Bahnsen, and Ken Gentry. It really ought to answer Princeton Seminary's Geerhardus Vos, whose book, *The Pauline Eschatology*, has also been conveniently ignored by dispensational scholars since its publication in 1930.

A modern dispensational systematic theology must discuss at least the following points:

1. The distinction between Israel and the Church
2. The distinction (if any) between the kingdom of God and the kingdom of heaven
3. The meaning of leaven (always evil or not?)
4. Biblical law and sanctification (law and grace)
5. The neutrality of "natural law" and Church Age politics
6. Where the Rapture is in Matthew 13 (continuity)
7. When the clock of prophecy starts ticking
8. How Hebrews 8 – Christ's priestly office – fits with the idea of reinstated sacrifices in the millennium
9. When the Church began: Acts 2, Acts 9, or Acts 28
10. How the gospel is a fulfillment of God's promise to rebuild David's tabernacle (Acts 15:14-16)
11. How literalism applies to stars falling to earth (Rev. 6:13)
12. How Revelation 12 can be future, given verse 11

9

DISPENSATIONALISM VS. SIX-DAY CREATIONISM

For in six days the Lord made heaven and earth, the sea, and all that in them is, and rested the seventh day; wherefore, the Lord blessed the sabbath day, and hallowed it (Ex. 20:11).

The first creative act refers to the dateless past, and gives scope for all the geologic ages.
Scofield Reference Bible (1909)[1]

Scripture gives no data for determining how long ago the universe was created.
New Scofield Reference Bible (1967)[2]

The Fourth Commandment makes it plain: *God created the world in six days,* not six ages. God rested the seventh day, not for an age. He hallowed this day, meaning that He set it apart. The very structure of the week is supposed to reflect the six days and one day pattern of God's first week. From the early days of the Christian Church, its Bible-believing religious lead-

---

1. C. I. Scofield, *Scofield Reference Bible* (New York: Oxford University Press, 1909), p. 3, note 2: Genesis 1:1.
2. *The New Scofield Bible* (Oxford, 1967), p. 1.

ers taught no other view of creation. Augustine wrote in the *City of God* concerning those people who believe in a long history of the earth: "They are deceived, too, by those highly mendacious documents which profess to give the history of many thousand years, though, reckoning by the sacred writings, we find that not 6000 years have yet passed" (XII.10). Mendacity, indeed!

Such was the opinion of Christian orthodoxy for almost seventeen centuries. But then in the late 1600's opinions began to change. As men began to study the geologic column in detail, they began to conclude that the world is much older than had previously been believed by Christians, though of course all religions not tied to the Old Testament had always denied that history is so short. The pagan presuppositions of all anti-biblical religions began to seep into the Church through sedimentary rocks, as it were.

A Loss of Faith

For fifty years prior to the publication of Charles Darwin's *Origin of Species* in 1859, Christian intellectuals steadily abandoned faith in a literal six-day creation. They extended the time frame of what was considered acceptable regarding biblical chronology. Writes evolutionist Michael Ruse:

> However, by 1859, even in Victorian Britain, nearly all intelligent and informed people realized that one could no longer hold to a traditional, Biblically inspired picture of the world: a world created by God in six days (of twenty-four hours each); a world of very, very recent origin (4004 B.C. was the favored date of creation, based on genealogies of the Bible); and, a world which at some subsequent point had been totally covered and devastated by a monstrous flood. Through the first half of the nineteenth century, scientific discovery after scientific discovery had modified these traditional beliefs.[3]

---

3. Michael Ruse, *Darwinism Defended: A Guide to the Evolution Controversies* (Read-

Dispensationalism vs. Six-Day Creationism

Darwin, of course, opened the floodgates of religious skepticism. A good example of the erosion of faith is the 1925 statement of Rev. James Maurice Wilson:

> Is it not evident that the vast change of our conception of the created universe has affected in general men's thought of the Creator? What was conceivable, credible, and fully believed by early Semites, as to the nature of a God ruling a small tribe in what was thought to be the sole created world – a conception long accepted on their authority – became inconceivable, incredible, and is frankly disbelieved in presence of the infinities of space now known to us. Our Christian conception of God, adopted from Jewish tradition, was in fact small and childish; and it was of a kind that would not bear indefinite expansion. It was stretched, and stretched, till it burst like a bubble and disappeared.[4]

> Most of the educated young people were, I think, in that stage of thought in November, 1859. We were, as I have said, evolutionists at heart. We had begun to realize the immense extent of the Sidereal Universe. It was incomparably more to us than it was to the writer of the first chapter of Genesis, who added incidentally that God "made the stars also". Lyell and others had also familiarized us with the age of the earth, its slow and gradual formation, and the long succession of forms of life on it.[5]

The immensity of the universe no longer impressed these evolutionists with the majesty of God the Creator. Instead, they interpreted the size of the universe in terms of the supposedly impersonal, meaningless processes of immense, uncreated time.

---

ing, Massachusetts: Addison-Wesley, 1982), pp. 285-86.

4. James Maurice Wilson, "The Religious Effect of the Idea of Evolution," in *Evolution in the Light of Modern Knowledge: A Collective Work* (London: Blackie & Son, 1925), p. 486.

5. *Ibid.*, p. 488.

God was shoved out of their mental universe. The result was predictable: the eventual decline of biblical orthodoxy.

Scofield's Shuffle

You might imagine that by 1900, every orthodox Christian scholar would have recognized the tight connection between the evolutionists' geological time frame and their rejection of biblical truth. You would be wrong. Virtually no leading theologian in any orthodox camp was steadfast in his defense of Bishop Ussher's chronology or anything remotely resembling it.

Into this wasteland came lawyer C. I. Scofield and his Reference notes in 1909. Beginning with his notes on Genesis 1:1, he gave away the biblical case for creationism. In note 2, he wrote: "The first creative act refers to the dateless past, and gives scope for all the geologic ages." This is exactly what the besieged defenders of the Bible had been arguing for over a century, and each generation saw them pushed into the wilderness of ever-greater compromise.

He adopted the so-called "gap" theory of creation. In between Genesis 1:1 and 1:2, there was a gap of an indeterminate period – in fact, a gap just long enough to allow Christians to fill in the latest theories of the geologic time frame. This supposedly removed from Christian scholars the necessity of dealing with biblical chronology prior to Adam. What such a strategy could not do, however, was to remove the stigma of the biblical account of creation, which places the creation of the sun, moon, and stars *after* the creation of the earth (Gen. 1:14-15). This problem passage was what led Rev. Wilson to sneer concerning the immensity of the universe, "It was incomparably more to us than it was to the writer of the first chapter of Genesis, who added incidentally that God 'made the stars also'."

Who would have invented the gap theory if uniformitarian theories of the geologic column had never appeared, or if Darwinism had never appeared? No one. It is obviously a half-hearted, half-baked attempt to escape one problem, *fossils*, without solving the really difficult exegetical problem for anyone who accepted uniformitarianism's geologic time frame: *the age of the earth in relation to the age of the sun.*

Henry M. Morris has called attention to the harm that Scofield's notes on the creation produced:

> While anti-evolutionism was strong among the fundamentalists, almost none of their leaders questioned Lyellian uniformitarianism and the geological-age system. The Scofield Reference Bible, originally published in 1909, had actually incorporated both these theories in its notes, while at the same time ignoring the critically important question of the universality of the Flood, and it had a tremendous impact on fundamentalists in many denominations.[6]

Scofield Lives!

In the *New Scofield Reference Bible* (1967), the editors kept all of the worst features of the Scofield notes on creation. Note 4 retains at least part of the original edition's note 2, "The first creative act refers to the dateless past." It drops the words, "and gives scope for all the geologic ages." This does not indicate any change in opinion on the part of the editors; it only covers up one of Scofield's more blatant concessions to uniformitarian geology. In note 2, they insist, "Scripture gives no data for determining how long ago the universe was created." It refers the reader to a note for Genesis 5:3: "Scripture does not reveal the exact date of Adam's creation." It then refers the reader to a note for Genesis 11:10: "Scripture does not provide data by which the date of the flood can be discovered."

Here is the game all the chronology compromisers play. First, they tell us that Scripture cannot give us the *exact* date of the creation, Adam, or the flood. Second, they sit passively while the evolutionists drive a chronological truck through this

---

6. Henry M. Morris, *History of Modern Creationism* (San Diego, California: Master Book Publishers, 1984), pp. 58-59.

gap that carries a cosmic time scale of *15 billion years*, give or take five billion. In fact, the compromisers deliberately invented this tactic of "insufficient Scriptural exactness" in order to allow the evolutionists to drive their truck right through the Church. They are like children playing a game of *dodge-a-truck* on a freeway, yelling, "Nyah, Nyah, you can't hit us!" This game always produces piles of dead bodies – personal, ecclesiastical, and educational – that are scattered all over the landscape.

In a 1982 book published by dispensationalist Moody Press, a group of dispensational scholars paid tribute to John Walvoord, the long-time president of Dallas Theological Seminary. Frederick R. Howe contributed an essay, "Creation and Evolution: The Continuing Confrontation." He listed four features of the biblical account of creation: (1) creation by a sovereign, triune God; (2) creation by divine fiat; (3) creation with boundaries (e.g., the concept of *kind*); (4) the accomplished work of creation, i.e., creation distinguished from providence.[7]

All well and good, but hardly complete. The gaping hole ("gap") in his list is the doctrine of the six-day creationism. The intellectual leaders of the dispensationalist movement continue to pay ultimate tribute to its major American distributor, lawyer Scofield, who naively sold out the movement to the evolutionists in 1909.

Should we be surprised to learn that Moody Press refused to publish Morris and Whitcomb's *The Genesis Flood* (1961) because it insisted on a six-literal-day creation scheme?[8] Should we be surprised that Dallas Theological Seminary has never offered a course defending the six-literal-day creation? Seminary professors are embarrassed by Genesis 1. None has built a curriculum around this crucial doctrine. Dallas is no worse than the others, but no better. Its financial supporters should demand much

---

7. Donald K. Campbell (ed.), *Walvoord: A Tribute* (Chicago: Moody Press, 1982), pp. 146-47.

8. Morris, *History of Modern Creation*, p. 154.

better. But they are afraid to insist that creationism be defended. Laymen still sit silent, and they continue to send in their checks. This has been going on for over half a century.

The co-author of *The Genesis Flood*, John Whitcomb, taught for decades at Grace Theological Seminary, which did maintain a defense of the six-day creation. In 1990, Whitcomb was fired, three months short of his retirement. He had complained once too often regarding what he viewed as the theological drift of the seminary.

Henry Morris is a fundamentalist and a dispensationalist. He has waged a lifelong defense of six-day creationism, and he has yet to convert a single seminary. He is the "odd man out" in modern dispensationalism, however. Scofield set the standard of dispensational compromise in 1909, and the vast majority of his academically certified followers have not departed from the received tradition. The sell-out continues.

The Triumph of Darwinism

Only one major conservative, seminary-based theologian in the nineteenth century publicly opposed Darwinism: Charles Hodge. He wrote *What Is Darwinism?* in 1874, and concluded that Darwinism is atheism. By the time he wrote his little book, Darwinian thought had begun to capture the colleges, academic departments, and intellectuals of the era. By 1900, Darwinism's triumph was institutionally complete.

In between, Christians played no part in the debate. The debate was between two forms of Darwinism: Social Darwinism and Statist Darwinism. The Social Darwinists argued that free market competition is analogous to competition in nature. Therefore, we should let this competition run its course, producing ever-stronger private business firms. The Statist Darwinists switched the debate from planless nature to planning man. Man, meaning elite scientists, now know the secrets of evolution. They can use this knowledge to design and direct scientifically the next stage of the evolutionary process. The politicians will carry out these plans. This view of Darwinism had become dominant by 1900.[9]

Darwinism was not confined to the geology department, the biology department, and the paleontology department. It spread outward from these fields in natural science into the social sciences and the arts. Above all, it spread into the field of law. In 1881, Oliver Wendell Holmes, Jr., made the evolutionary worldview the basis of his book, *The Common Law*. He eventually became a justice of the U.S. Supreme Court.

Since 1961, a few academic Christians have begun to defend the six-day creation in the natural sciences. The problem is, dispensationalism does not have a doctrine of biblical law. Thus, there is no attempt on the part of these dispensational six-day creationists to extend their view of origins into the social sciences and the arts. Three decades after *The Genesis Flood*, there is not a single college-level textbook by a dispensationalist that applies creationism to the social sciences, law, and the arts. Only the Christian Reconstructionists make these applications, precisely because they are not dispensationalists, although they are six-day creationists.[10]

The pietism and retreatism of traditional dispensationalism, which are the inevitable products of dispensationalism's view of social law and the future, have paralyzed the six-day creationists within the dispensational camp. These scholars have refused to take the creation vs. evolution battle out of the narrow confines of the natural sciences. Yet it was in these other academic disciplines that nineteenth-century Darwinism created a new view of God, man, law, and time, and a new civilization to match this Darwinian worldview. The battle has barely begun, yet the dispensational creationists seem almost unaware of the vast

---

9. Gary North, *The Dominion Covenant: Genesis* (2nd ed.; Tyler, Texas: Institute for Christian Economics, 1987), Appendix A: "From Cosmic Purposelessness to Humanistic Sovereignty."

10. Gary North, *Is the World Running Down? Crisis in the Christian Worldview* (Tyler, Texas: Institute for Christian Economics, 1988).

extent of the task that lies ahead. Why? Because they do not really believe that there is sufficient time remaining to the Church to complete this task.

Conclusion

The failure of the vast majority of dispensationalism's theologians to defend a six-literal-day creation is only one part of its intellectual paralysis. Meanwhile, the failure of the few dispensational six-day creationists to extend their doctrine of God's fiat creation into the social sciences and the arts constitutes another aspect of this paralysis.

The Darwinists knew what to do with their scientific alternative to Christianity's view of God, man, law, and time. Within one generation after the publication of *The Origin of Species*, they were completely victorious in the academic and intellectual world. In contrast, within one generation after the publication of *The Genesis Flood*, not one dispensational creationist scholar has produced a book in his own academic field on the application of six-day creationism, except in the natural sciences. (I must not be unfair; amillennial six-day creationists have been equally silent in the social sciences and the arts.)

The paralysis of dispensationalism has not yet been relieved, even by the most courageous of its academic representatives. Ideas have consequences. The idea of the imminent Rapture, the idea of the inevitable cultural defeat of the Church, and the idea that God's revealed law is annulled in this dispensation are bad ideas, and they have produced bad results.

To reconstruct theology, we must begin with the doctrine of the six-day creation. It points to the absolute sovereignty of God and the absolute distinction between God's being and creation. God spoke the world into existence, and He placed it under law. Man was given the dominion covenant: to serve as God's representative in history. The curse on the earth is progressively removed in history through the power of the resurrection: the biblical doctrine of corporate sanctification.

10

DISPENSATIONALISM VS. SANCTIFICATION

> *What doth it profit, my brethren, though a man say he hath faith, and have not works? can faith save him? If a brother or sister be naked, and destitute of daily food, And one of you say unto them, Depart in peace, be ye warmed and filled; notwithstanding ye give them not those things which are needful to the body; what doth it profit? Even so faith, if it hath not works, is dead, being alone. Yea, a man may say, Thou hast faith, and I have works: shew me thy faith without thy works, and I will shew thee my faith by my works. Thou believest that there is one God; thou doest well: the devils also believe, and tremble (James 2:14-19).*

John MacArthur, Jr., is one of the major figures in the dispensational world. He has a large church in southern California. His father started it, but he has expanded it. He is a popular speaker. He is also an author. When he speaks, a lot of people listen. When he writes, a lot of people read.

His book, *The Gospel According to Jesus* (Zondervan Academie Books, 1988) was one of 1988's best-selling hardback Christian books. It presented the case for Lordship salvation: the necessity of publicly accepting Jesus as Lord and then obeying Him, rather than a one-time verbal profession of faith in Jesus as Savior, followed by libertinism. The book created an immediate

Dispensationalism vs. Sanctification

sensation. Here was a major dispensationalist author who chose to have J. I. Packer, Calvinist theologian and neo-Puritan professor, write one Foreword, and James Montgomery Boice, Calvinist theologian and Presbyterian minister, write a second Foreword. But even more surprising, they both consented to write.

Something very peculiar was going on here.

The Issue is Obedience: Sanctification

Boice writes:

> . . . In *The Gospel According to Jesus*, MacArthur is not dealing with some issue or issues external to the faith, but with the central issue of all, namely, What does it mean to be a Christian? His answers address themselves to what I consider to be the greatest weakness of contemporary evangelical Christianity in America.
>
> Did I say weakness? It is more. It is a tragic error. It is the idea – where did it ever come from? – that one can be a Christian without being a follower of the Lord Jesus Christ. It reduces the gospel to the mere fact of Christ's having died for sinners, requires of sinners only that they acknowledge this by the barest intellectual assent, and then assures them of their eternal security when they may very well not be born again. This view bends faith far beyond recognition – at least for those who know what the Bible says about faith – and promises a false peace to thousands who have given verbal assent to this reductionist Christianity but are not truly in God's family (p. xi).

Boice then goes on to quote Matthew 10:22, the verse that defends the traditional Calvinist doctrine of the perseverance of the saints: "And ye shall be hated of all men for my name's sake: but he that endureth to the end shall be saved." Then he cites Luke 6:46: "And why call ye me, Lord, Lord, and do not the things which I say?" Then he cites Luke 9:23: "And he said to them all, If any man will come after me, let him deny himself, and take up his cross daily, and follow me." And finally, he cites Hebrews 12:14: "Follow peace with all men, and holiness, without which no man shall see the Lord."

You mean that the Bible teaches that without *holiness* – ethical set-apartness – the professing Christian's verbal confession of faith in Christ is of zero value? Worse: that his verbal profession in fact will testify against him eternally in the lake of fire? You mean to say, as MacArthur says, that

> Real salvation is not only justification. It cannot be isolated from regeneration, sanctification and, ultimately, glorification. Salvation is an ongoing process as much as it is a past event. It is the work of God through which we are "conformed to the image of His Son" (Romans 8:29, cf. Romans 13:11). Genuine assurance comes from seeing the Holy Spirit's transforming work in one's life, not from clinging to the memory of some experience (p. 23).

Oh, my! To say that this book caused great consternation in the "just confess Jesus as Savior, but not necessarily as Lord, and be eternally saved" camp is putting it mildly. Dr. MacArthur did more than launch a torpedo into the side of the good ship *Antinomianism*; he in fact detonated a charge from deep inside its bulwarks.

What Is the Target of His Attack?

His target is the theology (soteriology) of C. I. Scofield, Lewis Sperry Chafer, Charles C. Ryrie, Zane C. Hodges, and Col. R. B. Thieme, whose works MacArthur footnotes scrupulously and refutes thoroughly. It is a full-scale assault on the theological foundations of Dallas Seminary, *Moody Monthly*, and almost every independent Bible church and Bible college in the country.

Dispensationalism vs. Sanctification 175

Whose writings does he use in order to refute dispensationalism's ethics? Calvinist Presbyterians Benjamin B. Warfield, Geerhardus Vos, and J. Gresham Machen, Calvinist Baptist Arthur Pink, the Puritans, and Calvinist-charismatic Martyn Lloyd-Jones. Oh yes, and Ken Gentry, whose two books on the pre-70 A.D. dating of the Book of Revelation were published the next year, 1989.

Something *very* peculiar is going on here.

He starts out by announcing clearly that "salvation is by God's sovereign grace and grace alone. Nothing a lost, degenerate, spiritually dead sinner can do will in any way contribute to salvation. Saving faith, repentance, commitment, and obedience are all divine works, wrought by the Holy Spirit in the heart of everyone who is saved. I have never taught that some pre-salvation works of righteousness are necessary to or are any part of salvation" (p. xiii). So much for Arminianism, "free will," and the agreed-upon theology of 95% of those who call themselves evangelicals today. But he does not stop with the doctrines of total depravity and salvation by grace alone. He immediately goes to ethics: the doctrine of *progressive sanctification*:

> But I do believe without apology that real salvation cannot and will not fail to produce works of righteousness in the life of a true believer. There are no human works in the saving act, but God's work of salvation includes a change of intent, will, desire, and attitude that inevitably produce the fruit of the Spirit. The very essence of God's saving work is the transformation of the will that results in a love for God. Salvation thus establishes the *root* that will surely produce the *fruit* (p. xiii).

What is also astounding is that this dispensationalist author actually cites the very verses we Calvinists appeal to in demonstrating that God's grace includes *predestined* good works, Ephesians 2:8-10: "For by grace are ye saved through faith; and that not of yourselves: it is the gift of God: Not of works, lest any man should boast. For we are his workmanship, created in

Christ Jesus unto good works, which God hath before ordained that we should walk in them" (pp. 95-96). Fundamentalists almost never quote Ephesians 2:10. MacArthur does. He even refers the reader to James 2:14-26, the New Testament's premier passage on faith and good works.

Then MacArthur goes for the jugular. After affirming dutifully that "Dispensationalism is a fundamentally correct system of understanding God's program through the ages" (p. 25), *he then rejects on the same page the number-one thesis of dispensationalism, the distinction between ages of law and grace.*

> The age of law/age of grace distinction in particular has wreaked havoc on dispensationalist theology and contributed to confusion about the doctrine of salvation. Of course, there is an important distinction to be made between law and grace. But it is wrong to conclude, as Chafer apparently did, that law and grace are mutually exclusive in the program of God for any age.

Next, he goes after the traditional dispensationalist dichotomy between the Sermon on the Mount ("law for Israel and the Jewish-Christian Millennium only") and the Church Age. He cites Clarence Larkin's 1918 standard, *Dispensational Truth*, in which Larkin affirmed that the teachings of Jesus delivered in His Sermon on the Mount "have no application to the Christian, but only to those who are under the Law, and therefore must apply to another Dispensation than this" (p. 26). To which MacArthur replies:

> But that is a dangerous and untenable presupposition. Jesus did not come to proclaim a message that would be invalid until the Tribulation or the Millennium. He came to seek and to save the lost (Luke 19:10). He came to call sinners to repentance (Matthew 9:13). He came so the world through Him might be saved (John 3:17). He proclaimed the saving gospel, not merely a manifesto for some future age (p. 27).

Ideas Have Consequences

MacArthur tells us frankly what traditional dispensational theology's rampant antinomianism has produced: churches filled with immorality.

> One of the most malignant by-products of the debacle in contemporary evangelism is a gospel that fails to confront individuals with the reality of their sin. Even the most conservative churches are teeming with people who, claiming to be born again, live like pagans. Contemporary Christians have been conditioned never to question anyone's salvation. If a person declares he has trusted Christ as Savior, no one challenges his testimony, regardless of how inconsistent his life-style may be with God's Word (p. 59).

Who teaches such doctrines of "once saved, always saved, no matter what"? Col. Bob Thieme does. Yes, the man who had the world's largest tape ministry in the early 1960's. MacArthur cites Thieme's book, *Apes and Peacocks in Pursuit of Happiness* (1973): "It is possible, even probable, that when a believer out of fellowship falls for certain types of philosophy, if he is a logical thinker, will become an 'unbelieving believer.' Yet believers who become agnostics are still saved; they are still born again. You can even become an atheist; but once you accept Christ as savior, you cannot lose your salvation, even though you deny God" (Thieme, p. 23; MacArthur, pp. 97-98). So much for I John 2:19: "They went out from us, but they were not of us; for if they had been of us, they would no doubt have continued with us: but they went out, that they might be made manifest that they were not all of us."

Imputation and Confession

MacArthur did his best to refute Lane Hodges and others who proclaim that people are saved even though they refuse to proclaim Jesus as Lord. Proclaiming Jesus as savior is sufficient to get them into heaven. MacArthur denies this. He says that people must accept Jesus as Lord or else their sins will destroy the validity of their verbal confession.

Neither side in this debate understands the biblical doctrine of imputation. God imputes Christ's perfection to each person at the time of his or her conversion. That is, God declares judicially that the person is not guilty in His court because of the completed work of Jesus Christ in His substitutionary death. What MacArthur and his opponents do not discuss is the content of this judicial imputation. It is total. That is, the total perfection of Christ's ministry becomes the inheritance of the redeemed believer. *This means that Christ's public confession of His own work is imputed to the believer.* Christ is a legal representative, just as Adam was. His perfect confession becomes each believer's confession before God. It does not matter that the believer confesses imperfectly in history. He may or may not ever recognize that Jesus is His sovereign Lord, but Lordship salvation is inescapable judicially. *Jesus Christ makes the sinner's confession for him.* This is a neglected aspect of the biblical doctrine of representation, commonly called the substitutionary atonement.

The definitive sanctification – Christ's moral perfection – which the believer received through imputation at the time of his conversion cannot stay still. History is inescapable. We move from spiritual infancy to spiritual maturity. We work out the salvation that God extends to us. Thus, definitive sanctification leads to progressive sanctification in history. Progressive sanctification culminates in final sanctification on the day of final judgment. So, as Christians mature, their confessions are supposed to become more precise, and their behavior is more and more to reflect these ever-improving personal confessions. Thus, Hodges is correct: men do not need to confess Jesus as Lord in order to be saved. Thus, MacArthur is correct: if there is no evidence of progressive sanctification in the confessing church member's life, he is not saved, i.e., he was not the recipient of definitive sanctification. "Once saved, always saved" is true; but this does not mean that "once confessed, always saved" is true. The perseverance of the saints is a reality; the evidence that some men are not saints is that they refuse to maintain either their confession or the lifestyle which the Bible mandates for those who confess Christ as savior.

> Know ye not that the unrighteous shall not inherit the kingdom of God? Be not deceived: neither fornicators, nor idolaters, nor adulterers, nor effeminate, nor abusers of themselves with mankind, Nor thieves, nor covetous, nor drunkards, nor revilers, nor extortioners, shall inherit the kingdom of God (I Cor. 6:9-10).

Conclusion

The dispensationalists now face a major problem: one of their own has broken publicly with the traditional dispensationalism's antinomianism. Christians bought something in the range of 100,000 copies of his book – a huge number. Although he has not shown how, exactly, his view of law can be integrated into dispensationalism, he has nevertheless unleashed the power of God's law within dispensational circles. Once again, we see that the dispensational system is unraveling, and it is dispensational authors who are doing this work of deconstruction. They are revising the system to death. This is producing another layer of paralysis.

To escape the ethical paralysis of dispensationalism, MacArthur adopted a view of law and salvation which Calvinists J. I. Packer and James Boice could enthusiastically endorse. Once again, in order to become relevant, a dispensationalist has had to look for theological support from outside dispensationalism's camp. This is the fate of any movement that refuses to address publicly the ethical issues of the day.

11

THEOLOGICAL SCHIZOPHRENIA

[I wrote this in 1981 in order to warn my subscribers of a major shift in opinion among fundamentalists. It is worth reprinting as a primary source document of the times.]

Last summer, I had the opportunity of speaking at the National Affairs Briefing Conference, sponsored by the Religious Roundtable, and held in Dallas. It was a truly remarkable event. Over 15,000 people attended the final evening meeting, which gave them an opportunity to hear James Robison, the Fort Worth evangelist (and, in my view, the most effective large audience preacher in the English-speaking world), and R. W. Reagan, a political candidate. (Yes, I know. His name is Ronald Wilson Reagan. Each name contains six letters. The three names make 666. And we all know what 666 means! Or do we?)

The conference brought many of the nation's leading Protestant evangelists to the podium, along with senior retired Protestant military men and Christian political leaders, to speak to thousands of (mostly) Protestant laymen and ministers. The message was straightforward: it is the Christian's responsibility to vote, to vote in terms of biblical principle, and to get other Christians to vote. There can be no legal system that is not at bottom a system of morality, the speakers repeated again and again, Furthermore, every system of morality is at bottom a religion. It says "no" to some actions, while allowing others. It has a concept of right and wrong. Therefore, everyone concluded, it is proper for Christians to get active in politics. It is our legal right and our moral, meaning religious, duty.

You would think that this was conventional enough, but it is not conventional at all in the Christian world of the twentieth century. So thoroughly secularized has Christian thinking become, that the majority of Christians in the United States still appear to believe that there is neutrality in the universe, a kind of cultural and social "no man's land" between God and Satan, and that the various law structures of this neutral world of discourse are all acceptable to God. All except one, of course: Old Testament law. That is unthinkable, says the modern Christian. God will accept any legal framework except Old Testament law. Apparently He got sick of it 2,000 years ago.

So, when the crowd heard what the preachers and electronic media leaders were saying, they must have booed, or groaned, or walked out, right? After all, here were these men, abandoning the political and intellectual premises of three generations of Protestant pietism, right before the eyes of the faithful. So, what did they do? They clapped. They shouted "Amen!" They stood up and cheered.

These men are master orators. They can move a crowd of faithful laymen. They can even move a crowd of preachers. Was it simply technique that drew the responses of the faithful? Did the listeners just not understand what was being said? The magnitude of the response, after three days of speeches, indicates that the listeners liked what they were hearing. The crowds kept getting larger. The cheering kept getting louder. The attendees kept loading their arms with activist materials. What was going on?

[1993 note: a paradigm shift was in progress. It is still going on. Whenever it extends into dispensational circles, Rapture fever begins to subside.]

Victory

They were, for the first time in their lives, smelling political blood. For people who have smelled nothing except political droppings all their lives, it was an exhilarating scent. Maybe some of them thought they smelled something sweet back in 1976, but now they were smelling blood, not the victory of a safe, "born again" candidate like Jimmy Carter once convinced Christians that he was. They were smelling a "throw the SOB's out" victory, and they loved it. Only Reagan showed up. Carter and Anderson decided the fundamentalists wouldn't be too receptive to them. How correct they were.

But it was not simple politics that motivated the listeners. It was everything. Here were the nation's fundamentalist religious leaders, with the conspicuous exception of the fading Billy Graham, telling the crowd that the election of 1980 was only the beginning, that the principles of the Bible can become the law of the land, that the secular humanists who have dominated American political life for a hundred years can be tossed out and replaced with God-fearing men. Every area of life is open to Christian victory: education, family, economics, politics, law enforcement, and so forth. Speaker after speaker announced this goal to the audience. The audience went wild.

Here was a startling sight to see: thousands of Christians, including pastors, who had believed all their lives in the imminent return of Christ, the rise of Satan's forces, and the inevitable failure of the church to convert the world, now standing up to cheer other pastors, who also have believed this doctrine of earthly defeat all their lives, but who were proclaiming victory, in time and on earth. Never have I personally witnessed such enthusiastic schizophrenia in my life. Thousands of people were cheering for all they were worth – cheering away the theological pessimism of a lifetime.

Did they understand what they were doing? How can anyone be sure? But this much was clear: the term "rapture" was not prominent at the National Affairs Briefing Conference of

1980. Almost nobody was talking about the imminent return of Christ. The one glaring exception was Bailey Smith, President of the Southern Baptist Convention, who later told reporters that he really was not favorable to the political thrust of the meeting, and that he came to speak only because some of his friends in the evangelical movement asked him. (It was Smith, by the way, who made the oft-quoted statement that "God does not hear the prayer of a Jew." Ironically, the Moral Majority got tarred with that statement by the secular press, when the man who made it had publicly dissociated himself from the Moral Majority. He has since disavowed the statement, but he certainly said it with enthusiasm at the time. I was seated on the podium behind him when he said it. It is not the kind of statement that a wise man makes without a lot of theological qualification and explanation.)

In checking with someone who had attended a similar conference in California a few weeks previously, I was told that the same neglect of the Rapture doctrine had been noticeable. All of a sudden, the word has dropped out of the vocabulary of politically oriented fundamentalist leaders. Perhaps they still use it in their pulpits back home, but on the activist circuit, you seldom hear the term. More people are talking about the sovereignty of God than about the Rapture. This is extremely significant.

How can you motivate people to get out and work for a political cause if you also tell them that they cannot be successful in their efforts? How can you expect to win if you don't expect to win? How can you get men elected if you tell the voters that their votes cannot possibly reverse society's downward drift into Satan's kingdom? What successful political movement was ever based on expectations of inevitable external defeat?

The Moral Majority is feeling its political strength. These people smell the blood of the political opposition. Who is going to stand up and tell these people the following? "Ladies and

Gentlemen, all this talk about overcoming the political, moral, economic, and social evils of our nation is sheer nonsense. The Bible tells us that everything will get steadily worse, until Christ comes to rapture His church out of this miserable world. Nothing we can do will turn this world around, all your enthusiasm is wasted. All your efforts are in vain. All the money and time you devote to this earthly cause will go down the drain. You can't use biblical principles – a code term for Old Testament law – to reconstruct society. Biblical law is not for the church age. Victory is not for the church age. However, get out there and work like crazy. It's your moral duty." Not a very inspiring speech, is it? Not the stuff of political victories, you say. How correct you are!

Ever try to get your listeners to send you money to battle the forces of social evil by using some variation of this sermon? The Moral Majority fundamentalists have smelled the opposition's blood since 1978, and the savory odor has overwhelmed their official theology. So they have stopped talking about the Rapture.

But this schizophrenia cannot go on forever. In off-years, in between elections, the enthusiasm may wane. Or the "Christian" political leaders may appoint the same tired faces to the positions of high authority. (I use the word "may" facetiously; the Pied Pipers of politics appoint nobody except secular humanists. Always. It will take a real social and political upheaval to reverse this law of political life. That upheaval is coming.) In any case, the folks in the pews will be tempted to stop sending money to anyone who raises false hopes before them. So the Moral Majority fundamentalist preachers are in a jam. If they preach victory, the old-line pessimists will stop sending in checks. And if they start preaching the old-line dispensational, premillennial, earthly defeatism, their recently motivated audiences may abandon them in order to follow more optimistic, more success-oriented pastors.

What's a fellow to do? Answer: give different speeches to different groups. For a while, this tactic may work. But for how long?

An Inescapable Division[1]

Eventually, the logic of a man's theology begins to affect his actions and his long-term commitments. We will see some important shifts in theology in the 1980's. We will find out whether fundamentalists are committed to premillennial dispensationalism – pretribulation, midtribulation, or post-tribulation – or whether they are committed to the idea of Christian reconstruction. They will begin to divide into separate camps. Some will cling to the traditional Scofieldism. They will enter the political arenas only when they are able to suppress or ignore the implications of their faith. Men are unlikely to remain in the front lines of the political battle when they themselves believe that the long-term earthly effects of their sacrifice will come to nothing except visible failure. Others will scrap their dispensational eschatology completely and turn to a perspective that offers them hope, in time and on earth. They will be driven by the implications of their religious commitment to the struggles of our day to abandon their traditional premillennialism. Pessimistic pietism and optimistic reconstructionism don't mix.

This is not to say that consistent premillennialists cannot ever become committed to a long-term political fight. It is to say that *most* premillennialists have not in the past, and are unlikely to do so in the future. If they do, leadership will come from other sources, theologically speaking.

Three basic ideas are crucial for the success of any religious, social, intellectual, and political movement. First, the doctrine of predestination. Second, the doctrine of law. Third, the doctrine of inevitable victory. The fusion of these three ideas has led to the victories of Marxism since 1848. The Communists

---

1. I changed this subhead in 1993. Originally: Theological Schizophrenia.

believe that historical forces are on their side, that Marxism-Leninism provides them with access to the laws of historical change, and that their movement must succeed. Islam has a similar faith. In the early modern Christian West, Calvinists and Puritans had such faith. Social or religious philosophies which lack any one of these elements are seldom able to compete with a system that possesses all three. To a great extent, the cultural successes of modern secular science have been based on a fusion of these three elements: scientific (material) determinism, the scientists' knowledge of natural laws, and the inevitable progress of scientific technique. As faith in all three has waned, the religious lure of science has also faded, especially since about 1965, when the counter-culture began to challenge all three assumptions.

Modern fundamentalism has long since abandoned all three. The fundamentalists are divided on the question of predestination, but the majority are committed to Arminian views of God, man, and law. They believe in man's limited autonomy, or "free will." Furthermore, they have rejected biblical law as a guideline for social order. They argue that there is no explicitly Christian law-order in the era of the church, from Pentecost to the future Rapture into heaven of the saints. Finally, they are committed to eschatological pessimism concerning the efforts of the church, in time and on earth. Without a doctrine of the comprehensive sovereignty of God, without a doctrine of a unique biblical law structure that can reconstruct the institutions of society, and without a doctrine of eschatological victory, in time and on earth, the fundamentalists have been unable to exercise effective leadership.

The prospects for effective political action have begun to shake the operational faith of modern fundamentalists – not their official faith, but their operational world-and-life view. This shift of faith will steadily pressure them to rethink their traditional theological beliefs. The leaders of the Moral Majority will come under increasing pressure, both internal and external, to come to grips with the conflicts between their official theology and their operational theology.

It is doubtful that many of the leaders will announce an overnight conversion to the long-dreaded Calvinist faith. It is doubtful that they will spell out the nature of the recently rethought world-and-life view. But younger men will begin to become more consistent with their own theological presuppositions, and those who adopt the three crucial perspectives – predestination, biblical law, and eschatological optimism – will begin to dominate the Moral Majority movement. It will take time, and older, less consistent leaders will probably have to die off first, but the change in perspective is predictable. The taste of victory will be too hard to forget.

* * * * * * * * * * *

This newsletter appeared under the title, "The Eschatological Crisis of the Moral Majority," published in *Christian Reconstruction* (Jan./Feb. 1981).

Within a year after the Conference, James Robison had left the Baptist world and had adopted a radically pietistic form of charismatic theology. He publicly called for the abandonment of all confrontational rhetoric among Christians and began talking about the need for Church unity – with no mention of theology.

In 1989, Jerry Falwell shut down the Moral Majority, having absorbed about $60 million. Falwell, with his ministries $90 million in debt, returned to the Rapture theme in late 1992. (See Chapter 13.)

By 1992, Pat Robertson's Christian Coalition had become a growing force in local politics in the United States, gaining the ire of humanists who cried out against the "stealth politics" of Christian candidates. Activist Robertson, like activist Beverly LaHaye, does not dwell on the Rapture. He occasionally mentions it, but only occasionally (see Conclusion).

12

WHEN "BABYLON" FELL, SO DID DISPENSATIONALISM

[I sent this to my subscribers as a cover letter in September, 1991. I have not changed my opinions.]

Did you hear it? *Thud.* Babylon the Great is fallen! No, I don't mean the Soviet Union. I mean Jerusalem in 70 A.D.[1] The fall of the Communist Party in Russia and the break-up of the Soviet Union makes it clear that the USSR was *never* prophetic Babylon. (Dispensationalism: "Red alert! The Reds are gone. Russia's invasion of national Israel has been indefinitely postponed. *Damage control!*")

When KGB Group A refused to follow orders on Monday morning, August 19, 1991 – orders to arrest Boris Yeltsin and shoot him if he tried to escape – the end of Soviet Communism was only 63 hours away. So was the end of pop-dispensationalism's "ticking clock." Rapture postponed! *Popular dispensationalism is now in its terminal generation.*

As midnight approached on August 21, the Moscow crowd pulled down the statue of Felix Dzerzhinsky, the founder of the

---

1. See David Chilton, *The Days of Vengeance: An Exposition of the Book of Revelation*, Dominion Press, 1987, $24.95. P.O. Box 7999, Tyler, Texas 75711

Communist secret police. But it was not just the legacy of Karl Marx that was flattened beneath the image; it was also the legacy of Hal Lindsey. *Thud!* The difference is, Rev. Lindsey is still alive and well on planet earth.

Rev. Lindsey's book royalties are about to drop. *Rapture fever has subsided.* (Side note: his humanistic publisher, Bantam Books, is located at **666** Fifth Avenue, New York City. Odd.) Maybe he bought enough California real estate to sustain him in his "golden years," for he is not going to be raptured out of the "golden state." That "imminent" event has been put on indefinite hold. (Actually, it always was on indefinite hold [Acts 1:7].)

Failed Prophecies

What's a failed prophet to do? What would *you* do? Since 1855, dispensationalism's supposed experts in "fulfilled prophecy in our day" have told millions of their followers (i.e., victims) that the Rapture was just around the corner because Russia ("Magog") will soon invade Israel. Then came the establishment of the nation of Israel on May 14, 1948. The generation of the fig tree had begun! Only 40 more years until the Millennium! Only 33 more years until the absolutely Secret Rapture! 1981 is coming! Get ready! Get Set! . . .

No go; 1981 came and went. Nothing happened. The next major date was May 14, 1988, the 40th anniversary of the establishment of the State of Israel – the "generation of the fig tree," 1948-1988. May 14 came and went. Nothing happened. No Rapture. Again.

"No, no," said Edgar C. Whisenant in July, 1988, "it's going to be this September." September came and went. Nothing happened. "No, no," said Mr. Whisenant, "I forgot about the extra year in zero A.D. It's going to be in September, 1989." September, 1989, came and went. Nothing happened. In November, the Berlin Wall came down. A big problem was brewing. Where was national Israel's invader? *No invasion – no Rapture!*

But then came hope! Saddam Hussein invaded Kuwait on August 2, 1990. "Wait, wait!" the cries came from The Church of Paperback Sensationalism. (I call this theology dispen*sensationalism*.) "It really *will* be Babylon. It won't be Russia after all. We've been wrong since 1855.[2] No problem, though. We just need to shift a few gears. It's Iraq. Baghdad. The restoration of Babylon is almost here. It's coming soon!" Dallas Seminary professor Charles Dyer's book was published in January, 1991, *The Rise of Babylon: Sign of the End Time*. Babylon was on the map again! So was Dallas Seminary. Hot stuff!

Even before Dr. Dyer got into the race for royalties, retired Dallas Seminary president John Walvoord spotted a fabulous new market for his 1974 Armageddon prophecy book that had gone out of print. Once again, the gullible victims streamed into the book stores to get the inside dope. The cash registers hummed. Royalties flowed. One million copies of this resurrected potboiler had been sold by February (*Time*, Feb. 11, 1991).

But then a funny thing happened on the night of January 16, 1991. Our Air Force began the smashing of "Babylon." Over the next month, bombs smashed Iraq flat. Flatter than the collected works of Hal Lindsey. *Thud.* "It's revised edition time!"

Hoaxed Again!

The realization began to dawn on the hapless troops in the pews: *hoaxed again*. Again! *Nuts!* People don't like to be hoaxed. Christians don't like to be hoaxed in the name of Jesus. Fundamentalists love to be thrilled. They love sensationalism. But at some point, their resentment about being hoaxed overcomes their love of endlessly false prophecies.

---

2. John Cumming, *The End: Or, The Proximate Signs of the Close of This Dispensation* (1855), Lecture 7: "The Russian and Northern Confederacy."

When "Babylon" Fell, So Did Dispensationalism 191

Then came the week of August 19. *Thud.* Down went Dzerzhinsky's statue. Down went the dreams of the Communist Party's leaders. Boris Pugo shot his wife and killed himself. Marshal Akhromeyev committed suicide. Soviet Communism died. It's *over.*

So is Hal Lindsey's reputation as a prophet. So is John Walvoord's. Walvoord, at 80, lived to see it. I regard this as evidence that God has a marvelous sense of humor.

I wonder how it feels. To be a Communist who lives long enough to have seen this. To be a best-selling paperback book author whose specialty is false prophecies about Russia's coming invasion of Israel. To see the work of your life get flushed down the commode of history. ("This can't be happening. It just can't!") It must be painful. I hope so.

The day after Dzerzhinsky's statue crashed to the ground in what was then called Dzerzhinsky Square, but what will soon be called something else, Paul Crouch announced to his Trinity Broadcasting Network (TBN) viewers: "We need to get Hal Lindsey on the show to explain the meaning of what has happened." Indeed you do, Paul. Let him try to reconcile these events for your emotionally victimized followers. Let him play the "identify Babylon" game one more time. *Let's see Hal Lindsey dance the "Whisenant two-step."* It greatly resembles "Montezuma's two-step." In both dances, the pressure is intense. There will be dozens of Whisenant two-steppers in 1992, the year of the revised editions.

Rapture Postponed

It's all over. The curtain has come down. The Rapture has been postponed. Again. A dispensationalist can still argue that the inevitable invasion of Israel by Russia may take place in a hundred years or a thousand, but the troops in the pews have been told for 135 years that this event is imminent. The Rapture was due *at any moment* because Russia was going to invade the State of Israel in *any moment plus seven years.* "The clock of prophecy is ticking again!" shouted all those best-selling authors who never bothered to tell their hapless followers that according to original dispensational theology, the clock of prophecy will not start ticking until *after* the Rapture. It's "any-moment Rapture" vs. "ticking clock today."

Even John Walvoord couldn't resist those fabulous book royalties (1.6 million copies, as of August). He had to get back into the pop-dispensationalist parade. He announced that the clock of prophecy was again ticking (*USA Today*, Jan. 19, 1991). He abandoned the doctrine of the any-moment Rapture, which he had long taught. He thereby baptized Hal Lindsey's "just around the corner" eschatology. And then . . . *thud.* Goodbye reputation.

Smashed. *Smashed.* Smashed by Norman Schwarzkopf in January and by Boris Yeltsin in August. Flattened. Dead. "Rapture postponed indefinitely." What now?

Changes at Dallas Seminary

In 1991, Dallas Theological Seminary introduced a revised curriculum. Perfect timing, guys! I congratulate you. The new curriculum abandoned the original one that had emphasized dispensational eschatology, Greek, and Hebrew. It intensified the post-1978 curriculum shift, which had substituted an emphasis on psychology for eschatology. Now the seminary has introduced a so-called "tracking" system. Students can specialize from the beginning of their academic careers in this or that area of practical theology. They can pursue *Christian social relevance*, but apart from biblical law.

Dallas theologians need to explain exactly how Scofieldism can be the foundation of all this. They need to introduce each class with a week or two of verse-by-verse lectures on "Dispensationalism and this application." If they refuse to do this, class by class – and my "prophecy" is clear: they *will* refuse – then they have traded dispensational theology for practical theology. Dispensational theology was never practical; it rejects culture

When "Babylon" Fell, So Did Dispensationalism 193

and reform. It was to avoid questions of Christian social responsibility that dispensationalism was adopted by the fundamentalist world. *Any attempt to make Christianity socially relevant before the era of the Millennium is inescapably the implicit abandonment of dispensational theology.*

Rev. Tommy Ice (of "House & Ice" fame) may be willing to admit in private what this shift means, but dispensationalism's leaders won't discuss it in public. Tommy knows my prediction: if dispensational Christians become *psychological* or *operational* social activists, pretty soon they will quietly abandon their official dispensationalism. This is what is now happening at Dallas Theological Seminary. *We will see Dallas Theological Seminary become something very different*, just as Talbot Seminary did four years ago. Dallas' Board won't tell donors about this implication, of course. They want that continuing stream of income. *But Dallas Seminary has left operational dispensationalism behind*, and there is nothing that Bob Lightner can do about it in his freshman theology course. *Thud.*

Where will traditional dispensationalists – the "Scofield notes" people – now send their young men to be trained for the ministry? It's one thing to face this academic certification problem at the beginning of a movement (as Christian Reconstructionism does), but it's quite another to face it 160 years after a movement's founding. *The end is near.* It's just a matter of time. Dispensationalism's epitaph: "Died of a Self-Inflicted Wound: *Sensationalism*."

Suggested Revisions

Now, let it never be said that Gary North is "all criticism and no solutions." Here's a possible strategy to resurrect the theological corpse. Dispensensational theologians need only to identify a new enemy of national Israel. They need to identify a superpower nation that will soon invade the State of Israel. They need to identify a new "Beast, 666." How about . . .

George Bush? After all, on September 11, 1990, he told Congress:

> A new partnership of nations has begun. We stand today at a unique and extraordinary moment. The crisis in the Persian Gulf, as grave as it is, also offers a rare opportunity to move toward an historic period of cooperation. Out of these troubled times, our fifth objective – a new world order – can emerge: a new era, freer from the threat of terror, stronger in the pursuit of justice, and more secure in the quest for peace. An era in which the nations of the world, east and west, north and south, can prosper and live in harmony.

Got that, Constance? Hear that, Dave? *A New World Order*. A new era of prosperity. You know what to do now! I put it in your hands. (I'd put it in Jerry Falwell's hands, but he was the first fundamentalist leader to promote George Bush's political legitimacy, way back in 1984. To reciprocate, Mr. Bush spoke at the graduation exercises at Liberty University in 1990. It is not easy to get an incumbent President to speak at a non-Ivy League college's graduation. You have to pay more than a speaker's fee. Far more.)

Dispensationalists need to hear the sermons on the latest, greatest prophecy. "God's Antichrist nation is the good old U.S. of A. I can prove this from the Bible. I have this chart. Turn in your *Revised Scofield Reference Bible* to page. . . ."

But if we don't hear such sermons soon, then popular dispensationalism is as dead as Marxism-Leninism inside Russia. That is to say, *thud*.

13

THE STRANGE DISAPPEARANCE OF DISPENSATIONAL INSTITUTIONS

But sanctify the Lord God in your hearts: and be ready always to give an answer to every man that asketh you a reason of the hope that is in you with meekness and fear (I Pet. 3:15)

Where can traditional dispensationalists find answers? In 1985, there were three major theological seminaries that taught dispensational theology: Dallas, Grace, and Talbot. In the mid-to-late 1980's, Talbot very quietly replaced both its faculty and its theology. Not wishing to alienate its dispensational donors, it did not do this with fanfare, but it was done. Its new theology has been left undefined. The school is in transition.

On December 10, 1992, John J. Davis, the president of Grace Theological Seminary, sent out a form letter. It began, "Dear Friend of Grace Seminary," in good form letter fashion. President Davis spoke of "recent changes taking place here at the seminary." He mentioned the fact that "a rumor is usually half-way around the world before truth has his shoes on!"

This is true. In this case, however, "the truth, the whole truth, and nothing but the truth" is still being covered up, in good academic administrator fashion. He wrote:

Significant change rarely comes without significant pain and challenge. None of the seven full-time faculty contracts will be renewed for next year. [Italics in original]

You may have wondered why President Davis and the Board fired Professor John C. Whitcomb in 1990, when Whitcomb had only three months to go until retirement. Whitcomb was the only Grace Seminary faculty member with a reputation outside the campus, as the co-author of *The Genesis Flood*. Some people could not understand why he had been fired, and President Davis' official explanation was, to put it charitably, non-informative. Well, now we know. "Significant change" was in the works, and Dr. Whitcomb had been warning against it. He wound up analogous to John the Baptist: decapitated.

My friends, when the entire full-time faculty of an institution is fired in one shot, we are talking about something greater than rearranging the academic furniture.

Then President Davis went on: "*We will be discontinuing the Th.M. and Th.D. programs. . . .*" That is to say, Grace Theological Seminary is leaving the field of advanced academic studies. It will no longer grant an advanced *academic* theological degree. The other "practical" degrees will remain – degrees for men who want preaching jobs: Master of Divinity, Doctor of Ministry, etc. Also, *Grace Theological Journal* is being discontinued. In short, *Grace Theological Seminary has just committed suicide at the professional academic level.* The question is: Why?

In part, because Grace is facing universal pressures in theological education today. Small, struggling movements can no longer afford the luxury of full-time faculties that teach a handful of academic specialists. That is to say, they can no longer afford to pay their faculty members to reproduce themselves. They can no longer afford traditional academic certification. *Dispensationalism is becoming a small, struggling movement.* Paralysis has produced attrition. Attrition is steadily shrinking the dispensational movement. Yet no one inside admits this in public.

The Strange Disappearance of Dispensational Institutions 197

But this is only part of the story. President Davis then dropped this theological bombshell on page three of his form letter:

12. What are the mission and values of Grace Seminary?
Its mission is to: "develop Christian ministry leaders who can influence culture with an integrated biblical world and life view."

He re-stated this mission in his newsletter, *President to Pastor* (1st quarter 1993, p. 2). Question: When was the last time you heard a leader of a dispensational seminary speak of the need to influence culture? When was the last time you heard him call for "an integrated biblical world and life view"? I'll tell you: *the next time will be the first time.*

Where is Grace Seminary heading? I don't know. But this I do know: when a seminary president starts talking about "biblical world and life view," he is not talking about traditional dispensationalism. *He has moved to a new theological position, and he is planning to take the school with him.* This is what Talbot did in the late 1980's.

Of course, I could be wrong. President Davis is retaining the part-time faculty and hiring new full-time members. Perhaps members of this new faculty, including President Davis, have quietly developed a brand-new synthesis of Scofield's theology. Maybe they are about to introduce the long-awaited "new dispensationalism," whose theology leads to Christian cultural relevance and activism. This synthesis has never been published, of course. The present faculty's members have not mentioned it. But perhaps the long-awaited dispensational paradigm shift will be completed and presented in public in broad outline: culturally relevant dispensationalism. If so, its details will not be published in the *Grace Theological Journal*, since President Davis and his supporters on the Board have discontinued the journal. (Perhaps it will be resurrected during the millennium.) President Davis announced to the seminary's pastor-donors:

The restructuring we have announced to begin in the fall of this year [1993] involves both philosophy and method and reaffirms the primary focus of Grace Theological Seminary on preparation of ministry leaders.[1]

But what of the previously crucial task of defending dispensational theology? What of Grace's intellectual leadership within American dispensational churches? Silence. Dead silence.

I conclude that President Davis, like an earlier President Davis, is leading a secession movement within the Grace Brethren Church and American dispensationalism. *Grace Seminary has just seceded from historic dispensationalism.* Will he succeed? Probably. The younger donors are as embarrassed by traditional dispensationalism as the younger theologians are. This secession is visible at the top, but bureaucrats always count the costs of change well in advance. They think they know what the next generation will accept, and they have concluded that the seminary's donors will follow them into a theologically vague future.

Dallas Seminary is next. There is not one man remaining on that faculty who can or will answer Ken Gentry's book, *He Shall Have Dominion: A Postmillennial Eschatology* (Institute for Christian Economics, 1992). *We are hearing the silence of the lambs.* They have left the field of intellectual battle, to the extent that they were ever on it. Their continuing silence regarding O. T. Allis' refutation of dispensationalism, *Prophecy and the Church* (1945), indicates that they have never tried to respond intellectually to the challenges offered by professional theologians and scholars. Charles Ryrie's brief attempt to respond in *Dispensationalism Today* came twenty years too late, and was an ill-fated effort anyway. Besides, he disappeared from the Dallas faculty in the early 1980's under clouded circumstances. *Dallas Seminary's faculty members have become theological deaf-mutes.*

---

1. *President to Pastor* (1st quarter 1993), p. 1.

The Strange Disappearance of Dispensational Institutions 199

I predict that Jesus will not return by the year 2000, but it is highly likely that by that year Dallas Seminary will also have experienced a Talbot-like, Grace-like restructuring. Then where will all those faithful dispensational laymen recruit their pastors? If the pastors don't share the theology of the people in the pews, it's only a matter of time before the children of the people in the pews abandon Scofield and his revisors.

O Debt, *Here* Is Thy Sting!

Meanwhile, according to an Associated Press story (December 14), Jerry Falwell's Liberty University is $73 million in debt. I know from having spoken to one faculty member (who will leave soon) that the enrollment figures are no longer issued even to faculty members. They all can see what is coming: pink slips. Rev. Falwell has already told those faithful Christian people who bought Liberty University's bonds: *no more interest payments*. He has promised that someday the principal will be repaid. He has not said when.

The campus of Liberty University was valued at $55 million in 1990. That was when Rev. Falwell tried to sell government-subsidized development bonds to refinance the existing debt. The courts said no deal: separation of church and state. Today, Liberty University is valued at $5.2 million, the Associated Press report said. Why the decline? Because the estimated value of a school is based on the estimated value of its net income. The bricks and mortar of a college are white elephants: almost worthless except as a college. If a college declines in enrollment, the expected net income disappears. Hence, the 90% drop in the estimated value of the Liberty University campus in just two years.

Let's see: a $73 million debt with assets of $5.2 million. You know what that says to me? Payday isn't coming. Judgment day is. No, not the Rapture: the *rupture*. As in ban k*rupt*.

Meanwhile, his Old Time Gospel Hour is $16 million in debt. From 1979 to 1989, said the AP story, the Moral Majority absorbed a fantastic $69 million in donations from six million people. The Moral Majority was shut down in 1989, the year of George Bush's inauguration. (Rev. Falwell had publicly supported the idea of a Bush Presidency since 1984.) The AP story commented:

> In the blink of an eye, Mr. Falwell went from a central figure in the nation's stage to a bit player, burdened by enormous problems.

How would you feel at age 59 to have your life's visible legacy $90 million in debt, having defaulted on the interest payments, and with no visible means of your ministries' avoiding bankruptcy before you die? What kind of Christian testimony would you imagine that this presents? He has only two hopes: an early death or the Rapture.

So, what do we find? *He has been struck down once again with Rapture fever.* In his broadcast of December 27, he said that the Rapture will probably take place by the year 1999. But then he added that he also expects to live as long as W. A. Criswell, the legendary 83-year-old pastor of First Baptist Church of Dallas. Mixed chronological signals!

Meanwhile, First Baptist Church of Dallas, the nation's largest Southern Baptist church (28,000 on the rolls), is now $8 million in debt. It has had to cut back its television ministry. The story has recently been on the front page of the *Dallas Morning News*. It has once again lost a promising assistant pastor because Rev. Criswell has once again refused to give up preaching at the 11 a.m. service. The church keeps hiring the best replacement pastors it can find, promising them that they will soon lead the church. Fat chance. Then they quit. And the debt builds up.

In ministry after ministry, the story is the same. Debt. Enormous debt. *Debt for Jesus' sake.* From red letter edition Bibles (no creed but Christ, no law but love) to red ink: the story is repeated. Debt is the lure. Debt is the killer. "I have faith that God will bless this ministry later if I make a leap of faith now – with other people's money."

Jerry Falwell is a decent man. He just forgot the rule: "Owe no man any thing but to love one another" (Romans 13:8a). He was under grace, not biblical law, he thought. *Scofield strikes again!*

In 1982, I wrote an essay, "The Intellectual Schizophrenia of the New Christian Right." It was published in *Christianity and Civilization*. There I predicted the break-up of the New Christian Right. I argued that its politically activist stance could not be defended by its dispensational theology. One by one, the leaders of that short-lived phenomenon have faded away. Those few who remain rarely talk about eschatology. (In Beverly LaHaye's case, her husband talks about it; she doesn't. Not with 400,000 on her activist mailing list!)

Conclusion

I will say it again: *Dispensationalism is dying*. The leaders who write the paperback prophecy books won't admit it, but it's true. One by one, institutions that long maintained the old position have revised, restructured, and retreated from the intellectual battlefield.

This doesn't prove that theonomy is winning. It means that our most consistently antinomian, anti-victory, anti-activism opponents are retiring, in every sense. Sensational paperback books plus a Canadian tabloid newspaper filled with prophecies that never come true cannot preserve the old theology. Hype is not a substitute for scholarship.

It is just a matter of time. We have plenty of it. Dispensationalism doesn't. As those old travelogues used to end: "And so it's time to say, 'Sayonara, Scofield!' "

CONCLUSION

> *. . . ye are dull of hearing. For when for the time ye ought to be teachers, ye have need that one teach you again which be the first principles of the oracles of God; and are become such as have need of milk, and not of strong meat. For every one that useth milk is unskilful in the word of righteousness: for he is a babe. But strong meat belongeth to them that are of full age, even those who by reason of use have their senses exercised to discern both good and evil (Heb. 5:11-14).*

It is my contention that Christians today are in the same spiritual condition as the readers of the Epistle to the Hebrews in the author's day. They have become theological milk-drinkers who are content with the ABC's of faith. They are unskilled in the word of righteousness. They are out of shape judicially.

There is a reason for this. They hate three-quarters of the Bible: the law and the prophets. Hating God's law with all their heart, they also hate the thought of victory, which has been promised by God to those cultures that obey God's revealed law (Deut. 28:1-14). Hating victory in history, they necessarily have come to regard themselves as principled losers in history.

"Who is on the Lord's Side?" So asks a popular Protestant evangelical hymn. The correct answer, as far as modern evangelicalism teaches in public, is this: *historical losers*. For over two centuries, Protestant evangelicals have seen themselves as members of a culturally impotent Church and a religiously neutral civil order. They have had far greater faith in the civil order –

supposedly based on universal principles of natural law – than the Church. They have trusted the moral authority of the humanist State far more than they have trusted the moral authority of the Church. And why not? The humanist State is a winner in history. The Church is a loser. So say the theologians. The result is easily predictable: a Church filled with people who are unskillful in the word of righteousness, God's revealed law.

No better statement of this ethical position can be found than Norman Geisler's 1992 affirmation. Dr. Geisler received his Ph.D. in philosophy from a Jesuit university. He defends neutral natural law. He has devoted a large portion of his academic career to a public rejection of biblical law. Geisler is a dispensationalist: formerly a professor at Dallas Theological Seminary and formerly a professor at Jerry Falwell's Liberty University. He writes: "The religious right is at least as dangerous as the secular left. Religious theonomy (divine law) as the basis for human dignity can be as frightening as secular anarchy."[1] He assures us that "Theonomy is an unworkable ethical basis for government in a religiously pluralistic society, whether it be Muslim or Christian in form."[2] He insists: "Sooner or later the question arises: whose religious book will be the basis for the civil laws? It is sheer religious bigotry to answer: 'Mine.' "[3] Conclusion: *it is not sheer religious bigotry for secular humanists to answer, "Ours."* Dr. Geisler believes in the legitimacy of secular humanism's claim that civil law can be religiously neutral and morally valid. Dr. Geisler is a consistent dispensationalist: *he prefers to live under the civil banner of religious pluralism rather than under the civil banner of Jesus Christ.* So do his colleagues.

---

1. Norman Geisler, "Human Life," *In Search of a National Morality: A Manifesto for Evangelicals and Catholics*, edited by William Bentley Ball (Grand Rapids, Michigan: Baker Book House, 1992), p. 114. Mr. Ball is a Roman Catholic lawyer who specializes in defending Christian schools. Baker Book House is a Protestant publishing firm with a Calvinist slant. It publishes mainly amillennial books.
2. *Idem.*
3. *Idem.*

A Covenant of Historical Despair

There are five reasons why modern Christians take this grim view of their condition: history's losers. These reasons imitate perversely the Bible's five-point covenant model.[4]

First, the strength of God obviously cannot be trusted in history, for God brings defeat for His Church in history. The Arminians have explained the guaranteed defeat of the gospel in history as the outcome of man's free will. The evil in most men's hearts will not be overcome, we are told. Covenant-breakers will generally remain covenant-breakers until the final judgment. The Calvinists offer another explanation: God predestined the gospel to cultural failure before the world began. So, Christians have seen God as either unwilling to do what it takes to win in history or else determined to lose in history.

Dealing with such a God is a fearful thing. It means that the Church of Jesus Christ is filled with people who are religiously committed to their own cultural impotence in history. Who would trust such people with authority or power? No rational person would. So, Christians do not trust the judgments of local church officers. When rulings go against them, they transfer membership to another local church. Because they cannot escape judgment this easily in civil affairs, Christians demand the separation of Christianity from the State. They much prefer to live under the civil jurisdiction of God's enemies rather than under other Christians. They agree with Norman Geisler.

Third, they do not trust the Bible-revealed law of a God who has chosen them to be crushed in history. Who can trust the law-order of a God who will not bring victory to His Church in terms of that law-order? Christians have been told by their leaders for almost two millennia that the Old Testament is a discarded first draft, a judicial mistake. God used to judge history in terms of His law (Lev. 26; Deut. 28), but no longer.

---

4. Ray R. Sutton, *That You May Prosper: Dominion By Covenant* (2nd ed.; Tyler, Texas: Institute for Christian Economics, 1992).

Conclusion

Fourth, because God's revealed law is annulled in the New Testament era, so are the sanctions attached to that law, especially civil sanctions. Because God supposedly refuses to bring sanctions in history in terms of His law, Christians believe that they should not seek to bring civil sanctions in terms of God's law. After all, if God rewards covenant-breakers with victory in history and curses covenant-keepers with defeat in history, why should God's chosen representatives seek to bring negative civil sanctions against covenant-breakers in history? If God refuses to honor the system of historical sanctions in Leviticus 26 and Deuteronomy 28 in the New Testament era, why should His people honor Exodus 21-23: the case laws?[5]

Fifth, Because God supposedly promises to disinherit His Church in history, why should Christians pay any attention to the historical long run? After all, Keynes was correct: in the long run we are all dead. In history's long run, the Church will be embarrassed. Why sacrifice oneself for a lifetime to study what God's law requires, since all plans to impose God's law in history are at best utopian and at worst tyrannical? This is why social ethics has been the idiosyncratic pastime of a handful of Christians who have been taught to impose humanism on the Bible's categories, abandoning the Bible whenever it contradicts the latest humanist intellectual fad. This has been true for about 1,800 years.[6]

The Lure of Pretribulational Dispensationalism

Few people can function psychologically under the threat of inevitable historical defeat. The genius of pretribulation dispensationalism is its appeal to psychologically defeated people, whose name is legion in the modern Church because they have

---

5. Gary North, *Tools of Dominion: The Case Laws of Exodus* (Tyler, Texas: Institute for Christian Economics, 1990).

6. Cornelius Van Til, *A Christian Theory of Knowledge* (Nutley, New Jersey: Presbyterian & Reformed, 1969).

believed what they have been told for the last two centuries. Except for postmillennialism, which is believed by very few Christians, the other systems of eschatological interpretation offer only historical despair. But the pretribulational system offers a glimmer of hope in the darkness of historical despair, namely, an escape from history: the Rapture.

"We're under grace, not law." So runs the theology of most Protestants. But pretribulational dispensationalists assert a radical judicial discontinuity with both the past and the future. Today's Christians, they argue, have escaped the heavy moral burdens of law-enforcement in history, unlike Israel prior to the cross and also during the millennial era to come. *Victory in history is correctly seen by dispensationalists as Christians' ability to enforce God's law, bringing sanctions in terms of it, including civil sanctions.* But this ability supposedly has nothing to do with the Church during the Church Age. Christians therefore need not concern themselves with legal matters because in this dispensation, unlike the one behind us and the final one ahead, God's law has nothing to do with Christ's gospel.

This is a two-fold deliverance: from total defeat in history and from the responsibility to study God's revealed law and develop its principles in practice. Of course, the price of this rejection of the Church's victory in history and this rejection of responsibility is the open affirmation of the Church's cultural irrelevance. This affirmation leads to a rejection of any work that might produce victory or extend Christians' cultural responsibilities. It is not just that dispensationalists reject the Bible as a legitimate guide to social ethics in our dispensation; they reject the very legitimacy of studying social ethics. Why bother with social ethics? If three-quarters of the Bible is not a valid guide to ethics, then to become masters of social ethics, Christians must also become humanists: either natural-law humanists or some far worse variety. The Christian should ask himself: Why work hard for a lifetime in order to become just one more ethical humanist? The answer is obvious.

The dispensationalists are more consistent in their rejection of the task of developing Christian social ethics than other Protestant evangelicals are, but the reality is this: all of them have rejected the *motivation* to become a social ethicist (postmillennialism) as well as the *judicial foundation* of biblical social ethics (theonomy). They hate God's law. They hate personal and corporate responsibility. Therefore, they hate the idea of Christianity's victory in history, for corporate ethical conformity to God's law inevitably produces victory (Deut. 28:1-14).

Joining the Losing Side

Over four decades ago, Whittaker Chambers gave his reasons for his departure from the Communist Party. His book, *Witness* (1952), is the classic among many book-long testimonies by former American Communists. I bought the book in 1959, after it had gone out of print, in a book store run by the Forest Home Christian Conference Center in California. No one had bought that lone copy in seven years. I suspect that it had been put on the shelf because the book store manager thought it was a book on handing out gospel tracts. I don't know. What I do know is that no one had bought it. Chambers gave this explanation of his defection from the Party:

> In 1937, I repudiated Marx's doctrines and Lenin's tactics. Experience and the record had convinced me that Communism is a form of totalitarianism, that its triumph means slavery to men wherever they fall under its sway and spiritual night to the human mind and soul. I resolved to break with the Communist Party at whatever risk to my life or to myself and my family. Yet, so strong is the hold which the insidious evil of Communism secures upon its disciples, that I could still say to someone at that time: 'I know that I am leaving the winning side for the losing side, but it is better to die on the losing side than to live under Communism.' (p. 541)

Chambers was wrong: he had not left the winning side. But it took almost four decades for the world to know this for sure. God has granted us a mighty victory. He has removed a major enemy from our midst.

A few people may fight an "invulnerable enemy" out of principle, but very few will devote their lives to developing a theoretical alternative to it. Chambers surely didn't. He was content to bear witness to the terrible evil of Communism. He had no positive theology, no view of progress in history.

This is why eschatology is so important. What people believe about the earthly future greatly influences what they do in the present. We need Christians who are willing to devote their lives to overcoming Christ's enemies with something better, not just lay down their lives in a lost historical cause.

The Paralysis of Pessimism

A remarkable statement to this effect was made at the graduation exercises of Wheaton College's Graduate School. Josef Ton, a Romanian pastor, recounted his experiences. His statement appears in *Wheaton Alumni* (Aug./Sept. 1991).

> Let me illustrate the importance of understanding the times from my own experience. The communist disaster fell on my country when I was a teenager. For many years after that, my life was a battle for intellectual and spiritual survival under Marxist indoctrination and totalitarian anti-Christian terror. I struggled to understand the nature of that calamity, and the Lord gave me that understanding. In the forties, I wrote papers on the nature of the failure of communism. One of them, published under the title "The Christian Manifesto," landed me in six months of house arrest with harsh interrogations by the secret police. But for me the crucial moment came in 1977, when a friend of mine challenged me to set up an organization that would openly expose communism.
>
> Here is what I told him: "Communism is an experiment that has failed. It wasn't able to fulfill any of its many promises and

nobody believes in it any more. Because of this, it will one day collapse on its own. Now, why should I fight something that is finished? I believe that our task is a different one. When communism collapses, somebody has to be there to rebuild society! I believe our job as Christian teachers is to train leaders so that they will be ready and capable to rebuild our society on a Christian basis!"

To my surprise, here is what my friend said to me: "Josef, you are wrong. Communism will triumph all over the world, because this is the movement of the Antichrist. And when the communists take over in the United States, they will have no restraining force left. They will then kill all the christians. We have only one job to do: alert the world and make ready to die."

A few years later my friend was forced to leave Romania. He came to the U.S. and settled down. Then I was forced into exile, and I moved to the U.S. as well. Since then, my friend has not done anything for Romania. He simply waited for the final triumph of communism and the annihilation of Christianity.

On the other hand, when I came here in 1981, I started a training program for christian leaders in Romania. We translated Christian textbooks, and smuggled them into Romania. With our partners in the organization, The Biblical Education by Extension (BEE), we trained about 1200 people all over Romania. Today, those people who were trained in that underground operation are the leaders in churches, in evangelical denominations, and in key Christian ministries.

This is why those who hold to dispensationalism have not produced meaningful solutions to the social crises of our age. They reject biblical law. They overestimate Satan. They are without hope in history. They see no hope in any efforts by Christians before the Rapture to build a better world for tomorrow. When their social programs are consistent with their eschatology, their ministries become, at best, rescue mission operations.

This is why Christian anti-Communism is now dead. It died on August 21, 1991. Rest in peace! It was easy for dispensational pre-millennialists to be anti-Communists. It was impossible for them to offer a distinctly biblical alternative to Communism. They never did. They had to appeal to natural law or other "neutral" pagan systems. But it is not enough to be anti-sin; you have to have a pro-righteousness position. It is not enough to know what *not* to do; you have to know what to do. This is why the collapse of Communism is a great opportunity for Christians in Europe to begin reconstructing from the ruins left by Communism. Dispensationalism can play no major role in this reconstruction. It denies the legitimacy of reconstruction.

1988: The Doomsday Year for Dispensationalism

I wrote the first two issues of ICE's monthly newsletter, *Dispensationalism in Transition*, which began in January of 1988. I started this newsletter because I knew that 1988 was the year in which the dispensationally defined "Rapture" could not be delayed again if the movement was to retain the emotional commitment of its laymen, especially its brightest younger members, who are my selected targets. Dispensationalism's leaders had for almost four decades "bet the farm" on the State of Israel, which came into being in May of 1948. One generation after 1948, the pulp paperback theologians had repeatedly promised, the Rapture would surely take place. In fact, it was originally scheduled for 1981: 1948 + 40 - 7 (the seven-year tribulation period). A lot of dispensational prophets had assured their followers in 1980 or earlier that 1981 would be "the year." They bet wrong. There was one last chance: 1988.

Betting on the fact that the Rapture would not take place in 1988 – an exceedingly safe bet, theologically speaking – I started publishing the newsletter. I had an agenda in mind (as I usually do): *to challenge the leaders of the dispensational movement to engage in open theological combat*, something they had steadfastly refused to do since the mid-1960's. Furthermore, they had decided decades earlier to focus all their efforts on refuting other premillennialists and the amillennialists. They had written repeatedly that "postmillennialism is dead," and so had completely ignored the rise of the newer postmillennialism of the Christian Reconstruction movement. They had, in effect, built themselves a theological Maginot Line, with all its guns trained on rival "pessimillennialists." I knew enough about tactics to plan a Blitzkrieg around that line.

The Date-Setting Addiction

Little did I suspect that dispensationalism's "last hurrah" would begin that very spring, when Edgar C. Whisenant published his "two-books-in-one" paperback book, both of which appeared under several different titles, on 88 reasons why the Rapture would surely take place that September. Millions of copies were printed and distributed. Just about every dispensational church in America had members who were getting ready for the Great Escape. "Everything must be put on hold!"

Predictably, nothing happened. "Wait," said Whisenant in effect, "I forgot about the B.C to A.D. shift. I lost a year. I should have said 1989." No; he should have said nothing. But he had said enough. The egg on the dispensational movement's collective face would stick for a long time. Or so I thought.

But wait! There has been yet another reprieve. Pat Robertson's 1990 newsletter identified Israel's 1967 Six-Day War as the first time that Jerusalem was fully liberated from Gentile control, as prophesied in Luke 21:24. "The Six-Day War gave the Jews control over Jerusalem in June of 1967. That event started the cosmic clock ticking. The length of a generation in the Bible is 40 years. Ten is the biblical number of completion. Forty years from 1967 is 2007."

But that's not all. America was founded in 1607 at Jamestown. Now, if you take 40 (the number of years in a generation) and multiply it by ten (the number of completion), you get 400 years. "The end of the generation' of Gentile decline coincides with 10 'generations' of America . . . the 'completion' in biblical numerology of the most powerful Gentile nation the world has ever known. Just 17 years from now."[7]

This was enough to get me thinking. Let's see, if Bishop Ussher's chronology is correct, and the world was created in 4004 B.C., then 1996 will be the world's 6,000th birthday. Also, one day to the Lord is as a thousand years. Plus, only six days shall we labor. So, what is scheduled for 1996? It's obvious: a Presidential election in America. Now, if Pat could be elected President in '96, and again in the year 2000 (THE YEAR 2000!!!), he would get two full terms in office, and then, just 1260 days after his successor is inaugurated. . . .

Perhaps I am becoming too prophetic. But you can understand how my mind started working when I looked at the numbers. Just as Hal Lindsey did in 1970. And Whisenant did in 1988. And Walvoord did in 1990.

First, the Brain Goes Dead

In 1974, Aleksandr Solzhenitsyn was thrown out of the Soviet Union. After he arrived in the West, one of his constant themes was the general loss of faith in Marxism in the Soviet Union. No one believes in it any more, he insisted. It is a dead ideology. Nobody can defend it, and nobody wants to.

The lesson we have learned from the demise of original Marxism is this: *when a movement dies, it dies at the top first.* Its head goes soft before its body grows cold. The faithful members keep coming to church long after the leaders have abandoned the original faith. The seminaries depart from the faith; then the bureaucrats on the various church boards; then the pastors; and last of all the laymen. Their checks finance this defection, start to finish. Naive laymen refuse to recognize the obvious: when the spokesmen at the top, especially in the institutions of higher learning and pulpit certification, cease to defend the

---

7. *Pat Robertson's Perspective* (May-June 1990), p. 5.

original creed against all comers, the handwriting is on the wall for that denomination or group.

The Irreversible Shifting of Priorities

There is a progression in this slow defection. At first, the leaders think it is not worth their time to respond to serious intellectual challengers. They feel secure in their tenured and well-policed places of instruction. Besides, they are too busy seeking loans for new building projects. (The Soviet Union's experience after 1973 is analogous: *detente* plus Western credits.) They grow intellectually flabby.

Second, the institution seeks accreditation from a secular humanist or theologically liberal accrediting organization. Once accepted, it then adopts the "neutral" academic standards of the accrediting organization. It quietly downgrades the original educational and creedal standards, since tuitions are needed to pay off the debt. It begins to substitute less intellectually rigorous "Christian" psychology courses for systematic theology and the biblical languages. Its faculty begins to focus on general theological concerns – concerns of the academic guild – rather than the specifics of the older faith, meaning the creeds held by the dedicated supporters who financed the original buildings and paid the salaries for decades.

Third, the institution's original faculty members depart. They resign in disgust, or get fired, or simply retire quietly. They are steadily replaced by teachers who are certified (Ph.D., Th.D.) by liberals as being technically competent in their academic specialties. These new men make no systematic attempt to relate their specialties to the original theological formulas.

Talbot Theological Seminary no longer is staffed by hardcore dispensationalists. Grace Theological Seminary in 1990 fired John C. Whitcomb. The president of the seminary fired him just before Whitcomb was to retire – as symbolic an act as any bureaucrat ever devised. A form letter sent by the president in December, 1992, announced the firing of the entire full-time faculty as of June, 1993. Academic priorities are shifting.

But what of Dallas Seminary? Consider the 1989 prediction by Rev. Thomas D. Ice, a Dallas Seminary graduate and the co-author of *Dominion Theology: Blessing or Curse?* (1988):

> By the year 2000, Dallas Theological Seminary will no longer be dispensational. [Professional] priorities are elsewhere than the defense of systematic dispensationalism from external criticism.[8]

By the time Ice gave this interview to a Christian Reconstructionist magazine, his co-author, H. Wayne House, had left Dallas Seminary to join the faculty of a small Baptist college in Oregon. In 1992, he departed from that institution. House was always far more an activist than a theologian. His activist priorities have produced shifts in his theology, as we can see in his essay in the 1992 *Journal of The Evangelical Theological Society*.[9]

Question: Where will some fired-up dispensationalist attend seminary in a decade? After he enrolls, what will he be taught? Answer: not Scofield, Chafer, Ryrie, or Walvoord. This is why dispensationalism is experiencing a fundamental paradigm shift. The younger theologians who are engineering it are too wise to admit publicly what they are doing, and the older men who cannot stop the shift are too embarrassed to admit what is being done to them and their lifetime work. *They are being disinherited*: exactly what they predicted would happen to Christians in history. Theirs is a self-fulfilling prophecy.

Walvoord Responds With 1953 Classroom Notes

In the July-September, 1990, issue of Dallas Seminary's *Bibliotheca Sacra*, the major scholarly journal of dispensationalism, Dr. John Walvoord at last responded to Christian Recon-

---

8. Interview with Martin Selbrede, *Counsel of Chalcedon* (Dec. 1989).
9. See above, Chapter 7, Conclusion.

struction. Sort of. Specifically, he wrote a book review of Bahnsen and Gentry's *House Divided: The Break-Up of Dispensational Theology* (ICE, 1989). He neglected to mention its subtitle. That is not all he neglected. He neglected to review the book.

I occasionally exaggerate for effect. Not this time. In a two and a half page review, Walvoord referred to the book only in the first two paragraphs (eight lines, total) and in the next-to-the-last paragraph. He did not state its thesis, only that he "has read few books with more errors of fact and half-truths about the doctrines being considered." (He did not identify even one of these errors.) He said it is a "diatribe." Worst of all, he didn't identify my Publisher's Preface as the source of all this erroneous vitriol; instead, he blamed Bahnsen and Gentry exclusively – a slur against me, if there ever was one.

For the next two pages, he simply restated what sounds like 1950's-era class notes on the history of premillennialism. He continued the tactic that Dallas professors have used constantly: to deflect all criticism of dispensationalism by saying that the critics are simply hostile to premillennialism. "The debate against dispensationalism is a misguided one, because what is actually involved is the premillennial interpretation of the Bible." This is "the central issue." Central for whom?

Not for Bahnsen and Gentry, who were attacking dispensationalism, especially its antinomianism. Dr. Bahnsen's section of the book deals only with the question of biblical law. Walvoord never mentioned this. He challenged *House Divided* by arguing that the early Church held exclusively to premillennialism, a theory refuted successfully in a 1977 Dallas Seminary Th.M. thesis by Alan Boyd, which identified Walvoord as the source of this error. Walvoord's tactic is the traditional dispensational apologetic: keep the reader's attention focused on historic premillennialism, so that he will not consider either the origins (late) or peculiar theological views of dispensationalism, which no group in Church history held prior to 1830.

Almost the entire review is devoted to the Dallas Seminary version of the history of rival eschatologies. Finally, he did refer to *House Divided* again. And what he said can serve as an epitaph for dispensationalism:

> A reasoned answer to this book would require another book of equal size, which the reviewer does not intend to write. When Whisenant announced that the Rapture would occur in September 1988, many people suggested that this reviewer answer that teaching. His answer, however, was, "Just wait." As the alleged date of the Rapture came and went, that teaching was seen to be wrong. The same will be true of dominion theology.

So, Walvoord's answer also is: "Just wait." But at his age, one can hardly afford to wait. His followers, like Dallas Seminary's donors, have been waiting for generations. What kind of theological response is "just wait," when your critics have used your movement's mania for date-setting as one of the most obvious signs of its deformity? When the widely acknowledged theological leader of a movement can only respond "just wait" to a book as detailed and theologically rigorous as *House Divided*, that movement is drawing near to the end. *When dispensationalism's premier theological journal runs such a book review as if it were intellectually adequate, the movement is visibly brain-dead.*

Walvoord did what I never thought likely. He appealed to newspapers as the proof of his eschatology. Remember the words of Hal Lindsey: "Some of the future events that were predicted hundreds of years ago read like today's newspaper."[10] Now hear Walvoord: "One wonders how the writers of this book can read the newspapers with their accounts of increased crime and a decaying church and come up with the idea that Christianity is triumphant in the world." Here it is, in black and white: *newspaper exegesis*. Here is the dean of dispen-

---

10. Hal Lindsey (with C. C. Carlson), *The Late Great Planet Earth* (Grand Rapids, Michigan: Zondervan, 1970), p. 20.

sationalism, openly adopting Hal Lindsey's hermeneutics. And why not? He had already adopted Lindsey's ticking clock of prophecy.[11]

Note: Christian Reconstructionists say only that Christianity *will* be visibly triumphant some day, not that it is visibly triumphant today. But this is not the main point. Walvoord confirms what Bahnsen wrote in 1977 concerning dispensational theology. Bahnsen wrote: ". . . believers and unbelievers alike had been trained to interpret the Bible in terms of *extrabiblical* considerations (secular scholarship for the modernists, world events for the dispensationalists)." He called this phenomenon newspaper exegesis.[12] Walvoord's work conforms to this assessment.

Let me repeat my endless refrain: until a dispensational *theologian* decides to take us on in print, in a book-long defense of House, Ice, Scofield, Chafer, and, yes, Walvoord, we Reconstructionists know exactly where dispensationalism is headed: into oblivion.

Just wait.

A Terminal Generation

I ended my Preface with this syllogism:

Dispensational theology leads to moral paralysis. Moral paralysis produces intellectual paralysis. Intellectual paralysis produces institutional paralysis. Institutional paralysis produces extinction through attrition. Dispensationalism is now at this final stage. We appear to be witnessing the birth of the terminal generation – not the terminal generation of the Church of Jesus Christ but of dispensationalism.

The secondary self-inflicted wound of dispensationalism is its view of the future: the eschatologically guaranteed failure of the

---

11. *USA Today* (Jan. 19, 1991).
12. *Journal of Christian Reconstruction* (Winter 1976-77), pp. 52-53.

Church to fulfill the Great Commission during the so-called Church Age. The primary self-inflicted wound of dispensationalism is its antinomianism, best expressed in the slogan: "No creed but Christ, no law but love." This slogan is in fact a creed – a creed designed for and approved by adulterers: "no law but love." This creed has produced a stream of adulterers since 1980: men who have publicly affirmed their commitment to dispensationalism, several of them doing so on their cable television shows. Dispensational theologians may choose to shrug off the antics of these adulterers, as well as that serial polygamist who marries and divorces as if he were playing musical chairs. They may choose to say (as always, in private), "There is simply no relationship between dispensationalism's rejection of biblical law and the unending stream of sexual scandals that afflict our movement." But there *is* a relationship between sanctions and behavior. These adulterers are not immediately defrocked permanently by their churches. *No law but love!*

Dispensationalism is nearing the end of the road. Its academic defenders have departed to a better world. Its present academic representatives no longer write systematic theologies. They refuse to write scholarly monographs that show precisely how recent suggestions for revisions to their theological system actually fit together, and how these revisions will not undermine the received system. In the 1990's, all but one (Rev. Ice) have refused to respond in print to the intellectual challenges from those theonomic theologians who have been published by one or more of the publishing firms I control. Since at least 1965, they have played "let's pretend" and "the silence of the lambs." *What they are really playing is* **blind man's bluff.**

On January 5, 1993, a Dallas Seminary faculty member sent me a letter. It said, among other things:

> I have not paid much attention to your writings because you principally have been occupied with attacking us and misrepresenting our point of view. If you expect any scholarly response

to what you are doing, you are going to have to start defending your own point of view and giving us solid reasons for giving credence to what you are doing. I find this strangely lacking in your literature.

This is a very strange statement from a representative of a theological position that has produced nothing new since Charles Ryrie's *Dispensationalism Today* (1965), from a professor at the seminary that unceremoniously fired Ryrie over a decade ago. Misrepresentations, if they really are misrepresentations, are quite easy to prove. All it takes is a published, book-length response with line-by-line refutations. I offer as a fine example Bahnsen and Gentry's *House Divided*. They took apart the accusations of Dr. House and Rev. Ice, piece by piece. But academic dispensationalists have refused to respond to our supposed misrepresentations, except for Dr. House, and then (mysteriously) he was no longer on the Dallas Seminary faculty. Eventually, the younger faculty members learn a lesson: publicly defend the system from its critics, and you will find yourself unemployed. It is prudent to remain silent. And so they do.

Rapture Fever is my response to my challenger's accusation. If dispensational scholars have the material, and also have the willingness to enter into a public debate with me in the form of a series of books like this one, they should do so. Gentlemen, it really isn't very difficult to respond *if* you have done your homework. But when the intellectual representatives of a 160-year-old theological movement can muster only one book-length response in a decade – *Dominion Theology: Blessing or Curse?* – and then the men who offered it subsequently fail to answer the immediate book-length rebuttal – *House Divided* – a perceptive observer is tempted to conclude: "They just don't have the firepower! They are out of ammo." Indeed, they are.

Perhaps the Dallas professor who initiated the challenge will review *Rapture Fever* in *Bibliotheca Sacra*. Or perhaps he will prudently remain silent. One thing is sure: he will not write a book refuting the books I have financed since 1984. If he had been able to do this, he would have done it long before now.

This is why dispensationalism is paralyzed: *its theologians are intellectually unable to defend it.* This is not because they are stupid; it is because the dispensational system is incoherent. It is now visibly falling apart. Its official revisors are succeeding only in speeding up the disintegration process. Its time is short.

In 1988, Dallas Seminary allowed the full eight-volume set of Lewis Sperry Chafer's *Systematic Theology* to go out of print. The seminary allowed Scripture Press to print an abridged, two-volume version in 1988. In January, 1993, the full set was reprinted by Kregel, an independent publisher that specializes in reprints of out-of-print books. That the seminary did not bother to keep in print the only comprehensive dispensational systematic theology ever written indicates that a quiet shift is in progress there. This shift will eventually be felt in the churches that depend on Dallas Seminary to supply both their present intellectual leadership and their future pastors.

A movement needs a long-term offensive strategy and a contemporary defensive strategy in order to win. First, it needs a *strategy of replacement*: leaven. It must have a strategy to replace the dominant anti-Christian culture, plus all anti-Christian rivals and all those within Christianity who preach a different theology. Dispensationalism has never had a strategy of replacement because it preaches a theology of departure from history. Dispensationalism preaches that the Church, not anti-Christianity, will be replaced at the end of the Church Age. Its strategy has therefore been defensive: "Form a circle with the wagons!"

This defensive strategy is institutional, not intellectual. This leads us to the second weakness of dispensationalism. Dispensationalism has never produced a theologian who has been willing to serve as a critic of the critics, a defender against all attackers. The *strategy of silence* has always been the preferred strategy. Either the movement's theologians have not been confident about their ability to defend the system (which is surely the situation today) or else they have assumed that their followers are not readers of theological books, and therefore book-length criticisms by other theologians are dismissed as institutionally irrelevant. The dispensational movement at best throws up one book per half generation to defend the system. In the case of *Dominion Theology: Blessing or Curse?*, its academic co-author immediately began to retreat, both geographically and theologically. Dr. House may no longer be a dispensationalist; surely he no longer defends the traditional system with the fanatic though incoherent determination that Rev. Ice does. Ice is the dispensational movement's last visible defender; his newsletters reply to the system's major critics, namely, Christian Reconstructionists. No one else bothers to defend the system.

Without either a long-term strategy of cultural replacement or a strategy of rapid and comprehensive intellectual defense, a movement can recruit and retain only the less bright and less dedicated members of the next generation. This is the situation in which dispensationalists find themselves today.

My conclusion: *we are witnessing dispensationalism's terminal generation.* Just wait.

* * * * * * * * * * * *

For those of you who have been persuaded by my arguments, and also for those who are at least curious, I invite you to request a free six-month subscription to the monthly newsletter, *Dispensationalism in Transition*, written by Dr. Ken Gentry, the author of *He Shall Have Dominion*, *The Beast of Revelation*, and *Before Jerusalem Fell: Dating the Book of Revelation*. Since 1988, this newsletter has covered the issues that dispensational theologians refuse to discuss. To subscribe, write to:

Dispensationalism in Transition
P. O. Box 8000
Tyler, TX 75711

BIBLIOGRAPHY

This list serves as an extension to the issues I raised in this book. The serious reader is encouraged to read one or more of these books. He is also encouraged to search out published refutations of any of these works by dispensational theologians. The absence of such published rebuttals will reinforce my basic point: the intellectual paralysis which afflicts dispensational theologians. Seminary students should be especially diligent in discovering if their professors have read any of these books. Have they discussed any of these books in class? Are any of these books listed in any classroom bibliography? In short, is the academic black-out still in operation?

General Works on Eschatology

Boyer, Paul. *When Time Shall Be No More: Prophecy Belief in Modern American Culture.* Cambridge, MA: The Belknap Press of Harvard University Press, 1992. Professor Boyer holds the Merle Curti chair in history at the University of Wisconsin.

Clouse, Robert G., ed. *The Meaning of the Millennium: Four Views.* Downers Grove, IL: InterVarsity Press, 1977. Advocates of the four major views of the millennium present each case.

Erickson, Millard J. *Contemporary Options in Eschatology: A Study of the Millennium.* Grand Rapids, MI: Baker, 1977. Examines modern views of eschatology: the millennium and the great tribulation.

Works Defending Postmillennialism or Preterism

Adams, Jay. *The Time Is At Hand.* Phillipsburg, NJ: Presbyterian and Reformed, 1966. An amillennial, preterist interpretation of the book of Revelation.

Alexander, J. A. *The Prophecies of Isaiah, A Commentary on Matthew* (complete through chapter 16), *A Commentary on Mark,* and *A Commentary on Acts.* Various Publishers. Works by the nineteenth-century Princeton Seminary Old Testament scholar.

Boettner, Loraine. *The Millennium.* Revised edition. Phillipsburg, NJ: Presbyterian and Reformed, (1958) 1984. A classic study of millennial views, and a defense of postmillennialism.

Brown, John. *The Discourses and Sayings of Our Lord* and commentaries on *Romans, Hebrews,* and *1 Peter.* Various Publishers. Brown was a nineteenth-century Scottish Calvinist.

Campbell, Roderick. *Israel and the New Covenant.* Phillipsburg, NJ: Presbyterian & Reformed, (1954) 1981. A neglected study of principles for the interpretation of prophecy. Campbell examines major themes of New Testament biblical theology. The book is easy to read; its chapters are short; the biblical references are numerous.

Chilton, David. *The Days of Vengeance: An Exposition of the Book of Revelation.* Ft. Worth, TX: Dominion Press. A massive postmillennial commentary on the book of Revelation. (New address: P. O. Box 7999, Tyler, TX 75711.)

Chilton, David. *The Great Tribulation.* Ft. Worth, TX: Dominion Press, 1987. A popular exegetical introduction to the postmillennial interpretation of this important but long-fulfilled prophecy. (New address: P. O. Box 7999, Tyler, TX 75711.)

Chilton, David. *Paradise Restored: A Biblical Theology of Dominion.* Ft. Worth, TX: Dominion Press, 1985. A study of prophetic symbolism, the coming of the Kingdom, and the book of Revelation. Deeply exegetical. (New address: P. O. Box 7999, Tyler,

TX 75711.)

Clark, David S. *The Message from Patmos: A Postmillennial Commentary on the Book of Revelation*. Grand Rapids, MI: Baker, 1989. A brief preterist and postmillennial commentary.

Davis, John Jefferson. *Christ's Victorious Kingdom: Postmillennialism Reconsidered*. Grand Rapids, MI: Baker, 1986. A biblical and historical defense of postmillennialism by a professor at Gordon-Conwell Seminary.

DeMar, Gary and Peter Leithart. *The Reduction of Christianity: A Biblical Response to Dave Hunt*. Ft. Worth, TX: Dominion Press, 1988. A detailed critique of the pietist and openly retreatist pop-dispensational theology of best-selling author and accountant Dave Hunt. Also, an historical and biblical defense of postmillennialism.

Edwards, Jonathan. *The Works of Jonathan Edwards*. 2 volumes. Edinburgh: The Banner of Truth Trust, (1834 ed.) 1974. Volume 2 includes Edwards' "History of Redemption." Edwards is generally regarded as America's most influential theologian. He was a defender of postmillennialism.

Gentry, Kenneth L. *The Beast of Revelation*. Tyler, TX: Institute for Christian Economics, 1989. A preterist study of the identity of the beast in Revelation.

Gentry, Kenneth L. *Before Jerusalem Fell: Dating the Book of Revelation*. Tyler, TX: Institute for Christian Economics, 1989. A Th.D. dissertation of the dating of Revelation: prior to A.D. 70.

Gentry, Kenneth L. *The Greatness of the Great Commission: The Christian Enterprise in a Fallen World*. Tyler, TX: Institute for Christian Economics, 1990. A thorough presentation of the comprehensive nature of Christ's call to world evangelism.

Gentry, Kenneth L. *He Shall Have Dominion: A Postmillennial*

Eschatology. Tyler, TX: Institute for Christian Economics, 1992. A comprehensive statement for postmillennialism and against premillennialism and amillennialism.

Henry, Matthew. *Matthew Henry's Commentary*. 6 volumes. New York: Fleming H. Revell, (1714). A popular commentary on the whole Bible by a still-popular seventeenth-century theologian.

Hodge, A. A. *Outlines of Theology*. Enlarged edition. London: The Banner of Truth Trust, (1879) 1972. A nineteenth-century introduction to systematic theology: question-and-answer form.

Hodge, Charles. *Systematic Theology*. 3 volumes. Grand Rapids, MI: Eerdmans, (1871-73) 1986. A standard Reformed text by Princeton Seminary's most renowned nineteenth-century theologian. Volume 3 includes a discussion of eschatology.

Kik, J. Marcellus. *An Eschatology of Victory*. N.p.: Presbyterian and Reformed, 1975. Preterist exegetical studies of Matthew 24 and Revelation 20.

Murray, Iain. *The Puritan Hope: Revival and the Interpretation of Prophecy*. (Edinburgh: Banner of Truth, 1971). Historical study of postmillennialism in England and Scotland, beginning in the eighteenth century.

North, Gary, ed. *The Journal of Christian Reconstruction*, Symposium on the Millennium (Winter 1976-77). Historical and theological essays on postmillennialism.

North, Gary. *Millennialism and Social Theory*. Tyler, TX: Institute for Christian Economics, 1990. A study of the failure of premillennialism and amillennialism to deal with social theory as an explicitly biblical enterprise.

Owen, John. *Works*, ed. William H. Goold. 16 volumes. Edinburgh: The Banner of Truth Trust, 1965. The seventeenth-century Puritan preacher and theologian; volume 8 includes several sermons on the Kingdom of God, and volume 9 contains a preterist sermon on 2 Peter 3.

Rushdoony, Rousas John. *God's Plan for Victory: The Meaning of Postmillennialism*. Fairfax, VA: Thoburn Press, 1977. A short theological study of the implications of postmillennialism for economics, law, and reconstruction.

Rushdoony, Rousas John. *Thy Kingdom Come: Studies in Daniel and Revelation*. Phillipsburg, NJ: Presbyterian and Reformed, 1970. Exegetical studies, full of insightful comments on history and society.

Shedd, W. G. T. *Dogmatic Theology*. 3 volumes. Nashville, TN: Thomas Nelson, (1888) 1980. A nineteenth-century Reformed text in systematic theology.

Strong, A. H. *Systematic Theology*. Baptist postmillennialist of late nineteenth and early twentieth centuries.

Sutton, Ray R. "Covenantal Postmillennialism," *Covenant Renewal* (February 1989). Discusses the difference between traditional Presbyterian postmillennialism and covenantal postmillennialism. Published by the ICE, P. O. Box 8000, Tyler, TX 75711.

Terry, Milton S. *Biblical Apocalyptics: A Study of the Most Notable Revelations of God and of Christ*. Grand Rapids, MI: Baker, (1898) 1988. Nineteenth-century exegetical studies of prophetic passages in Old and New Testaments; includes a complete commentary on Revelation.

Vos, Geerhardus. *The Pauline Eschatology*. Grand Rapids, MI: Eerdmans, (1930) 1952. A scholarly examination of the eschatological writings of Paul, written by the Bible-believing scholar who first developed orthodox biblical theology: the idea that the Bible's presentation of the gospel develops over time, but without any change in meaning, as liberals argue.

Vos, Geerhardus. *Redemptive History and Biblical Interpretation*. Edited by Richard Gaffin. Phillipsburg, New Jersey: Presbyterian & Reformed, 1980. These shorter essays deal with biblical theology and eschatology. Chapters 1-7 deal with eschatology.

Postmillennialism and the Jews

De Jong, J. A. *As the Waters Cover the Sea: Millennial Expectations in the Rise of Anglo-American Missions 1640-1810*. Kampen: J. H. Kok, 1970. A general history of millennial views; throughout the text it mentions the importance of prophecies concerning the Jews.

DeMar, Gary and Peter Leithart. *The Legacy of Hatred Continues: A Response to Hal Lindsey's **The Road to Holocaust*** (Tyler, TX: Institute for Christian Economics, 1989. A brief but thorough refutation to Hal Lindsey's claim that all nondispensational eschatologies are anti-Semitic. Lindsey has never replied in public to this book, published one month after his *The Road to Holocaust*. He did not revise any of its numerous factual errors in the subsequent paperback edition. Prior to the publication of *The Road to Holocaust*, he refused repeatedly to meet individually in private with either Gary North or Gary DeMar, although both men formally requested such a meeting.

Fairbairn, Patrick. *The Prophetic Prospects of the Jews, or, Fairbairn vs. Fairbairn*. Grand Rapids, MI: Eerdmans, 1930. Nineteenth-century scholar Fairbairn changed his mind about the conversion of the Jews. This volume reproduces his early arguments for the historic postmillennial position, and his later arguments against it.

Schlissel, Steve and David Brown. *Hal Lindsey and the Restoration of the Jews*. Edmonton, Alberta, Canada: Still Waters Revival Books, 1990. A Jewish-born Reconstructionist pastor responds to Hal Lindsey's claim that Christian Reconstruction is anti-Semitic. Schlissel's work is combined with David Brown's work which demonstrates that *postmillennialism* is the "system of prophetic interpretation that historically furnished the Biblical basis for the most glorious future imaginable for the Jews!"

Sutton, Ray R. "A Postmillennial Jew (The Covenantal Structure of Romans 11)," *Covenant Renewal* (June 1989). Sutton has a conversation with a postmillennial Messianic Jew.

Sutton, Ray R. "Does Israel Have a Future?" *Covenant Renewal* (December 1988). This examines several different views of Israel's future, and argues for the covenantal view.

Toon, Peter, ed. *Puritans, the Millennium and the Future of Israel: Puritan Eschatology 1600-1660*. Cambridge: James Clarke, 1970. A detailed historical study of millennial views with special attention to the place of Israel in prophecy.

Works Critical of Pre-Tribulational Dispensationalism

Allis, Oswald T. *Prophecy and the Church*. Phillipsburg, NJ: Presbyterian and Reformed, 1945. A classic comprehensive critique of the theology of dispensationalism by a postmillennialist Old Testament scholar. It has never been refuted and is rarely mentioned by dispensational scholars.

Bacchiocchi, Samuele. *Hal Lindsey's Prophetic Jigsaw Puzzle: Five Predictions That Failed!* Berrien Springs, MI: Biblical Perspectives, 1987. It examines Lindsey's failed prophecies.

Bahnsen, Greg L. and Kenneth L. Gentry. *House Divided: The Break-Up of Dispensational Theology*. Tyler, TX: Institute for Christian Economics, 1989. A detailed response to the book by H. Wayne House (then of Dallas Seminary) and Thomas Ice, *Dominion Theology: Blessing or Curse?* It includes a comprehensive discussion of eschatological issues written by Gentry.

Bass, Clarence B. *Backgrounds to Dispensationalism: Its Historical Genesis and Ecclesiastical Implications*. Grand Rapids, MI: Baker, 1960. A massively researched history of dispensationalism, with focus on J. N. Darby. The book is compact: 184 pages.

Bell, William Everett. "A Critical Evaluation of the Pretribulation Rapture Doctrine in Christian Eschatology." Ph.D. dissertation, New York University, 1967. This is by far the most thorough critical analysis of the theological failures of the pretrib position's developers and defenders.

Boersma, T. *Is the Bible a Jigsaw Puzzle: An Evaluation of Hal Lindsey's Writings*. Ontario, Canada: Paideia Press, 1978. An examination of Lindsey's interpretive method, and an exegesis of important prophetic passages.

Bray, John L. *Israel in Bible Prophecy*. Lakeland, FL: John L. Bray Ministry, 1983. An amillennial historical and biblical discussion of the Jews in the New Covenant.

Brown, David. *Christ's Second Coming: Will It Be Premillennial?* Edmonton, Alberta, Canada: Still Water Revival Books, (1876) 1990. A detailed exegetical study of the Second Coming and the Millennium by a former premillennialist who became postmillennial.

Cox, William E. *An Examination of Dispensationalism*. Philadelphia, PA: Presbyterian and Reformed, 1963. A critical look at major tenets of dispensationalism by former dispensationalist who became amillennial.

Cox, William E. *Why I Left Scofieldism*. Phillipsburg, NJ: Presbyterian and Reformed, n.d. A critical examination of major flaws of dispensationalism.

Crenshaw, Curtis I. and Grover E. Gunn, III. *Dispensationalism Today, Yesterday, and Tomorrow*. Memphis, TN: Footstool Publications, (1985) 1989. Two Dallas Seminary graduates take a critical and comprehensive look at dispensationalism.

DeMar, Gary. *The Debate Over Christian Reconstruction*. Ft. Worth, TX: Dominion Press, 1988. A response to Dave Hunt and Thomas Ice after their 1988 debate with Gary North and Gary DeMar. Includes a brief commentary on Matthew 24. The book was co-published by American Vision, Atlanta, GA. Audiotapes and a videotape of this debate are available from ICE, P. O. Box 8000, Tyler, TX 75711.

DeMar, Gary. *Last Days Madness*. Atlanta, GA: American Vision, (1991) 1993. A study of numerous false prophecies made by dispensationalists, and the demoralizing effects that such false prophecies produce on those who believe them.

Feinberg, John A. *Continuity and Discontinuity: Perspectives on the Relationship Between the Old and New Testaments*. Westchester, IL: Crossway, 1988. Theologians of various persuasions discuss relationship of Old and New Covenants; evidence of important modifications in dispensationalism.

Gerstner, John H. *A Primer on Dispensationalism*. Phillipsburg, NJ: Presbyterian and Reformed, 1982. A brief critique of dispensationalism's "division" of the Bible.

Jordan, James B. *The Sociology of the Church*. Tyler, TX: Geneva Ministries, 1986. Chapter entitled, "Christian Zionism and Messianic Judaism," contrasts the dispensational Zionism of Jerry Falwell, et. al. with classic early dispensationalism.

MacPherson, Dave. *The Incredible Cover-Up*. Medford, OR: Omega Publications, 1975. A revisionist study of the origins of the pre-trib rapture doctrine. He traces it to private revelations in 1830 by a 20-year-old mystic and follower of Edward Irving, Margaret Macdonald.

MacPherson, Dave. *The Unbelievable Pre-Trib Origin*. Kansas City, MO: Heart of America Bible Society, 1973. MacPherson's initial publication defending his thesis regarding Margaret Macdonald.

MacPherson. *The Great Rapture Hoax*. Fletcher, NC: New Puritan Library, 1983. Additional evidence of the unconventional account of the origins of the pre-trib position.

Mauro, Philip. *The Gospel of the Kingdom*. Boston: Hamilton Bros., 1928. Mauro accuses dispensationalism of having broken with Church history.

Mauro, Philip. *The Seventy Weeks and the Great Tribulation.* Swengel, PA: Reiner Publishers, n.d. A former dispensationalist re-examines prophecies in Daniel and the Olivet Discourse.

Miladin, George C. *Is This Really the End?: A Reformed Analysis of The Late Great Planet Earth.* Cherry Hill, NJ: Mack Publishing, 1972. A brief postmillennial response to Hal Lindsey's prophetic works; concludes with a defense of postmillennial optimism.

Provan, Charles D. *The Church Is Israel Now: The Transfer of Conditional Privilege.* Vallecito, CA: Ross House Books, 1987. A collection of Scripture texts with brief comments.

Vanderwaal, C. *Hal Lindsey and Biblical Prophecy.* Ontario, Canada: Paideia Press, 1978. A lively critique of dispensationalism and Hal Lindsey by a preterist amillennialist.

Weber, Timothy P. *Living in the Shadow of the Second Coming: American Premillennialism 1875-1982.* Grand Rapids, MI: Zondervan/Academie, 1983. This touches on American dispensationalism in a larger historical and social context.

Wilson, Dwight. *Armageddon Now!: The Premillenarian Response to Russia and Israel Since 1917.* Tyler, TX: Institute for Christian Economics, (1977) 1991. A premillennialist historian studies the history of failed dispensational prophecy. He warns against "newspaper exegesis."

Woodrow, Ralph. *Great Prophecies of the Bible.* Riverside, CA: Ralph Woodrow Evangelistic Association, 1971. An exegetical study of Matthew 24, the Seventy Weeks of Daniel, and the doctrine of the Anti-Christ.

Woodrow, Ralph. *His Truth Is Marching On: Advanced Studies on Prophecy in the Light of History.* Riverside, CA: Ralph Woodrow Evangelistic Association, 1977. An exegetical study of important prophetic passages in Old and New Testaments.

Zens, John. *Dispensationalism: A Reformed Inquiry into Its Leading Figures and Features*. Nashville, TN: Baptist Reformation Review, 1973. Brief historical and exegetical discussion by a (then) Reformed Baptist.

Theonomic Studies in Biblical Law

Bahnsen, Greg L. *By This Standard: The Authority of God's Law Today*. Tyler, TX: Institute for Christian Economics, 1985. An introduction to the issues of biblical law in society.

Bahnsen, Greg. *No Other Standard: Theonomy and Its Critics*. Tyler, Texas: Institute for Christian Economics, 1991. A detailed response, point by point, to dozens of critics of Bahnsen's earlier defenses of theonomy.

Bahnsen, Greg L. *Theonomy in Christian Ethics*. Nutley, New Jersey: Presbyterian and Reformed, (1977) 1984. A detailed apologetic of the idea of continuity in biblical law.

DeMar, Gary. *God and Government*, 3 vols. Atlanta, GA: American Vision, 1991. An introduction to the fundamentals of biblical government, emphasizing self-government.

Jordan, James. *The Law of the Covenant: An Exposition of Exodus 21-23*. Tyler, TX: Institute for Christian Economics, 1984. A clear introduction to the issues of the case laws of the Old Testament.

North, Gary. *The Dominion Covenant: Genesis*. Tyler, TX: Institute for Christian Economics, (1982) 1987. A study of the economic laws of the Book of Genesis.

North, Gary. *Moses and Pharaoh: Dominion Religion vs. Power Religion*. Tyler, TX: Institute for Christian Economics, 1985. A study of the economic issues governing the Exodus.

North, Gary. *Political Polytheism: The Myth of Pluralism*. Tyler, TX: Institute for Christian Economics, 1989. A 700-page critique of the myth of neutrality: in ethics, social criticism, U.S.

history, and the U.S. Constitution.

North, Gary. *The Sinai Strategy: Economics and the Ten Commandments*. Tyler, TX: Institute for Christian Economics, 1986. A study of the five-point covenantal structure (1-5, 6-10) of the Ten Commandments. Includes a detailed study of why the Old Covenant's capital sanction no longer applies to sabbath-breaking.

North, Gary. *Tools of Dominion: The Case Laws of Exodus*. Tyler, TX: Institute for Christian Economics, 1990. A 1,300-page examination of the economics of Exodus 21-23.

North, Gary. *Westminster's Confession: The Abandonment of Van Til's Legacy*. Tyler, TX: Institute for Christian Economics, 1991. Refutes, chapter by chapter, the criticisms offered in Westminster Seminary's *Theonomy: A Reformed Critique*. North shows that the seminary has returned to natural law theology in order to defend political pluralism. North says that this is by far his best polemical book. Rushdoony has publicly said so, too. It reprints H. L. Mencken's 1937 obituary of J. Gresham Machen.

North, Gary, ed. *Theonomy: An Informed Response*. Tyler, TX: Institute for Christian Economics, 1991. A 400-page symposium refuting Westminster Seminary's *Theonomy: A Reformed Critique*. Essays by DeMar (3), Gentry (3), Sutton, North, and Rev. John Maphet.

Rushdoony, Rousas John. *The Institutes of Biblical Law*. Nutley, New Jersey: Presbyterian and Reformed, 1973. The foundational work of the Christian Reconstruction movement. It subsumes all of biblical law under the Ten Commandments. It includes three appendixes by Gary North.

Sutton, Ray R. *That You May Prosper: Dominion By Covenant*. Tyler, TX: Institute for Christian Economics, (1987) 1992. A detailed study of the five points of the biblical covenant model, applying them to church, state, and family. Sutton is president of Philadelphia Theological Seminary (Reformed Episcopal).

SCRIPTURE INDEX

Genesis
1:1   166
1:2   72, 166
1:14f   166
1:26ff   66, 68, 119-20
1:28   xxiii, 69
5:3   167
9:1ff   66
9:5   142
9:5f   146
9:7   xxiii
11:10   167
47:16   114

Exodus
5:19ff   40
18   65
20:11   163

Leviticus
2:1ff   150
26:3ff   120

Numbers
14:2ff   61

Deuteronomy
4:5ff   91

8:17f   xxi
8:18   62
28:1ff   62, 71, 83, 120, 202, 207
28:15ff   71

I Samuel
2:30   xxii
8:15   114

II Samuel
12:13   107

I Kings
18   105

II Kings
2   105

Psalms
2:11f   xix
23:1ff   76
25:12ff   77
25:13   60, 120
37:9   77, 120
37:11   120
37:22   77
50:10   112

110:1f   78-79

Proverbs
12:23a   14
13:22   xxiii

Isaiah
42:20ff xxiv

Ezekiel
43:19   50n

Daniel
2:34   30
9:24ff   21

Hosea
6:6   50

Zechariah
13:8f   36

Matthew
5:5   xiii, 77, 120
5:13   1
5:14   91
5:32   159
6:10   xiv, 94
6:31   xii
6:33   xii, xiii
9:13   176
10:22   173
13:20   99
13:24f   185
13:13ff 150
13:33ff 139

13:36ff 85-86
13:38ff 99
15:25ff 96
16:18   xviii
18:15ff 159
21:43   xii, xiii, 142
24:32ff 51, 90
28:18ff 66, 88
28:18   63

Mark
6:7   xvi
12:ff   110

Luke
6:46   173
9:23   173-74
12:47f   xxi
14:28ff ix
19:10   176
19:13   63
21:20ff 43, 90
21:24   211
22:29ff xx, 111

John
1:12   xxii
2:18ff   44
3:17   176
3:36   xii, 93
14:12ff 120

Acts
1:8   xvii
1:10ff   89
5:16   xvii
17:6   82

Romans
3:23	x
6:23	x
8:29	174
13:8	201
13:11	174
16:20	xvii

I Corinthians
6:9f	ix, xi, 179
6:11	xi
10:13	xviii
11:27ff	81
12	1n
13:11	53
15:20ff	xix
15:22ff	79-80
22:26	79-80

II Corinthians
6:2	37

Ephesians
1:17ff	xvii
2:8ff	175-76
2:10	39
5:1ff	ix, xv
5:1ff	78

Philippians
2:12	xvi

Colossians
1:10ff	xviii
1:15ff	94
3:2	64

II Timothy
3:6f	58
3:13	116

Hebrews
1:2	48
5:11ff	202
9:15f	48
9:22ff	48-49
12:14	174

James
2:14ff	172
2:14ff	176
4:17	xviii

I Peter
3:15	195

II Peter
1:19	78

I John
2:3	xvi
2:19	177
3:22	xvi
5:2	xvi

Revelation
20:7ff	71
8:7ff	71
9:15, 18	71

INDEX

abortion, xxxii, xxxv, 13, 141, 160
activism, xxxiv-xxxv, 102, 119
Adam, xix
adultery, 218
Allis, xxxi, xxxiv, 25, 46, 103, 147, 158
Amish, 117, 128
Antichrist, 54
antinomianism, 121, 174
apostles, 82, 89
Aquinas, Thomas, 95
Arabs, 30
Armageddon, 37
army (Satan's), xvi
attrition, xxiv, 217
Augustine, 164
authority, 113
autonomy, 110, 113

Baghdad, 190
Bahnsen, Greg, 130, 215, 217
Beast, xxiii, 51-53, 84
beatitudes, xiii
Bell, William E., 46
benefits, xii-xv, xvii
Blaising, Craig, xiii-xiv, 132, 145

blind man's bluff, 218
Bloom, Ed, 131
blueprints, 123, 134
Boice, James, 173-74
Boyd, Alan, 78n, 153, 215
bread, xiv
bureaucracy, 64-65
Bush, George, 194

Caesar, 110-11
Captain Jesus (see Christ)
Carlson, C. C., 1
carrot juice, 56
Carter, Jimmy, 4, 182
Chafer, Lewis, 220
Chambers, Whitaker, 207-8
Chilton, David, 133-134
Christ
    bureaucrat, 65, 135-36
    Captain Jesus, 9-10, 14, 88
    coin, 111-12
    commandment, xvi
    commandments, 120-21
    confession, 178
    Creator, 94
    Lord/Savior, 176-78
    loser?, xix, 74
    morning star, 78

One World State, 97
power, 63, 64-65, 75, 113
representation, xix, xx
resurrection, xix
right hand of God, 79-80
rule of, xix
sits tight, 79
stand pat, 140
Christian Reconstruction, 74
Church
    bystander, 66
    city on a hill, 91
    defeat of, 65-66
    history &, 119
    kingdom &, xii, xiii
    loser?, 203
    matures, xx
    millennium, 65
    "night shift," 78
    Parenthesis, xxvi
    rulership, xx
    victory, 69
Church Age, xxxi, 6, 11, 22, 87, 104, 139, 150-51
Church fathers, 153
citizenship, 117
city on a hill, 91
civilization, 63 (see kingdom)
clock of prophecy, 21-23, 31-32, 56-57, 191-92
college, xxv-xxvii
Communism, 207
confidence, xxii
confidence in man, 71
continuity, 84-85
cost, ix, xi, xv-xvi, xxiii
covenant, 142, 204-5
covenant lawsuit, 120-21

covenant model, 133-34, 135, 142
creation, 167-68
creationism, xxviii-xxix, 12
creed, 218
Criswell, W. A., 200
crumbs, 96
Cumbey, Constance, 57

Dallas Theological Seminary
    abortion, 141, 160-61
    black-out, 135, 156-57
    blind man's bluff, 218
    creationism, 72, 168
    curriculum, 108
    curriculum, 1991, 192
    deaf-mutes, 198
    defections, 131
    Ice's prediction, 145
    Lindsey &, 159
    monkey strategy, xxxii
    questions about, 17
    shifting, 193
    silence of, 5, 14, 20, 129, 131, 132, 160-61, 198, 219
    transformation, 1970's, 131
Daniel, 21
Darby, John N., 105, 137,
Darwin, xxvii, 164, 165
Darwinism, 73, 169-70
Davis, John, 67, 195
deaf-mutes, 198
death, 105
death penalty, 146
debt, 199-201
despair, 96
dirty little secret, xxxi

dispensationalism
  activists, 16-17, Chap. 11
  adulterers, 218
  appeal of, 205-7
  attrition, xxiv-xxvii, 196, 217
  bureaucracy, 135-36
  clock of prophecy, 21-23, 31-32, 191-92
  collapse of, 22-23
  covenant model of, 204-5
  defections, 160, 213-14
  defensive, 6, 220
  dirty little secret, xxxi
  dispensensationalism, 20
  division, xxxiv
  final stage, xxxv
  flame-out, 157
  history of, 3-5, 153-54
  Ice &, xxxiv
  incoherent, 220
  inferiority complex, xxvi
  killer marathon, 1988, 104
  law, xxvii, xxix, 82-83, 121, 140-41
  law/grace, 176
  leadership gone, 6
  lecture notes, 154-55
  Lord's Prayer, 76
  Maginot Line, 211
  optimism?, 98-99
  paradigm shift, 160-61, 197, 214
  paralyzed, xxxi, Chaps. 1, 2, 3
  pessimism, 99
  philosophy of history, 98
  postmillennial language, 99
  responsibility &, 192-93
  retreatist, 104
  sanctification, 172-79
  scholarship, xxix-xxx, xxx-xxxi
  scholarship &, xxix
  sensationalism, 20, 26, 28
  silence, xxxi-xxxii, 158 (see also silence)
  social ethics, 119, 206-7
  suicide of, 28
  systematic theology, 162
  ten commandments, 83
  terminal generation, xxxv, 3, 15, 18, 220
  theological heart, 24
  theologically dead, 102-3
  time, xxix
  time perspective, 86-88
  view of God, 32
  withdrawal, 8
Dispensationalism in Transition, 210, 220
dispensensationalism, 20
dominion, 99-100, 124
dominion covenant, 66, 68
dominion theology, 129
donors, 157, 198, 212
duties, ix
Dyer, Charles, 34, 107, 190

economics, xxviii
education, 96n, 128
Elijah, 105
Emperor's clothes, 147
end times, 47-51
entropy, 62
escape religion, 42

Index

eschatology, 43-44, 121-22
eternal life, x-xi
eternity, 93-94
ethics, 206
evangelicalism, xxxii
evangelism, 35-38, 41, 91, 122

false prophets, 54
Falwell, Jerry, 187, 194, 199-201
F.B.I., x
final judgment, 74, 79-80
footstool, xix, 79
foreign policy, 31
fundamentalism
   defense, 9
   despair, 96
   divided, 9
   fed up, 9
   law, 94-95
   Rapture fever, 88
   Roman Catholic, 97
   time perspective, 115
   two storeys, 95-97, 100, 101-2
   withdrawal, 8

"gap" theory, xxix, 72-73, 166-67
Geisler, Norman, 42, 203
Genesis Flood, 168, 170, 171
ghetto, xxv, 8, 10, 110-28
ghostwriter, 1-2
gift, xi, xxi
God, x, 68-69
good works, xxii, 175-76
Gorbachev, 107
gospel, 63, 64, 65-66, 77
   (see also Great Commission)
gospel tracts, 4-5
grace, 176
Grace Seminary, 108, 195-99
Graham, Billy, 182
Great Commission, xxiii, 41, 64, 88
Great Tribulation
   Daniel's 70th week, 21
   date of, 45, 52
   good works &, xxii
   Jews perish, 4, 35-38
   past event, xxiii

Halsel, Grace, 36n, 37n
head transplants, 55
heaven, xv, 94, 96, 105
helicopter escape, 87-88
history, 119, 178
hoax, 190-91
Hodge, Charles, 169
holiness, 174
Holmes, O. W., 170
House, H. Wayne, 129-44
   date of Revelation, 44
   death penalty, 146
   Dominion Theology, 129, 221
   kingdom, xiv-xv, 144
   "night shift" religion, 78
   retreat, 221
   silence, xxxiii, 220
Howe, Frederick, 168
humanism, xxv-xxvii, xxxii, 9, 92-93, 128, 203
Hunt, Dave
   dating Revelation, 44-45
   defeat is inevitable, 70, 77, 99

dispensationalism fading, 59
dominion, 99-100, 124
helicopter man, 87-88
imminent Rapture, 89
King must be present, 80
New Age & Reconstruction, 73-74
recruitment & suicide, 122
reforms are hopeless, 89-90
Whatever Happened? 105
Hussein, Saddam, 190

Ice, Thomas D.
Dallas Seminary, 145, 214
House &, 129, 221
last defender, xxxiv, 221
premillennial ethics, 83, 92
Whitby myth, 152
imputation, 178
inferiority complex, xxvi
inheritance
earth, xvi, 77, 120
kingdom, xiv, xv
personal, xxi-xxii
saints', xvii
Iraq, 20, 25, 34, 107, 190
irrationalism, 92
Israel, State of, 27-28, 31, 35-38, 190-91, 211
(see also Jews)

Jerusalem, 43, 45, 49, 70, 97
Jesus (sse Christ)
Jews, 35-38, 42
John the Baptist, 196
Johnson, S. Lewis, 83, 131

Kant, Immanuel, 92
Keynes, John Maynard, 42
KGB, 188
kingdom
all creation, 94
Caesar's, 110-11
Church &, xii, xiii
civilization, xiv, xxii, 85
cost, xv-xvi
footstool, xix
God's vs. Christ's, xx
God's vs. heaven, xiii-xiv
House (1992), xiv-xv, 144
inheritance, xiv
inner only, 139
judgment rendered, 111
politics &, 40-43
representation, xix
Satan's vs. God's, xviii
Scofield, xiii
seek first, xii
Kirban, Salem, 54-58
Kuhn, Thomas, 6
Kuwait, 190

Lalonde, Peter, 100
Larkin, Clarence, 176
last days, 45, 47-51
Latin, 114-15
Lattage, Beverly, 187
law
commandments, xvi
dispensational, xxvii, xxix
fundamentalism vs., 94-95
gospel &, 206
grace, 95, 176
inheritance, xv
kingdom, xv

natural, xxvii, 95, 97, 113, 141, 210
  rejection of, 83
  victory, 206
  victory &, 202
  "wisdom," 140-41
leaven, 139, 150-51
lecture notes, 154-55
Lewis, David Allen, 40-42
Liberty University, 194, 199-201
Lindsey, Hal
  anti-semitism, xxxiii
  Dallas Seminary, 159
  fading, 59
  ghostwriter, 1-2
  inside dope, 3
  lack of confidence, 149
  Late Great Planet Earth, 1
  newspapers, 22, 216
  prophet, 18
  publisher (666), 189
  pusher, 3
  response to, 159
Lord's Prayer, xiv, 76, 94
Lord's Supper, 80-81
losers, 202

MacArthur, John, 172, 175-78
Macdonald, Margaret, 105, 137
MacPherson, Dave, 137-38, 153
Maginot Line, 211
Man of Sin, 45
McClain, Alva, 139, 98
McGee, J. Vernon, 100
meek, xiii
Migne, J.P., 115
milk-drinkers, 202

Milton, John, 140
Montezumas' two-step, 191
Moody Press, xxix, 168
Moral Majority, 183, 184, 199-200
Morris, Henry, xxix, 73, 167
motivation, 66
murder, 142
Murray, John, 146

National Affairs Briefing Conference, 180-87
Nato, 30
Natural law, xxvii, 95, 97, 113, 141, 210
Nero, 52
Neuhaus, Richard, 42
neutrality, 42, 95, 151, 181
New Age, 73-74, 74, 80
New World Order, 194
newspaper exegesis, 22-23
newspapers, 216
night shift, 78
Noah, 142
Nobel, David, xxv

obedience, xviii
occultism, 39
Owen, John, 152

Packer, J. I., 173
padded cell, 119
Pamona College, xxvii
paradigm shift
  defensive mentality, 6
  delayed deliverance, xxxv
  evidence, 15-16
  Grace Seminary, 197

intellectual, xxxi
moral, xxxv
process of, 6-8
questions, 11-14
Parenthesis, 23
(see also Church Age)
Passover, xx
Pentecost, 149-51
Pentecost, J. Dwight, 136
perfection, 178
pessimillennialism, 62, 126
pessimism, 67-71, 82-83, 99, 182
Pharisees, 43, 112
pietism, 102, 185
pluralism, 95, 102, 117
polishing brass, 100
politics, 4, 8, 13, 40-43, 95, 117, 181, 182
positive feedback, xxi, 62
postmillennialism, 71, 73-74, 119, 124, 126, 138
power, xvii, xix
power religion, 42
premillennialism, 98, 153
progress, 61, 62, 73,
prophecies, 19-20, 123-24, 189-90
prophecy, 43-44
prophecy clock
(see clock of prophecy)
Puritanism, 138
Puritans, 62

Rapture
any moment, 23-25, 58
date, 210
delayed 1,950 years, 89
deliverance, 206
fading, 102
false hope, 105
helicopter escape, 87-88
impossible, 85
missing word, 183
passivity, 4
politics &, 182-83
postponed, 29-31, 191-92
responsibility vs., 60
Russia &, 27-29, Chap. 12
shelved, 1980, 4
Rapture fever
blessed hope, 75
contagious, 2
Falwell, 1992, 200
ghetto, 10
heart, 22
inside dope, 2-3
newspaper exegesis, 22
older generation, 88
played out?, 18
rationalism, 92
Reagan, 54, 180
scrambled theology, 90
subsided 1991, 189

responsibility
blessings &, ix
clock of, 39
dispensationalism vs., 109, 128, 192-93
escaping, ix, xxiii, 60
resisting Caesar, 111
victory, xx-xxi, 86
wisdom, xviii
representation, xix, 178
rescue mission, 67

restoration, xxiv
resurrection, xix
Revelation, 44-45
revolution, 140
Robertson, Pat, 187, 211
Robison, James, 180, 187
Roe vs. Wade, xxxii, 13, 141
Romania, 208-9
Ruse, Michael, 164
Russia, 27, 31, 188-89, 190-91
Ryrie, 46, 118, 131, 147-48

sacrifices, 48
Sadducees, 43
sanctification
   corporate, 171
   definitive, 178
   dispensationalism vs., 172-79
   progressive, 175
Santa Claus, 76
Satan
   army, xvi
   covenant, 121
   earthly rule, 80
   power, 69-70
   power of, xvii
   representation, xix
   victor, 65-66
Saucy, Robert, 148
Sauer, Erich, 147
Schaeffer, Francis, 9
schizophrenia, 42
Schnitger, David, 84, 104, 134
scholarship, xxix, xxvi
Scofield, C. I.
   apostles' rule, xx
   "At hand," 23
   creation, 163
   "gap theory," xxix, 72-73, 163, 166
   kingdom, xiii
   kingdoms, xx
   sacrifices restored, 50n
   sayonara, 201
   shuffle, 166-67
secession, 198
secular, 95, 100
secular clergy, 97
secularism, xxvi
seminaries
   abortion &, xxxii
   Big Three, 5
   black-out, 155-57
   donors, 157
   paradigm shift, 14-15
   silence, 34, 109
sensationalism, 20, 26, 28, 59, 193
signs, 58
silence
   Dallas Seminary, 5, 14, 20, 129, 131, 132, 158, 160-61, 198, 219
   dispensationalism, xxxi-xxxii, 221
   Grace Seminary, 198
   leaders, 125
   Lindsay's teachers, 2
   social theory, 141
   strategy, xxxi-xxxii, 220
   suicidal, xxxv, 160
sin, xviii, 12-13
Smith, Bailey, 183
social ethics, 92, 119, 206-7

Solzhenitsyn, A., 212
Soviet Union, 27, 188-89, 212
  (see also Russia)
stars, 71
State, 203
State of Israel
  evangelism in 35-38
  Russia &, 27-29, 31, 190-91, 211
state universities, xxv-xxvii
stick men, 132
Strauss, Lehman, 82
success, 185-86
suicide squads, 122
Sutton, Ray, 133-34, 156, 204

technology, 5
temple, 44, 48, 50
ten commandments, 83
terminal generation, xxxv, 84, 104
Thieme, Bob, 177
Tiberius, 111-12
time, 47, 61, 86-88, 94, 115, 126
Ton, Josef, 208-9
Truman, Harry, 125
trust & obey, xvi

utopia, 63, 70, 126

Van Til, Cornelius, 93

victory, xix-xxi, 202, 206
Vos, Geerhardus, 162

wagons, 9
Waltke, Bruce, 131
Walvoord, John
  anti-reform, 63
  clock of prophecy, 21, 24
  House Divided review, 215-17
  Iraq, 20, 25-26
  "just wait," 216
  millennial saints, 136
  moral law, 66-67
  pessimism, 68
  postmillennialism & liberalism, 72
  Rapture before he dies, 109
  "realist," 68, 75, 82, 98
  rescue mission, 67
  reviews Wilson, 20
  Soviet Union, 191
Westminster Seminary, 159-60
Wheaton College, 208
Whisenant, Edgar, 54, 56, 104, 189-90, 191, 211
Whitby, Daniel, 138, 151-52
Whitcomb, John, 169, 196
white flag, 66
Wilson, Dwight, 19-20, 32
Wilson, James, 165
wisdom, xvii, xviii, 140-41

MY CHALLENGE TO DALLAS SEMINARY

Gentlemen, your institution has not produced a systematic theology since your founder, Lewis Sperry Chafer, wrote his in 1948. Even so, he failed to answer O. T. Allis' book, *Prophecy and the Church* (1945). You refused to keep Chafer in print after 1988. Your continuing silence is the symbol of your dilemma. So is the inability of each generation to produce a detailed systematic theology which answers your many critics.

It is time for you as a faculty to produce a systematic theology. It is my opinion that there is insufficient agreement at Dallas Seminary for such a project to be completed. So, I now offer you this challenge. You are required to sign a statement of faith annually. The faculty needs to pay two or three members to write an 800-page defense of that statement. Make it clear to your students, the seminary's donors, and the Board of Trustees that this statement of faith can be defended in a scholarly, biblical manner. This will make it clear to pastors and laymen that somebody, somewhere is able to defend the dispensational system. As you know, I don't think anyone is.

I predict that you will not accept this challenge because you dare not do it. You are not agreed on what dispensationalism teaches. If you become specific, you will blow up the seminary. If you remain silent, you will forfeit whatever leadership you retain in the dispensational community. So, you can no longer afford to remain silent, yet you dare not become specific.

And so I leave it at this: there is no longer anyone who will go into print with a comprehensive dispensational systematic theology. The reason is simple: the dispensational system is so flawed that its defenders are embarrassed by it. It is time for its mute defenders to quit pretending otherwise.

Intellectual talent is scarce in evangelical Protestantism. We need theologians who are willing to commit all their intellectual gifts to the defense of the faith. If you cannot in good conscience and with all your strength commit to dispensationalism, it is time to adopt another position – one you can commit to.

A THREE-YEAR STRATEGY FOR PASTORS

If the message of this book has persuaded you, you now have a major problem: How to convey its message to your congregation, but without losing most of them and without getting fired. This can be done, but not overnight.

Warning: You are not yet ready to lead your congregation out of bondage in antinomian Egypt and through the wilderness, any more than Moses was when he fled into the wilderness. You must begin to develop a strategy of secession from cultural bondage: the humanist-pietist alliance. Your goal: **to make activists out of half your congregation within 36 months.**

First, you must devote the next three years to serious theological study, probably the most serious study in your life. You must read at least thirty of the books listed in the bibliography, but above all, Oswald T. Allis' *Prophecy and the Church*. Nothing less than thirty books will do. While you do this, you must re-read the entire Bible, once per year, minimum.

Second, you can't beat something with nothing. It is not sufficient to know what is wrong with dispensationalism. You must also know which theological system is correct. Find out. Think through your entire theology and restructure it, point by point, as you read through the Bible. But don't preach your theological discoveries as you make them. Be patient. Wait.

Third, do not announce to your congregation next Sunday, "I've switched my theology!" Instead, do what Grace Theological Seminary has done: **substitute practical theology for dispensational theology.** Start preaching a two-year series of 6-part sermons on any of these topics: evangelism, family discipline, getting a better job, managing your finances, Christian education, or a dozen others. Make Christian activists out of your congregation: salt and light for Christ. Projects!

Finally, pray about your strategy for 15 minutes each day. When you receive answers, enlist church activists to help you. For other suggestions, contact me: Box 8000, Tyler, TX 75711.

A THREE-YEAR STRATEGY FOR LAYMEN

I assume that you have finished reading *Rapture Fever*. You may be persuaded that I am correct. You may be persuaded only that I may be correct. Now you must find out.

You must locate a copy of O. T. Allis' *Prophecy and the Church*. When you do, get out your Bible and start reading Allis. You must verify every doubtful thing he says by looking up the Bible passages he cites as proof. This will persuade you.

Then what? If you are a member of a dispensational church, do not go running to your Christian friends shouting, "Look what I've found!" They will not believe you. Your message undermines everything they have been taught about God's law, the Church's future, and their personal responsibility. The price of accepting your newly discovered and not yet fully understood beliefs is too high. They will not yet pay it. Wait.

Second, sit down and map out a personal program of Christian service that will reflect what you now say you believe about God's law, the Church's future, and your responsibility. Talk is cheap; personal self-discipline is expensive. Count the cost.

You need to return to God a token payment for the grace He has bestowed on you. Search for an area of service in which your talents uniquely qualify you, and begin to serve: five hours a week, ten hours a week, or whatever. Become a productive citizen in God's city on a hill. Actions speak louder than words.

If you can no longer bear responsibility-rejecting preaching in your local church, quietly transfer to another congregation without leaving resentment behind. If you stay, work slowly to persuade others, one by one, by your service. (The odds are against you.) **Do not become a complainer or a conspirator.** Two or three years from now, when your light shines brightly before men, and some of them come to you for advice as to how they can better serve God, help them to find their niche of service. If (and only if) they ask you how your Christian life was changed, tell them about *Rapture Fever*. If they become Christian activists, they will become operational postmillennialists.

ABOUT THE AUTHOR

Gary North received his Ph.D. in history from the University of California, Riverside, in 1972. He specialized in colonial U.S. history. He wrote his doctoral dissertation on Puritan New England's economic history and the history of economic thought. A simplified version of this dissertation has been published as *Puritan Economic Experiments* (Institute for Christian Economics, 1988).

In the late 1960's, he and R. J. Rushdoony founded what has become known as the Christian Reconstruction movement, also known as theonomy.

He is the author of approximately 35 books in the fields of economics, history, and theology. His first book, *Marx's Religion of Revolution*, appeared in 1968. His *Introduction to Christian Economics* appeared in 1973, the year he began writing a multi-volume economic commentary on the Bible, which now covers Genesis, Exodus (three volumes), and Leviticus. He was the general editor of the Biblical Blueprints Series (1986-87), a 10-volume set.

Beginning in 1965, his articles and reviews have appeared in over three dozen newspapers and periodicals, including the *Wall Street Journal, Modern Age, Journal of Political Economy, National Review*, and *The Freeman*.

He edited the first fifteen issues of *The Journal of Christian Reconstruction*, 1974-81. He edited a *festschrift* for Cornelius Van Til, *Foundations of Christian Scholarship* (1976). He edited two issues of *Christianity and Civilization* in 1983: *The Theology of Christian Resistance* and *Tactics of Christian Resistance*. He edited *Theonomy: An Informed Response* (1991).

He is the editor of the monthly financial newsletter, *Remnant Review*. He writes two bi-monthly Christian newsletters, *Biblical Economics Today* and *Christian Reconstruction*, published by the Institute for Christian Economics.

He lives in Tyler, Texas, with his wife and four children.

QUESTIONS THAT DEMAND ANSWERS

Why are the children of dispensationalists steadily abandoning the faith? (xxv-xxx)
How did Jimmy Carter and Ronald Reagan change American dispensationalism? (4)
Have dispensational seminaries abandoned dispensationalism? (5, 195-99)
What is Rapture fever? (9-10)
What are the ethical questions that dispensationalists refuse to answer? (12-14)
What are the signs that dispensational leaders have switched? (15-16)
What six questions does Dallas Seminary need to answer? (17)
What is dispen**sensation**alism? (20)
What is the clock of prophecy, and is it ticking? (21-23)
Has the Rapture been postponed indefinitely? (29-31)
Why do dispensational ministries refuse to preach the gospel to Israelis? (35-38)
Does dispensationalism produce retreatism and pessimism? (40-43, 63-71, 81-82)
Why are the Last Days *not* the End Times? (47-51)
Did Jesus actually teach the pre-tribulation Rapture? (85-86)
Why are dispensationalists in league with humanists? (95-97)
Why did 1988 undermine modern dispensationalism? (106-8, 210-11)
Why have dispensational leaders defaulted intellectually (124-27)
Why has no dispensationalist written a history of dispensationalism? (153-55)
Why have dispensational theologians rejected the six-day creationism? (166-69)
Have dispensational laymen become schizophrenic? (180-84)
What ever happened to the USSR's invasion of Israel? (188-90)
What is the lure of dispensationalism? (205-7)
Is dispensationalism in its terminal generation? (217-21)